SOUL QUALITIES: THE ART OF BECOMING

WITH STUDY GUIDE

D. A. WILLIAMS

BALBOA.PRESS
A DIVISION OF HAY HOUSE

Balboa Press books may be ordered through booksellers or by contacting:

Balboa Press
A Division of Hay House
1663 Liberty Drive
Bloomington, IN 47403
www.balboapress.com
1 (877) 407-4847

Because of the dynamic nature of the Internet, any web addresses or
links contained in this book may have changed since publication and
may no longer be valid. The views expressed in this work are solely those
of the author and do not necessarily reflect the views of the publisher,
and the publisher hereby disclaims any responsibility for them.

The author of this book does not dispense medical advice or prescribe the use
of any technique as a form of treatment for physical, emotional, or medical
problems without the advice of a physician, either directly or indirectly. The
intent of the author is only to offer information of a general nature to help
you in your quest for emotional and spiritual well-being. In the event you use
any of the information in this book for yourself, which is your constitutional
right, the author and the publisher assume no responsibility for your actions.

Any people depicted in stock imagery provided by Getty Images are
models, and such images are being used for illustrative purposes only.
Certain stock imagery © Getty Images.

Print information available on the last page.

Cover Artwork by Charlotte E. Jones

ISBN: 978-1-9822-4423-1 (sc)
ISBN: 978-1-9822-4426-2 (e)

Balboa Press rev. date: 04/14/2020

To the Holy Spirit, who revealed to
me my karmic patterns,
the Grace to override the ego, and the
transformation of my mind through
Forgiveness, Repentance, Atonement, Renewal,
Awareness, and Restoration. My
Purpose is to awaken others from the dream
world to reality through the Power of
The Holy Spirit. I Am grateful for my new
reality, my Divinity - The Light.

Becoming is the possibility of change in a thing that exists; suitable or appropriate for a particular person or in a certain situation; fitting (Merriam-Webster). Everything in this world is constantly changing and becoming, nothing is permanent. Spiritual activism are consistent intentional practices resulting in positive tangible and measurable change. Through the power of the Holy Spirit we **become** emissaries (advocates) for change. The intent of *Soul Qualities* is to inspire spiritual activism and to **become** who we are created to be. When I was a child, I talked like a child, I thought like a child, I reasoned like a child; when I became a (wo)man, I did away with childish things (1 Corinthians 13:11 AMP).

becoming is the possibility of change or of change that
exists somehow appropriate for a particular person or in a
certain situation living (Wittman Schelsky)? everything in
this world is complex... change... and becoming, as long
is remaining... and final arrival... increase... immortal
practice... involves... in positive, tangible, and meaningful
change, through the promise of the Holy Spirit, we become
enthusiastic (advocates) for course. The human being... God's
is to inspire spiritual nurture and to become who we are
(parenthesis). When I was a child, I talked like a child, I
thought like a child, I reasoned like a child, when I became
a woman I put away childish things (1 Corinthians
13:11 AMP).

CONTENTS

D

E

F

G

H

I

K

L

M

N

O

P

R

S

T

V

W

INTRODUCTION
SOUL QUALITIES

Soul Qualities associates the meaning of Adinkra philosophy and concepts with spiritual principles. The meaning of Adinkra symbols are visual representations of the traditions, proverbs and values of the Akan, one of the largest ethnic groups in Ghana and Cote d'Ivoire in West Africa. Adinkra artform has existed for over 200 years with thousands of symbols and combinations. The beauty of the geometric shapes and designs of Adinkra symbols have spiritual and cultural meanings.

Soul Qualities is not a book on the history of Adinkra or the Akan. *Soul Qualities* is a twenty-year project that includes the book *Soul Qualities: The Art of Becoming*, *Adinkra Note Cards*, *Scriptural Gems*, and *Adinkra Jewelry by Focused Art*. The purpose of *Soul Qualities* is to connect the meaning of Adinkra symbols with spiritual principles and practice.

Soul Qualities: The Art of Becoming pinnacles forty spiritual principles that coincide with the meaning of an

Adinkra symbol. The anatomy of a soul quality includes spiritual principle, soul inquiry, soul practice, and prayer.

Soul Quality

Sunsum (soon-soom) or **SOUL** is an immaterial force that gives the body life, energy, and power; spirit; life; vitality; being; essence. Sunsum is the Akan symbol of spirituality, spiritual purity, and the cleanliness of the soul. Divine qualities include creativity, order, affirmation, truth, right action, and balance. Soul qualities heighten the practice of gratitude, humility and praise and encourages conscious choice, responsibility, awareness, vision, and clarity. Divine qualities faith, discipline, commitment, courage, and patience are essential to right relationship.

Soul Inquiry

Hwehwemudua (scheweb-scheweb-meu-doo-ah) or **SOUL INQUIRY** is the Akan symbol of a measuring rod to inspire excellence, quality, and critical examination. Test and evaluate yourselves to see whether you are in the faith and living your lives as committed believers (2 Corinthians 13:5 AMP). Examine the 'why and how' of core thoughts, words, and actions. Out of the heart flows life's issues (Matthew 15:19 AMP). Self-examination and self-assessment tailors' spiritual practice.

Soul Practice

Nkyinkyin (n-chin-chin) or **SERVICE** is the action of helping or doing work for someone and contributing to the welfare of others. Akan symbol represents selfless devotion to service and ability to withstand hardships. Spiritual practice is service and creates a space for growth. Practice makes mastery. Spiritual practice creates peace and harmony. Be meditation, right action, prayer, stillness, and gratitude. The purpose of *Soul Qualities* is to create and demonstrate Greatness by tailoring a spiritual practice to your life style. *The Art of Becoming* is a process.

Soul Prayer

Aban (ah-ban) or **PRAYER** is spiritual communion with God, the Creator of the Universe. Akan symbol represents strength, seat of power, authority and magnificence; Great Fortress. Affirmative prayer is gratitude and elevated thinking. Collective prayer is a powerful spiritual practice. Consider the collective consciousness of an affirmative prayer for family, community, and world. Affirmative prayer is the right use of the mind.

The brain can train for optimal physical performance, and can also train for heightened spiritual awareness. *Soul Qualities* fuses the antiquity of African spiritual traditions and culture into the realm of the modern world. Adinkra is the possibility of personal, family, community, and global evolution by integrating the wisdom of Adinkra with spiritual practice.

Soul qualities are gifts from The Divine – to have is to give.

Peace and Blessings

D A Williams

Serenity Prayer

God grant me the serenity to accept the things I cannot change; courage to change the things I can; and wisdom to know the difference. Living one day at a time; enjoying one moment at a time; accepting hardships as the pathway to peace; taking, as He did, this sinful world as it is, not as I would have it; trusting that He will make all things right if I surrender to His Will; that I may be reasonably happy in this life and supremely happy with Him forever in the next. Amen.

- *Reinhold Niebuhr (1892-1971)*

1

ACCEPTANCE AS A SPIRITUAL PRACTICE

Acceptance. The act of taking or receiving something offered; favorable reception; approval; favor; the act of harmonizing. A feeling of oneness and sharing a common spirit. Akan symbol of agreement, togetherness, and unity.

Acceptance is judgment free. When we accept people for who they are, the energy we waste in attempting to change others can be used to enjoy their uniqueness. Our thoughts about others create fear, anxiety and frustration. Is it possible to let go of the thoughts that keep us stuck in the past and future? Letting go is liberation. Stop being worried or anxious, uneasy, and distracted about your life... who of you by worrying can add one hour to the length of his life (Matthew 6:25-27 AMP)? Acceptance creates a space for peace.

Acceptance is on the soul level with full attention, appreciating life, nonjudgment, humility, embracing love, and no expectation of a response from others. You do what you do because it feels right for you. Awareness is directly related to how you accept the present moment.

Who are you? False images and pretense originate from the ego. Clinging to a façade and building on the concept of a false Self is not your true Self. We cling and build to conform to societal norms in order to be accepted. Creating a false self is like building a foundation on sand, similar to social media profiles that create a false reality – an illusion. Let go and accept your authentic Self. Be who you are with no reservations, be your authentic Self.

Accept and embrace the truth of spiritual principles (peace, strength, freedom, understanding, joy, love). Acceptance is a knowing that all is well even when you cannot see how things will turn out. Realize that someone somewhere is taking care of things without little effort on your part; the peace of God which transcends all understanding (Philippians 4:7 AMP). Accept the past and present, and do not worry about the future.

The pathway to acceptance is peace. No stress, fear, or drama. When we practice acceptance, events and situations pass through us with no resistance from our mind and body; no clinging. Being right is over-rated when it alienates and causes conflict and confusion. Don't waste your energy, use life situations to grow spiritually.

Soul Inquiry

What do I do to be accepted by others?

Am I willing to be wrong, even when I think that I am right?

How do I struggle with the things that have already happened?

How do I accept the presence of God in all things?

How do I demonstrate God's acceptance of me?

What spiritual principles do I see working in my life?

Can I accept who I am in this moment?

How do I accept others?

Who am I pretending to be?

How do I judge others?

What are my preconceived notions that cause me to accept or reject others?

When do I cling?

Why and how do I resist the present moment?

Do I assert my will in opposition to others?

How often do I exert my energy on worrying about the past and future?

What does stress look like in my life?

What are my stress triggers?

Soul Practice

When caught up in a strong belief, needing to be liked, to be right about something, or stuck in a strong emotion, ask Self, Could I let it go? Letting go and accepting, happens in the mind and body. First ask yourself if it is possible to let go. In recognition of the possibility, something happens in the body - a deep sigh, a muscle spasm, or a release of tension you might not have ever known was there. We don't need to know or understand where a belief comes from in order to change it. Observe or witness the mind and body's response to accepting the present moment.

Write a heartfelt love letter to yourself, scent the paper with your favorite essential oil, place dried flowers or crystals in the envelope – make it special. Include everything you love about you - beauty, strength, energy, intelligence, sensuality – write only about your Goodness. Mail it. Receive the letter as if it came from a secret admirer or love interest - set the ambiance when you read it. Create ways to demonstrate the love you have for you.

Ask the question, Who am I? This question prods your awareness in examining your true Self.

Don't take anything personal (Ruiz). Don't respond to naysayers because their agenda is not about you; it is about them. People act according to their level of awareness.

Affirmation: I surrender to the power of truth and the presence of the Holy Spirit in my life.

Affirmation: I am totally independent of the good and bad opinions of others; I am beneath no one; I am fearless in the face of any and all challenges.

How do you demonstrate acceptance and letting go? Develop your own spiritual practice.

Peace and Many Blessings

Prayer

Dear Father,

Help me to temper my mouth – that I choose my words with purpose. Give me the wisdom and knowledge to express my feelings clearly and directly. Give me the discipline to control my mouth and to speak words of peace and love. Help me avoid vain, disloyal, and double-mindedness in my thoughts, speech, and actions. I desire a pure heart and mind that meditates on Your principles and laws. I love Your teachings, instructions, and revelations. Guide my mouth to words of forgiveness. You are my place of quiet retreat; I wait for Your Word to renew me. Let my words be few, but the power be revealed through Your Holy Spirit. I take delight in You. You are All Mighty and Powerful and I look to You with joy. You hear my prayers and You help me do what I promised. Love is the goal of my life. I am alive in my life because of Your grace. You are my Father, find me where You want me to be. I am supremely happy with You, now and forever. I am ever so grateful. In You, I move, I live, and have my being. Thank You Father. Amen.

2

AFFIRMATION AS A SPIRITUAL PRACTICE

Affirmations. A call to action. The act or an instance of affirming; state of being affirmed; the assertion that something exists or is true; a statement or proposition that is declared to be true; a solemn declaration. Akan symbol of authority and action.

An affirmation is intelligent self-talk with purpose, power, encouragement, motivation, and conviction. Affirming is the process of harmonizing with God's blessings and provisions. We are responsible for our lives through our thoughts and speech. Speak words of forgiveness, peace, and grace. Think and speak on good things. Whatever is true, whatever is honorable and worthy of respect, whatever is right and confirmed by God's word, whatever is pure and wholesome, whatever is lovely and brings peace, whatever is admirable and of good repute; if there is any excellence, if there is anything worthy of praise, think continually on these things [center your mind on them, and implant them in your heart] (Philippians 4:8 AMP). Affirmations plug us into the power Source – God. Affirming your good reduces the habit of negative self-talk. Words are things; words create. Speak encouraging and positive statements that support your prayers, moving you closer to peace, love, wisdom, and forgiveness – soul qualities. Like music, words create tone, harmony, and vibration. According to scientific research, positive affirmations, prayer, and gratitude boosts our energy potential and affects us on a cellular level. As we think in our hearts, that is who we become (Proverbs 23:7 AMP). There is power in the spoken word.

Affirmations clear the mind from years of negative programming. Everything we say is an affirmation – positive or negative. The tongue can speak words that bring life or death. Those who love to talk must be ready to accept what it brings; Words kill; words give life; they're either poison or fruit—you choose. Death and life are in the power of the tongue, and those who love it and indulge it will eat its fruit and bear the consequences of their words (Proverbs 18:21 AMP). Speak about what you want for yourself and others, and if necessary, bridle the tongue. Words are things. The goal of affirmations is to change your thinking and as a result, a change in behavior occurs. The process is thought-to-speech-to experience. You will also decide and decree a thing, and it will be established for you; And the light [of God's favor] will shine upon your ways (Job 22:28 AMP). The establishing is not up to us, we leave the establishing to God and focus on intention. Even if we cannot see how our request can manifest, decree it anyway. Do all you can do, and leave the rest to God - He is our source and supply. Demand and supply; you affirm your desires and God establishes them. Watch your thoughts, and if necessary, make a course correction on negative, limited thinking. Doubt and unbelief delays God's blessings. Whatever things you ask for in prayer [in accordance with God's will], believe [with confident trust] that you have received them, and they will be given to you (Mark 11:24 AMP). Our thoughts attract our experiences and the promise of God is to manifest our desires. God always works on our behalf. You are the thinker that creates the thought and creates the thing.

Affirmations should create positive feelings and be stated in the present moment, be spoken with conviction and belief, be spoken with emotional energy, state what is true for you, state your desire and intention, bring you joy and happiness, establish a desire, state that a thing exists - I am attracting; I love the thought; I feel excited; I am thrilled; I love feeling; I am overjoyed; I am happy that; I am elated.

You are powerful and responsible for your life situations. Decide for yourself what you desire to experience. Don't doubt your progress or process, and keep believing for the best. Be careful what you think. Watch over your heart with all diligence, for from it flow the springs of life (Proverbs 4:23 AMP).

Soul Inquiry

What do I say and believe about my life?
What do I intend for myself?
What do I want?
What are my passions and desires?
Do I express myself clearly and directly?
What is it that I want for myself and family?

Soul Practice

For optimal results, commit to an affirmation practice at least daily (approx. 30 minutes). Listen to your affirmations on a recorder during the day, or as an auto suggestion before sleep. At sleep time, the mind is relaxed and less resistant. Commit your affirmations to memory. Affirmations reprogram years and generations of negative programming. Affirmations are the right use of the mind.

When stating affirmations, make a conscious effort to breathe slowly and deeply during inhales and exhales. Conscious breathing is powerful and results in mind/body balance. Although there are basic guidelines for constructing affirmations, create affirmations that feel right for you. The "I AM" empowers the affirmation. The goal is to select words that arouse positive emotions. God is experienced through the heart, not the intellect.

Every morning for 30 days, look into your eyes, in the mirror and say "I love you; I really love you." Your mind responds to what you say and believe, and within days your body will reflect what you affirm.

How do you affirm your goodness to Self, God, and others? Develop your own spiritual practice.

Peace and Many Blessings

Prayer

Dear Father,

My desire is to do the best I can do in all situations, and give You all glory, honor, and praise. I do not compare myself with others. I look to You for approval and I never grow tired of doing good. You provide all good things to Your servants at Your appointed time. All that is good comes from You and I thank You for opportunities to serve You. You are my place of safety, my fortress, my God, I trust in You and am ever so grateful for the rewards of Your Holy Spirit in my life: love, joy, peace, patience, kindness, goodness, faithfulness, gentleness, and self-control. I live the way Your Spirit leads me. I speak openly, and I am grateful for Your peace that is beyond my understanding. Love is the goal of my life. I am alive in my life because of Your grace. You are my Father, find me where You want me to be. I am supremely happy with You, now and forever. I am ever so grateful. In You, I move, I live, and have my being. Thank You Father. Amen

3

AUTHENTICITY AS A SPIRITUAL PRACTICE

Authenticity. Real; not copied; true and accurate; not false or imitation; excellence, genuine, bona fide; authentic implies being fully trustworthy. Akan saying: He who does not know the real design will turn to an imitation.

It is better to have heart without words than words without heart (Gandhi). Authenticity is living from the heart; whole-heartedness. Being authentic is to know your truth and to have the courage to show up with integrity, genuineness, honesty, and without pretense.

Be the answer and be willing to be who you are, even if it is unpopular, because you are unique. Discover your talent or gift and let it shine. Be positive, and be the best you can be. You are what God created you to be. Be true to yourself.

Being authentic is not an easy task in a culture bombarded with images of who we need to be. Advertisement, music, peers, number of friends on Facebook, number of followers on social media, entertainers as idols, and expectations of family, friends, and peers dictate our thoughts and actions. Authenticity is sacrificed for being 'liked' and accepted by others. Each one must carefully scrutinize his own work [examining his actions, attitudes, and behavior], and then he can have the personal satisfaction and inner joy of doing something commendable without comparing himself to another (Galatians 6:4 AMP). Who others expect us to be may cause anger, eating disorders, depression, unhappiness, physical ailments, anxiety, addiction, resentment, and grief. Other's expectations and our need for acceptance results in dis-ease. Be more interested in the Creator's acceptance of you, than how others feel about you. Search me [thoroughly], O God, and know my heart; test me and know my anxious thoughts (Psalm 139:23 AMP). We can be 'one hundred' with our Creator because our God knows and sees our heart.

Soul Inquiry

Who am I and why am I here?

How do I remain authentic and not drift back to pretense?

What distracts me from being authentic?

What has God called me to do; what is my gift or talent?

Do people know how I really feel about them?

What is my foundation of truth?

What do I know for sure?

What do I believe, and why?

Soul Practice

Affirmation: I am totally independent of the good and bad opinions of others, I am beneath no one, I am fearless in the face of any and all challenges (Chopra 2003).

Make a Vow of Authenticity: To have and to hold, for better or worse, richer or poorer, sickness and health, till death do us part. Be devoted to who you are.

Become who you were created to be and let go of the expectations of others. Find your truth and live it. No one can tell you what your truth is. We are created as diverse as the fish, flowers, and birds; God loves diversity. Becoming your true self is becoming authentic.

How do you develop the courage to be authentic in a culture that encourages you to fit in? Develop your own spiritual practice.

Peace and Many Blessings

Prayer

Dear Father,

In this moment I recognize that there is within me a perfect Self in You. A Self that is strong, unlimited and peaceful. A Self that is faithful, all-knowing, all loving, serene, calm, compassionate, and happy through Your Grace. In this present moment of awareness, I ask You, to release me from the influence of deceptive intelligence. I accept the covering of Your magnificence, You are my Father. Through the Grace and Power of the Holy Spirit, I AM good, innocent, strong and pure. Your will be done through me, as me. The love that originates from You to me, and from me to others is a GREAT power. Within Your Power, all negativity turns to good, peace and love. I receive Your Light and continue to look forward. I envision the unlimited possibilities for love of Self and others. Guide and direct my path. Love is the goal of my life. I am alive in my life because of Your grace. You are my Father, find me where You want me to be. I am supremely happy with You, now and forever. I am ever so grateful. In You, I move, I live, and have my being. Thank You Father. Amen

4

AWARENESS AS A SPIRITUAL PRACTICE

 Awareness. The state or condition of being aware; having knowledge; consciousness; cognizant; informed; alert; knowledgeable; sophisticated. Awareness of and connection to a Supreme Being. Akan symbol of the presence of God. literal meaning: An Altar of God.

Awareness means to be awake to our inner and outer world. Awareness is listening to our inner dialogue without judgment. Awareness allows us to be conscious of the ego (self) and soul (Self). In expanded awareness, we experience insights, discernment, intuitions and visions. Everything is meaningful and no experience is wasted. In awareness, the soul leads, and ego is reduced to a subordinate role. Awareness is where we do the real work for peace and freedom.

The person looking in the mirror today is the same person in the mirror at age 5, 10, 20, and 60. Ask the question: "Who am I? Who sees what I see, and who hears what I hear?" You are not your name, occupation, ethnicity, body, past, title, or thoughts because when these things change – your essence does not change. Although the body image changes over time, our essence remains intact. Who we are and why we are here is no longer a mystery. We are awareness.

Witness your thoughts through self-observation. There is a voice in your head that talks constantly. The voice is the ego talking about anything and everything in relationship to the self. "I like that...I don't like that...Why did they forget me...What about me...I should have said... Why don't they like me...I don't like that..."? There is never peace or contentment when the ego- self has a problem with everything. Spend a day with the voice inside your head, personify that voice and make it your roommate. Witness the endless chatter regarding the 'I/me' dialogue with problems, complaints, and disturbances. Don't fight the ego, question it. As you become aware of the unending chatter in the mind, say, "That's not me."

The experience of the Holy Spirit is peace love, mercy, forgiveness, and compassion – the opposite of the ego. The Holy Spirit is subtle and less demanding than the ego. Identify and practice the qualities of the Holy Spirit by vigilantly monitoring your thought processes. For as a man or woman thinks in their heart and soul, that is who they are (Proverbs 23:7 AMP). Fix your thoughts on what is true, and honorable, and right, and pure, and lovely, and admirable (Philippians 4:8 AMP). Think about things that are excellent and worthy of praise. Affirm – Your will be done on earth as it is in heaven (Matthew 6:10 AMP). Allow your soul, your higher Self, to be guided by the Holy Spirit.

Expanded awareness empowers us to sense and resolve problems and challenges because we are connected to the Source. Expanded awareness is the sacred path where 'I/me/mine' fades to the background. In addition to our five senses, we see more of what is available and have access to limitless possibilities. The scripture advices: Be still and know (recognize, understand) that I am God. (Psalm 46:10 AMP). Awareness occurs when we silence the mind in stillness. Awareness is not something we do, but a way of being. We are all part of God, the Holy Spirit – for in Him we live and move and exist [that is, in Him we actually have our being] (Acts 17:28 AMP). Our core quality is awareness, and the seed of awareness is available to all.

Soul Inquiry

Who am I and why am I here?
Am I aware of the voice inside my head?
What is the voice saying?
Who is the one that is listening to the voice?
What are my repetitive patterns of behavior?
Am I aware?

Soul Practice

Hugging Meditation: Practice breathing in and breathing out, recite "Breathing in, I know that life is precious in this moment. Breathing out, I cherish this moment of life." Smile at the person in front of you, expressing your desire to hold him or her in your arms. Then open your arms and begin hugging. Hold each other for three in – and out-breaths. Bring your body and mind together to produce your total presence (awareness (Hanh).

Affirmation: I am the one who sees out there. I am the observer, experiencer, the witness. I am changeless, timeless, invisible, and intangible. I am present at the seat of the soul. I look out and I am aware of the events and thoughts that pass before me with detachment. I sit in the seat of the soul; the seat of consciousness (Zukav).

Witness your ego-dominated behaviors and transition to the spiritual principles of the Holy Spirit. The soul is the Divine characteristic of the physical body. The ego contradicts the role of the soul, which is Higher Awareness. Keep track of your thoughts and eventually there will be a shift from ego-based to soul-inspired thoughts and actions. The goal is to modify the ego's role from a dominant to a subordinate status. Higher awareness produces soul qualities when we do the work by practicing spiritual principles. Create a new reality by making a shift from ego to the soul and allow the Holy Spirit to direct your life. Expand your God qualities, listed below, by practicing spiritual principles:

EGO	SOUL
Fear	Love
Judgment	Non-judgment
Selfish	Selfless
Rude/ Disrespect	Kindness
Guilt/Shame	Forgiveness
Separation	Unity
Appearance	Substance
Turmoil	Peace
Competition	Individual Expression
Rejection	Acceptance
Conquest	Peace
Toxic	Purity
Pessimism	Contentment
Criticism	Acceptance

How do you shift your awareness from being ego-based to soul-inspired? Develop your own spiritual practice.

Peace and Many Blessings

Prayer

Dear Father,

I carefully determine what pleases You and take no part in the worthless deeds of others. I will not be carried away by the errors of people and lose my own secure footing. Their evil intentions will be exposed when Your light shines. Your light makes everything visible and I grow in Your grace and knowledge. My purpose is to bring glory to You on earth by completing the work You gave me to do. Your will be done. Bring me into Your everlasting glory. I am humble, gentle and patient with others and my desire is to lead a life worthy of You. I keep my mind on whatever is true, whatever is respected, whatever is right, whatever is pure, whatever can be loved, and whatever is well thought of. And I give thanks for these things and continue to do the things I learned from You. I receive Your peace beyond my understanding. My intentions are tested to see if I am living by faith, and I acknowledge Your grace. Your Holy Spirit renews my thoughts and attitudes and my intent is good and helpful. My words are an encouragement to those who hear them. My hands are used for good work, and I am generous to others in need. Help me to be kind to others, tenderhearted, forgiving others, just as You forgive me. Love is the goal of my life. I am alive in my life because of Your grace. You are my Father, find me where You want me to be. I am supremely happy with You, now and forever. I am ever so grateful. In You, I move, I live, and have my being. Thank You Father. Amen.

5

BALANCE AS A
SPIRITUAL PRACTICE

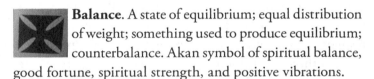 **Balance**. A state of equilibrium; equal distribution of weight; something used to produce equilibrium; counterbalance. Akan symbol of spiritual balance, good fortune, spiritual strength, and positive vibrations.

A balanced life requires moderation in rest and activity. Rest and activity are instinctual in lower animals; however, humans override balance by excess and irregularity. Our fast pace lifestyles become out of balance when we override our instincts and natural rhythms. Research indicates that there are physical benefits to a balanced lifestyle. On average, 7-8 hours of sleep, normal weight (not > 20% overweight and not < 5% underweight), physical exercise, moderate drinking, and no smoking are good indicators of longevity. These habits add years to our lives by retarding the aging process, and preserving order and balance (Chopra).

Balance requires a range of flexibility and spontaneity, and can be measured on a continuum. To find your center, you may need to go from one extreme to the other. Balance involves a process of exploring, developing, and nurturing the physical and spiritual self. Follow your energy by listening to your inner voice. To be balanced is to be in tune with being and doing. Sometimes it is necessary to do nothing - to be, and there are times when action is required. Try new things when you are inspired by people and projects. Trying new things is an opportunity to explore new interests, be guided by the Holy Spirit, and to seek the will of God for your life.

Balance in a spiritual context includes the following: love God with all your heart (Mark 12:30 AMP) through worship, love your neighbors and others (James 2:8 AMP) through ministry, share God's message of grace with others (Mark 13:10 AMP), and teach and grow through the practice of discipleship (Matthew 28:18-20 AMP). Pass on to others what you learn. Experiencing God's grace increases your responsibility to others. Every experience is an opportunity to tell others about God's grace, power, and glory. Share your knowledge and bless others with your insight. You are a witness to the grace and greatness of God.

To be balanced in loving God, loving others, sharing God's message of grace, and daily spiritual practice, explore the areas in your life that are underdeveloped. Don't allow people to lead you down a path that results in spiritual imbalance. Balance God's purpose for your life and examine your faith. Study and do your best to present yourself to God approved, a workman [tested by trial] who has no reason to be ashamed, accurately handling and skillfully teaching the word of truth (2 Timothy 2:15 AMP). Practice spiritual principles regularly and evaluate your spiritual health. Identify a spiritual partner and grow together through fellowship. As iron sharpens iron, so one man sharpens [and influences] another [through discussion] (Proverbs 27:17 AMP).

Soul Inquiry

Who am I and why am I here?

How do I apply spiritual practices in my life with family and community?

How do I maintain a balanced physical and spiritual life?

How do I share my experiences with others as a teaching tool?

Do I need a spiritual checkup?

Assess your present schedule of praise, prayer, gratitude, service, spiritual practice and study.

What is your present spiritual status?

How much time do I spend on my spiritual life?

Do I have a spiritual partner?

Soul Practice

Record your life lessons in a journal and review them periodically. Write down and share your faith in regards to your challenges, joy, pain, blessings, and disappointments. Thoughts become clear and meaningful when we write them down. A journal is beneficial to you and others.

Develop a small reading group. Pray, encourage, and support one another.

Balance your time with the people you love. List all the significant people in your life and schedule quality time with each person. See or call that person(s). Balance your time and be busy doing what matters.

Blessed are the balanced, they shall outlast everyone. Balance regulates internal and external peak efficiency. Being balanced is a combination of relaxation, play, and nurturing. According to scientific research, regularity and good habits arrests the aging process. Develop a process to balance your physical and spiritual lifestyle.

How do you balance God's purpose for your life? Develop your own spiritual practice.

Peace and Many Blessings

Prayer

Dear Father,

Restore your fortunes and have compassion on me. Search my heart and reveal my faults — my desire is to have a clean heart. I love You with all my mind and heart and with all my being. You set before me life and death, the Blessings and the curses; I choose life that I may live. You are faithful in keeping all Your promises. You are my Father and I depend on You to keep Your covenant of loyalty with me for a thousand generations. I choose life so that my children and their children's children will live. You are life itself. I choose the true road. Your road signs are at every curve and corner. I grasp and cling to Your Word; You lay out for me a course and I look for Your guidance. You chose me to love, and placed me in the world to bear fruit. As Your fruit bearer, whatever I ask, You give. I live freely, animated and motivated by Your Holy Spirit. I choose to be led by the Spirit. I am supremely happy with You, now and forever. I am ever so grateful. You are my Father, find me where you want me to be. In You, I move, I live, and have my being. Thank You God. Amen.

6

CHOICE AS A SPIRITUAL PRACTICE

Choice. An act or instance of choosing in awareness; choice is right action; something that is preferred or preferable to others; knowledge and prudence; the best part of something. Taking care and making a choice to adhere to good counsel. Akan symbol of wisdom, knowledge, and obedience.

Choice is a teacher when we are aware of why we choose our behaviors, friends, activities, food, attire, music, etc. When our decisions are based on social conditioning, automatic responses, and past experiences, they are not true choices. Habitual responses are learned behaviors, not choices. Choice only occurs in awareness. When we are unaware, choice is an illusion. We don't choose dysfunction - choice is a conscious act and requires a higher degree of consciousness. Domestic violence, eating disorders, oppression, depression, racism, and sexism are conditioned responses. Choices perceived as wrong can be reframed as lessons learned; no experience is wasted. Making choices to fit in, is the lowest level of choice. Learn the lesson, and in the future, make another choice. See life as a win-win and potentially self-correcting.

We think more about the past and future than the present moment. Research studies show, that as adults, 25,000 hours of conditioning from childhood affect our thought processes daily. Insanity is doing the same thing over and over again and expecting a different result (Albert Einstein). Seek to understand and qualify your actions. Automatic responses and conditioned patterns are changed overtime through awareness, but we cannot change what we do not see. Make a conscious choice to be aware, watch habitual reactions, and be open to change. Choices made from the level of the ego encourages drama, competition, and conflict. Overcome drama, conflict, and competition with forgiveness, peace, and cooperation. Jesus' proclamation of forgiveness on the cross was - Father, forgive them; for they do not know what they are doing (Luke 23:34 AMP). Forgiveness is a difficult choice, but possible through the power of the Holy Spirit.

Make choices based on intention. When making choices, ask the questions: What are my intentions in making this choice? How will this choice affect me and others? Is this choice for the good of all concerned? When examining the quality of your choices, align with the Holy Spirit. The energy of the Spirit is love, wisdom, unity, compassion, and acceptance – *soul qualities*. Responsible choice takes into account what is seen on the physical plane, and also the unlimited possibilities from intuition, gut feelings, and visions.

Your choices move you closer to the ego or the Holy Spirit. Temptation is an opportunity to grow when we allow the Spirit to enlighten us. God-consciousness provides insight before acting. When tempted, Jesus chose to move closer to the Spirit – The Word (Matthew 4:1-11 AMP). His deeper awareness superseded all physical temptation (breaking His fast; testing God by exhibiting arrogant behavior; and worshipping Satan). Keep the purpose of your life as your driver, and motivator when making decisions. Be clear on who you are and why you are here.

True choice is a spiritual teacher when we act from a state of awareness. Practice awareness in your actions/reactions. Identify when a choice is made from past conditioning - fear, loneliness, regret, revenge, anxiety, and hurt. With every choice there are consequences. Make choices based on *soul qualities*, and generate love and compassion for self and others. Our mind is conditioned by the past and we choose what is familiar. Patterns of dysfunction, conflict, pain, and insanity are habitual reactions, not conscious choices. No one chooses dysfunction or insanity. Free the choice maker and act in collaboration with the Holy Spirit - God's will.

Soul Inquiry

Am I morally justified to make this choice?
What past choices benefited me and others?
Who am I and Why am I here?
Who will this choice help or harm?
Is this what I have always chosen, is it automatic or habitual?

Has this choice worked in the past and what are my alternative choices?

Do I trust the Holy Spirit?

Is this choice based on my Highest principles?

What do I want?

Am I looking inward for direction?

Soul Practice

All choices have good or bad consequences. Make a list of crucial choices you've made over the past five years. Think of one 'bad' thing that resulted from a 'good' choice and one 'good' thing that resulted from a 'bad' choice. 'Good' and 'bad' are labels. Choice consists of a variety of scenarios, some things we can foresee and others are hidden. Our paths are not linear and predictable. Our level of awareness and how we respond to the choices we make have deeper meanings. Take an opportunity to choose a vertical path.

Set a list of values that are basic for who you are and why you are here (love, kindness, truth, compassion, wisdom, acceptance, etc.) and develop daily practices. Track your progress by journaling.

Have an accountability partner that can 'check' you when your choices are less than desirable. An accountability partner provides support, feedback, and insight.

Practice awareness. Identify when a choice is made from past conditioning. Once you track patterns of behavior, you have an option to make changes. Recognizing a choice is a choice.

Affirmation: Your will be done (Matthew 26:42 AMP), Find me where you want me to be.

Are your choices intentional and aligned with the Holy Spirit? Or are they a result of past conditioning? Develop your own spiritual practice.

Peace and Many Blessings

Prayer

Dear Father,

I call to you with all my heart. Open my eyes so that I can see the wonderful things in Your teachings. I will study Your laws. Help me learn and understand Your commands. I will do my best to follow Your instructions. You are the one who gives me the desire. Not only do I love Your guidance, but I also honor it. Let me always say what is true. I am Your servant and You do good things for me. You did what You promised to do. Give me the knowledge to make wise decisions. I trust Your advice. With Your hands, You made me and helped me become what I am. Your Word is like a lamp that guides my steps, a light that shows the path I should take. You are my Father, find me where You want me to be. I am supremely happy with You, now and forever. I am ever so grateful. In You, I move, I live, and have my being. Thank You God, Amen.

7

CLARITY AS A SPIRITUAL PRACTICE

Clarity. The quality of being understood in a very exact way; the quality of being easily seen or heard. Preparation to face changes with faith and assuredness, knowing that you have what it takes to stand. Akan symbol of fortitude. Literal meaning: Wind-resistant house.

Clarity is a sense of peace and well-being in the midst of chaos and confusion, and the ability to discern the truth. Clarity is to know why you do what you do, and to understand the cause and effect of conscious choice. When we are clear, our energy is focused on our purpose. The goal of a spiritual life is clarity.

Being clear is knowing what you want, and how to ask for it. We don't ask for what we want because we believe that our request will not be heard. The Word reminds us: You do not have because you do not ask [it of God] (James 4:2 AMP). Never be afraid to ask for what you want. Make a commitment to communicate clearly and directly. Be clear in what you want and what you don't want. Clarity in speech results in a clear direction.

Clarity is an internal process. Examine what you feel and why, verbalize your feelings, and know that you are not your feelings. Being emotional is an opportune time to discover the truth about what you feel. Seek the reason for the emotional disturbance, keeping the focus on you, not on others. Be responsible for what you allow in your life and make a commitment to make choices with your best interest in mind. Life experiences are teaching opportunities. If there is no change in behavior, there is no growth. When we are clear, distractions have minimal impact on our inner peace. Clarity requires trust, and the byproduct of clarity is peace of mind.

Soul Inquiry

What am I feeling and why am I feeling it?
Why doesn't this feel right?
What's troubling me?
When do I say yes when I want to say no?
What is my purpose?
What are my intentions?
Do I ask but doubt I will receive?

Soul Practice

Affirmation: I acknowledge what I want and what I feel and I express my feelings clearly and directly, with kindness.

Cry with an agenda. Write out what you are feeling. The goal of crying with an agenda is to gain clarity about what troubles you. Personify the energy of confusion, anger, depression, resentment, and defensiveness. Respond by declaring, "That's not me." Then, find your center of peace, be clear, and expect the best. Know that it shall also come to pass that before you call, He will answer; and while you are still speaking, He will hear (Isaiah 65:24 AMP).

How do you maintain clarity in the midst of chaos and confusion? Develop your own spiritual practice.

Peace and Many Blessings

Prayer

Dear Father,

I praise You. You are full of mercy, the God of all comfort. You comfort me every time I have trouble. You give me the strength to comfort others with the same comfort You give me. My eye is on the goal and You move me onward. I am off and running, and I will not turn back. I place You in charge of my work, and what You've planned will take place. I commit everything I do to You and I trust You to help me. You vindicate me and Your justice shines on me like the noonday sun. I enter by faith into what You have planned for me. I stand in the wide-open spaces of Your grace and glory, standing tall and shouting Your praise. I develop patience that strengthens me, keeping me alert for whatever You will do next. Your grace is sufficient and You fill my life with Your Holy Spirit! I experience Your Truth, and the Truth will free me. I will not grow tired of doing good, but will stand strong. I wait on You, and my strength is renewed. I mount up with wings like eagles; I run and am not weary; walk and not faint. You open the eyes of the blind, and You lift up those who are bowed down. You love those upright in heart and in right standing with You. I am convinced and sure of this very thing, that You began a good work in me, and will continue developing and perfecting that good work until full completion in You. You are my Father, find me where You want me to be. I am supremely happy with You, now and forever. I am ever so grateful. In You, I move, I live, and have my being. Thank You Father. Amen.

8

COMMITMENT AS A SPIRITUAL PRACTICE

Commitment. A promise to do or give something; loyalty; the attitude of someone who works very hard; an agreement or pledge to do something in the future. To make a commitment to God, family, and Self. I Am I my brother's keeper. Akan symbol of brotherhood, safety, and solidarity. Literal meaning: An enclosed or secure house.

Commitment is unwavering focus, faithful, all in, and dedicated to a desired course of action. Being committed to an end result begins with developing a process, and repeating the process until you get the desired result. Commit your way to the LORD; Trust in Him also and He will do it (Psalm 37:5 AMP). It takes time to give God our best. Commitment requires that we put our butt on the line, our entire self, regardless of the amount of time is involved. Do the thing until something happens; until you see results. Believe God is working on your behalf.

Napoleon Hill, author of *Think and Grow Rich*, and

You Can Work Your Own Miracles, reveals that his *Science of Success* philosophy took 20 years to complete. Hill's time was committed to research, theory and practice without monetary benefit or recognition. Deepak Chopra (2004) highlights three levels of commitment in *The Book of Secrets* - from half-hearted commitment to 'all-in' passion. First, quitting when you meet your first obstacle. Second, going into a situation conquering a few obstacles and then quitting. And third, going into a situation to master it. The Journey to becoming who we are created to be takes time, but the benefits are generational.

Challenges are opportunities for growth when we focus on the end result. There are no easy steps to spiritual maturity. We are encouraged to commit our works to the LORD [submit and trust them to Him], and our plans will succeed [if we respond to His will and guidance] (Proverbs 16:3 AMP). Be committed until you see the victory. Be committed to your spiritual growth and who you are created to be.

Soul Inquiry

How do I stay committed?

Stand for nothing; fall for anything (el-Hajj Malik el-Shabazz). What do I stand for?

How far reaching are my commitments – are they for me or do others benefit?

Who am I committed to becoming?

What price am I willing to pay for the end result in time and energy?

What am I willing to do to get what I say I want?

How long will I wait for the end result?

What does success look like?

Soul Practice

Track your spiritual growth by recording insights and life lessons. Share with others what you learned about life and relationships. Your life is preparation for greatness that benefits you and others. Review your journal often to keep a firm grip on your commitments.

Develop a process of self-motivation. Use affirmations to stay motivated. Encourage and motivate yourself through positive self-talk. If you need external motivation, find a coach or a support group.

In 15 words or less, write down or verbalize your commitment for the day or week. Develop a strategy and commit to it.

Affirmation of Greatness: I come from greatness, I attract greatness, I am greatness. I look for the evidence of my greatness; greatness attracts greatness.

Commit to practicing the qualities of the Holy Spirit – *soul qualities*. Select a *soul quality* (love, courage, mindfulness, commitment, faith, etc.) and commit to a practice until you get the expected results – practice makes mastery.

Commit to becoming what God created you to be. Commit to the habit of sharing your gift with others. Commit to daily spiritual practices. Developing a habit takes time - repetition is the mother of skill.

How do you stay motivated to your commitments? What is the "why" of your commitment? Develop your own spiritual practice.

Peace and Many Blessings

Prayer

Dear Father,

Reveal to me my imperfections and to recognize Your good works in me. I can do nothing good without You. You provide countless opportunities to demonstrate what I have learned. Thank you for the courage to forgive others as You forgive me. I am in awe of Your Blessings and Your gifts in myself and in others. I ask that I be aware of my heart condition, because out of my heart are the issues of life. Examine my heart; my desire is that my heart remain open to love and Your Light. Give me the courage to ask the questions and listen for Your voice of Truth. Guide and direct my path. My desire is to humble myself to serve others, and the courage to be kind, caring, and mindful of others and Self. Love is the goal of my life. I am alive in my life because of Your grace. You are my Father, find me where You want me to be. I am supremely happy with You, now and forever. I am ever so grateful. In You, I move, I live, and have my being. Thank You Father. Amen.

9

COURAGE AS A SPIRITUAL PRACTICE

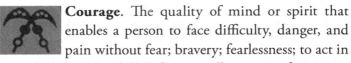**Courage**. The quality of mind or spirit that enables a person to face difficulty, danger, and pain without fear; bravery; fearlessness; to act in accordance with one's beliefs, especially in spite of criticism. Courage is demonstrated in one's behavior and character. Courage is required in becoming who you are created to be. Akan symbol of authority and heroic deeds.

What does courage look like? Courage is defined as strong, valiant, and unbending to the world's influence. If you do not have courage you cannot be who you are created to be. It takes courage to do what is right, it takes courage to examine your thoughts and behaviors. It takes courage to discard what is not working. Lack of courage is a character flaw. Right action is courageously submitting to the guidance of the Holy Spirit - the Will of God. Self-inquiry is a courageous act. You cannot change the not so good, if you are unaware. Find the courage to look at what you do; the good and not so good. No one is perfect, we all have shortcomings. Have the courage to let go of the things that are not beneficial to yourself and others.

Courage is an internal process. It takes courage to practice spiritual principles when others think it is a waste of time. Our feelings can be reduced to two emotions - love and fear. The fear of being wrong, alone, not knowing, and lack of control, damages our ability to move forward. The guidance of the Holy Spirit is our Helper, Advocate, and Protector. Be strong and let your hearts take courage, all you who wait for and confidently expect the LORD (Psalm 31:24 AMP). To be vulnerable and to move forward anyway is courageous. Have the courage to grow without question, hesitation, or complaint. Courage is trusting God and letting go of a false sense of control.

Courage is asking the hard questions, and the patience to wait for the answers, regardless of challenges and hardship. Have the courage to ask the question, "Who am I and why am I here?" It takes courage to examine what is true by doing your own independent investigation. Study and do your best to present yourself to God approved, a workman [tested by trial] who has no reason to be ashamed, accurately handling and skillfully teaching the word of truth (2 Timothy 2:15 AMP). Courage is bringing all of who you are to the present moment – do it afraid.

Soul Inquiry

Who is my model of courage?
Who do I admire and why?
What do I do in response to fear?

What decisions need to be made to move forward?
Do I have the courage to forgive myself and others?
What is it that I believe is wrong with me?
What is it that I refuse to admit about myself?
Do I have the courage to love?
Do people know my authentic Self?
Am I unkind?
Do I demonstrate my truth or deceive others?
Do I stand up for wrongdoing?
Am I aware and responsive to the feelings of others?

D. A. Williams

Soul Practice

What will it take to move forward to an abundant life? Abundance is not the bank account, house, car, investments, but something more. Write the word 'ABUNDANCE' on a sheet of paper and circle it. Then draw six lines from the abundance circle and list six things that will make your life abundant and happy at this present moment. Under each item, write actions you could do right now, and have the courage to do them (Chopra). Move forward on all levels of life and document your experience.

Assemble a small group and begin to have a dialogue about the spiritual part of who you are. Ask the question "Who am I and why am I here?" Share your coincidences. Have conversations that are deeper than the weather, politics, Facebook, entertainment, and celebrities in the news. The goal is to discover a deeper reality and spiritual connection. Have conversations with family members and friends about who you are and why you are here. Reveal your feelings about friendship, family and God to others.

Do you know someone who lives authentically, shines their light on others, and shares their gifts? Describe that person's core qualities. Find the courage to live an authentic life; live out loud. Don't die with your gift inside you.

Have the courage to discover the source of your pain. Have the courage to admit that you know what you know even when others disagree. Have the courage to be kind and to love others. Have the courage to live an authentic life. Have the courage to grow without question, doubt or resistance. And as for [the rest of] you, believers, do not grow tired or lose heart in doing good [but continue doing

46

what is right without weakening] (2 Thessalonians 3:13 AMP). The purpose of life is to develop the divinity within – find the courage.

Courage is a test of character. How do you exercise courage? Develop your own spiritual practice.

Peace and Many Blessings

Prayer

Dear Father,

You will instruct me and teach me the way to go and You counsel me with Your eye upon me. Create in me a clean heart, O God, and renew a right, persevering, and steadfast spirit in me. We are created in Your image and likeness; male and female, You created us. You created heaven and Earth, all things seen and things unseen, all things were created through You and for You. All Your creation is good, and nothing is to be thrown away if received with thanksgiving. You are worthy, Oh God, to receive the glory and the honor and dominion. You are good to all, and Your tender mercies are over all Your works. I am supremely happy with You, now and forever. I am ever so grateful. You are my Father, find me where you want me to be. In You, I move, I live, and have my being. Thank You God. Amen.

10

CREATIVITY AS A SPIRITUAL PRACTICE

Creativity. The quality of being creative; the ability to transcend traditional ideas, patterns, and relationships, to produce innovative ideas and methods; imagination. A spider demonstrates its resourcefulness and creativity by weaving an elaborate web for survival. Akan symbol of wisdom, creativity, and the complexities of life.

The Creative process occurs through our thought processes. We are most successful when we are co-creators with the Creator of the Universe - God. The process of creation is thought, to speech, to manifestation. Feel good about who you are and who you want to become. We are counseled, whatever is true, whatever is honorable and worthy of respect, whatever is right and confirmed by God's Word, whatever is pure and wholesome, whatever is lovely and brings peace, whatever is admirable and of good repute; if there is any excellence, if there is anything worthy of praise, think continually on these things [center your mind on them, and implant them in your heart] (Philippians 4:8 AMP). Thoughts are things; thought is energy, and creativity molds energy. Practice the habit of good thoughts and you will create a master piece.

Emotions connect us to a deeper level of our being and play a key role in the creative process. The energy of thought coupled with emotions is a powerful creative tool. Emotions are from the heart and connect the mind /body. Watch over your heart with all diligence, for from it flow the springs of life (Proverbs 4:23 AMP).

Author Esther and Jerry Hicks refer to feelings as our "Emotional Guidance System" (Hicks, 2004). Our concept of good and bad is determined by our level of consciousness. Our objective is to identify what we feel at this present moment and improve that feeling. The mind/body responds specifically to feeling and emotion, and with the help of the Holy Spirit we are elevated to Christ/God consciousness. Use the energy of thoughts and feelings to create your best life.

Soul Inquiry

Be creative. What am I living for?

What am I thinking/feeling this present moment?

What emotion is connected to my best thought?

How much time do I give to how I feel?

How do I feel about what I feel? Good or bad? Empowered or disempowered?

Do I draw my power from others, environment, or within?

What is my best life scenario?

Soul Practice

Keep a Creativity Journal and list your ideas. Write the unfolding of your story - your Ideal Scene. Include every stage of your life; feelings of well-being; and think on good things - see the end at the beginning.

Monitor your day-to-day experience and open a creative space through silence and nature. Creation occurs in silence. Make time to watch the sunrise, sunset, ocean, and mountains. Nature nourishes the soul.

Be creative in practicing spiritual principles and notate your results. Keep a journal, and develop your own spiritual practices. Create prayers and affirmations, and share your wisdom. To have is to give. Take others on The Journey.

Create a Vision Board.

Live creatively and set high standards for your personal, home, and work life. Use your energy, excitement, and enthusiasm to spark your creativity. Find your passion. Know what makes you feel alive, passionate, and energetic, and follow your creative energies. When you find your stream of joy, what will you create? Create a you that radiates peace, harmony, and abundance.

How do you create and maintain a life of peace and harmony with self, family, friends, co-workers, community, and the world? Develop your own spiritual practice.

Peace and Many Blessings

Prayer

Dear Father,

You are my strong safe place, my rock, and where I am, You are. I will always have hope and I will praise You more and more. You are right and good, as the heavens are high. You have done great things, O God. Who is like You? I will call out for joy when I sing praises to You. You have set my soul free. You watched over me from the day I was born. My praise is always of You. I will tell about how right and good You are all day long. Guide and protect Your people and keep us safe. I am supremely happy with You, now and forever. I am ever so grateful. You are my Father, find me where you want me to be. In You, I move, I live, and have my being. Thank You God. Amen.

11

DETACHMENT AS A SPIRITUAL PRACTICE

Detachment. The act of detaching; disengage; surrender; disunite. Freedom from prejudice, partiality, and other people's opinions. Detach from the past, live in the present, and enjoy the here and now. Akan symbol of freedom, peace, and forgiveness, and avoidance of conflict. Literal meaning: Bite not one another.

Detachment is living in the present without social pressures and self-limitations. When we detach, we are not affected by the demands and expectations of other people's opinions and agendas. Detach from the way things are, how things used to be, or how you want things to be. Detach from the past and take advantage of the now – the present is available with new opportunities.

Detachment is an internal process, liberating ourselves from past conditioning. We no longer are conformed to this world [with its superficial values and customs], but are transformed and progressively changed [and mature spiritually] by the renewing of our mind [focusing on godly values and ethical attitudes], so that we may prove [for ourselves] what the will of God is - that which is good and acceptable and perfect [in His plan and purpose for us] (Romans 12:2 AMP).

Detach from other people's opinions, gossip, blame, and rejection. What other people think about you is not about you – people live in their own world and everything is all about them. For our struggle is not against flesh and blood [contending only with physical opponents], but against the rulers, against the powers, against the world forces of this [present] darkness, against the spiritual forces of wickedness in the heavenly (supernatural) places (Ephesians 6:12 AMP). God's image, your image, and the world's image of you are different. Know who you are in relationship to the Creator of the Universe.

Do what you do for the joy of doing it and detach from the outcome. Detachment does not mean you abandon your goals or intentions. What detachment means is that between your intention and the outcome, you are open to the possibility of better outcomes – unlimited possibilities. Develop an inner integrity that is above manmade laws by doing what you do to the best of your ability.

Soul Inquiry

How do other people's opinions effect who I am and what I do?

Do I define myself and others by their material gain or lack thereof?

What is success?

Do I have heart-centered standards?

How do I feel when I invest in others and things do not turn out as planned?

Can I surrender my hopes and dreams when they do not coincide with the Will of God?

How do I handle disappointment?

Do I expect awards and recognition for my services?

Am I free from other peoples' opinions?

Am I willing and able to do my best in every situation?

Am I interested in self-mastery?

How does God see me?

Soul Practice

Cultivate a high moral code. Be morality and intelligence; not just moral and intelligent. Don't take anything personal (Ruiz).

Affirmation: I am moral, profitable, and ingenious extraordinaire, regardless of what any institutional transcript, or bank statement says (Dyer).

See every experience as new; don't dull your experience with past expectations. Be enthusiastic, curious, and open to new possibilities.

Develop an internal guidance system based on truth, guided by the Holy Spirit. Your actions make the difference if your intent is for the greater good; God. How do you remain free from social pressures of the past and future? Develop your own spiritual practice.

Peace and Many Blessings

Prayer

Dear Father,

You provide me with every good thing I need to live a GREAT life. Teach me to be understanding and fair in everything I do. Teach me how to live and how to act in every circumstance. I become wise by trusting and worshipping You because You are all wise and knowing. Pour out Your Spirit of wisdom upon me and make me wise. Because of Your grace and kindness, I live in peace, safety, and unafraid. I am ever so grateful. I am supremely happy with You, now and forever. You are my Father, find me where you want me to be. In You, I move, I live, and have my being. Thank You Father. Amen.

12

DISCIPLINE AS A SPIRITUAL PRACTICE

Discipline. Self-control; self-mastery; self-censorship. Self-mastery requires discipline and discipline comes from doing. Couple discipline with mercy and patience. Akan saying: Seriousness of one's deeds is demonstrated by one's actions, not appearance.

Spiritual disciplines are guide posts that move us to our higher purpose. How do we develop the discipline to practice the spiritual disciplines (forgiveness, gratitude, courage, prayer, trust, humility, meditation, mindfulness)? There is no magic formula - discipline comes from doing. Discipline requires determination, resourcefulness, and planning. Discipline results in clarity of thought and focus. A few errors in judgment repeated everyday move us off course, in contrast, intentional disciplines practiced daily will keep us on track. First step toward self-discipline begins with self-knowledge. Know the 'why' of your actions. Awareness is the key to change, and 'why' is the catalyst that drives behavior. Examining your thoughts, emotions, and actions might be challenging, but do it anyway - for who you are becoming.

Develop spiritual disciplines that counter worry, fear, anger, and unforgiveness. Spiritual disciplines (acceptance, courage, love, forgiveness) bring peace - the peace of God [that peace which reassures the heart, that peace] which transcends all understanding, [that peace which] stands guard over our hearts and our minds in Christ Jesus (Philippians 4:7 AMP).

The more we practice compassion, we become compassionate. The more we practice love, we become loving. In comparison, we become a better hater when we continue to hate, and the angrier we are, the better we are at getting angry.

Discipline is like a self-apprenticeship. Channel your spiritual disciplines from hand to heart by creating positive thoughts, intentions, and actions – not just for yourself, but for the greater good. Become less preoccupied with controlling others and your environment. If anyone thinks himself to be religious [scrupulously observant of the rituals of his faith], and does not control his tongue but deludes his own heart, this person's religion is worthless, futile, and barren (James 1:26 AMP). Self-restraint is necessary in an ego-driven culture where the dictum is 'Do your own thing.' By nature, we lack self-control.

Research indicates that doing a new thing for 28 days will change behavior. The mind needs consistent repetition to make changes, the 'why' of making and maintaining change is a driver motivator, and crucial for meaningful change. The longer you do a thing, the better you get – practice makes mastery. The Holy Spirit is present to correct our behavior if we are willing and able to exercise self-discipline.

Soul Inquiry

Do I want to be a disciple?

In what areas of my life do I lack discipline?

Who am I becoming, and is that okay?

How do I bring spiritual disciplines into my daily life?

When am I challenged to control my anger?

What's on my heart?

What spiritual disciplines do I need?

Soul Practice

Become a spiritual disciple: Select a spiritual principle (*soul quality*) and be the principle in action for at least one week. Study every aspect of the spiritual principle. Keep it in the forefront of your mind, look for opportunities to practice the principle, write about it, contemplate/meditate on how you are willing and able to execute the principle in all your activities. Visualize yourself practicing/living the spiritual principle. Live the energy of the principle. Become the principle.

Recognize when you are successful at mastering a spiritual discipline. Share your process with someone on the Journey.

What spiritual practice keeps you centered when you face challenges? Develop your own spiritual practice.

Peace and Many Blessings

Prayer

Dear Father,

Because of Your grace and mercy, my mind and soul have become one with You. Your transformation of the renewal of my mind connects me with You and lifts me to a Higher consciousness - God consciousness. My evolution yokes my mind and soul with You and guides me on the path of always feeling good. I seek Your goodness, You are my Source — my God — and You have a divine design for my life and I find joy in it. You keep the promises You made to me and I worship You. I will listen to You with all my heart and look for Your guidance and protection. I turn my heart toward You, and hear Your word saying, "This is the way, walk in it." When I turn to the right or to the left You are with me. Teach me what I should know to be right and fair. Teach me Your way and give me understanding and give me the wisdom to turn my eyes away from things that have no worth. I desire to be all You created me to be and You give me new life because of Your rightness and goodness. You provide me with truth, discernment, love, knowingness, awareness — all that I need to live in Your light. Your hands made me and put me together and my soul is strong in Your power and grace. You are a lamp to my feet and a light to my path. Open my eyes so that I may see the great things you have planned for me, my children and my children's children. I desire to understand Your way so that I will talk about Your great works. Love is the goal of my life. I am alive in my life because of Your grace. You are my Father, find me where You want me to be. I am supremely happy with You, now and forever. I am ever so grateful. In You, I move, I live, and have my being. Thank You Father. Amen.

13

EVOLUTION AS A SPIRITUAL PRACTICE

Evolution. A process of gradual growth, progressive change or development. Spiritual evolution is living the qualities of the Holy Spirit – peace, compassion, forgiveness, and love; *soul qualities*. Akan symbol of the omniscience and omnipresence of God.

Evolution as a spiritual practice refers to an awareness and transformation of the soul through the power of the Holy Spirit. Non-judgment, forgiveness, love, compassion, joy, inner peace, and meditation are transpersonal qualities. Transpersonal is beyond personal and refers to a Higher level of awareness. Darwin's theory of evolution focuses on changes in physical traits over time. *Soul qualities* are evolutionary, placing the Holy Spirit as the driver of thought and action.

In spiritual evolution, the soul and the Holy Spirit are close partners. The soul is pure energy and is the life force of every living thing - from a butterfly to a blade of grass. The physical world consists of our physical body, and the non-physical or nonlocal world consists of the soul. A merging of the local and nonlocal takes place in spiritual evolution - Your will be done on earth as it is in heaven (Matthew 6:10 AMP). The qualities of the Holy Spirit are the fruits of the Spirit. The result of His presence within us is love [unselfish concern for others], joy, [inner] peace, patience [not the ability to wait, but how we act while waiting], kindness, goodness, faithfulness, gentleness, self-control (Galatians 5:22,23 AMP). *Soul qualities* act as a catalyst to our evolution. During the process of spiritual evolution, the ego takes a subordinate position to the Holy Spirit and we become the fruits of the Spirit, demonstrating elevated qualities of awareness, acceptance, discipline, creativity, and peace. Spiritual evolution is flowing with the Spirit.

Unlike Darwin's theory of ape evolving into man, spiritual evolution is not linear. Utilizing the mind for activities such as prayer, conscious breathing, contemplation, praise, and meditation are evolutionary practices that move us in an upward, vertical direction. The goal of spiritual evolution is to move closer to the Holy Spirit, closer to God. Evolution is a renewal of the mind where we are continually renewed in the spirit of our mind [having a fresh, untarnished mental and spiritual attitude], putting on the new self [the regenerated and renewed nature], created in God's image, [godlike] in the righteousness and holiness of the truth [living in a way that expresses to God our gratitude for our salvation] (Ephesians 4:23, 24 AMP). Evolution is expanded awareness – there are no boundaries.

Spiritual evolution is choosing to integrate the soul with the qualities of the Holy Spirit. We can choose to evolve and be aware, or not. Be alert and sober of mind (1 Peter 5:8 AMP) and listen – your ears will hear a word behind you, "This is the way, walk in it," whenever you turn to the right or to the left. (Isaiah 30:21 AMP). We were not created to be less than, we are created for greatness. You cannot be who you have come to the planet to be unless you develop and live *soul qualities*.

Spiritual evolution is spiritual intelligence. In your process of spiritual evolution, give others a space to change - when we evolve, others evolve.

Soul Inquiry

Am I listening to my Higher Self, or am I self-absorbed and self-important?

Do I communicate truth and love?

How do I demonstrate the fruits of the Spirit?

Who am I and why am I here?

Do I pay attention to coincidences?

Am I living my Highest potential?

How do I assist others in their evolutionary process?

How do I trust my inner being?

D. A. Williams

Soul Practice

Affirmation – I come from greatness, I believe in greatness, I am greatness. Integrity All Manifesting Graciously Rising Evolving All Together. I AM GREAT both human and Divine.

Spiritual practices are connections to the Source - God. The Holy Spirit wants to give you the desires of your heart. Be curious, passionate, and nurturing. Find the sacred in everyday life. Find out who you are at the soul level by developing a meditation practice (See *Meditation as a Spiritual Practice*).

What actions or states of elevated consciousness have you experienced in your spiritual evolution? Develop your own spiritual practice.

Peace and Many Blessings

Prayer

Dear Father,

Open my eyes and give me the courage to practice faith, to serve others, as I serve You, and to keep me true to Your Highest vision for my life. I cultivate spiritual principles, and develop enthusiasm, always encouraging others. Give me the wisdom and understanding to know that faith is power, faith is cultivated by direct experience, faith is a higher state of consciousness, faith is simple trust and confidence in You. All things are possible with You and You are always with me, and are waiting for me to rise Higher. You will meet me where I am, in the present moment. Love is the goal of my life. I am alive in my life because of Your grace. You are my Father, find me where You want me to be. I am supremely happy with You, now and forever. I am ever so grateful. In You, I move, I live, and have my being. Thank You Father. Amen.

14

FAITH AS A SPIRITUAL PRACTICE

Faith. Confidence or trust in a person or thing; belief in God or in the doctrines or teachings of religion; in truth; indeed. Akan saying "A child of the Supreme Being, I do not depend on myself. My illumination is only a reflection of His."

Faith is a spiritual power. We have faith in the natural laws of the Universe. Our basic faith is in the law of order, cause and effect, and the law of probability. We know the sun will rise and set, the moon cycles, and the law of gravity is tried and true. This type of faith provides us with a sense of stability. Faith as a spiritual practice refers to faith as the assurance (title deed, confirmation) of things hoped for (divinely guaranteed), and the evidence of things not seen [the conviction of their reality—faith comprehends as fact what cannot be experienced by the physical senses] (Hebrews 11:1 AMP). The evidence of faith is practice – what we think, do, and say. Faith and works are close partners.

Faith is not an idea or philosophy. Faith is demonstrated by confident expectation. Through practice, faith becomes a knowing. Faith is an action word - keep moving forward with your dreams and ideals until something happens. Faith is knowing [with great confidence] that God [who is deeply concerned about us] causes all things to work together [as a plan] for good for those who love Him, to those who are called according to His plan and purpose (Romans 8:28 AMP). Look for the deeper meaning in coincidences, be thankful, and keep moving forward one step at a time. Use every experience as a character-building exercise, always demonstrating love, kindness, mindfulness, and peace. Faith and experience are partners.

Faith is measured by quality, not quantity. Jesus counsels, If you have [confident, abiding] faith in God [even as small] as a mustard seed, you could say to a mulberry tree [which has very strong roots], 'Be pulled up by the roots and be planted in the sea'; and [if the request was in agreement with the will of God] it would have obeyed you (Luke 17:6 AMP). Jesus recognizes the power of faith and belief numerous times in The Word (Matthew 9:2 AMP; Matthew 9:22 AMP; Matthew 9:29 AMP; Matthew 8:10 AMP; Matthew 15:28 AMP; Mark 2:5 AMP; Mark 5:34 AMP; Luke 17:19 AMP). The mind has the capacity to heal the body when there is a confident expectation of the outcome. Faith is seen in what we think, say, and do. Enthusiasm inspires, generates positive energy, and stirs the soul.

Doubt is powerful because we tend to believe only what we see, but faith keeps us true to our vision.

Soul Inquiry

What is the Will of God for my life?
What is the quality of my faith?
What are the tools of my faith?
What do I have faith in?
What is the evidence of my faith?
Do I know the promises of God?
Can I trust that life is working on my behalf?
What role does faith play in my life?
What do I believe and why?
Who am I becoming?
What is my life vision?
Am I preparing to meet opportunities for success?
Do I substitute external rewards over inner growth?
Am I growing spiritually?

Soul Practice

Take inventory of your thoughts and habitual behaviors. What do you think about how you treat you and how others treat you? How much time do you spend on social media, watching television, and reading? What is the program content? Is it awe inspiring, drama-filled or violent? Do you believe you deserve better? If not, why not? Look for patterns and write them down a journal. The answers to the above questions will provide insight regarding the quality of your faith. What you accept from others is an indication of what you believe about you.

Treat your life as if you are weaving a tapestry. Create a masterpiece through your thoughts (faith) and behaviors (works). Combine faith with practice and ask the Holy Spirit for guidance.

What role does faith play in your daily life? Develop your own spiritual practice.

Peace and Many Blessings

Prayer

Dear Father,

You are a God of forgiveness, grace, mercy and compassion. You are slow to anger and full of loving kindness. Even though I rebelled against Your Will and did not wholeheartedly ask for forgiveness, You favored me. I pray to You, and my disobedience is forgiven; You have not abandoned me. I worship and glorify You for Your mercy and loving kindness, and I turn from my wickedness and place value in Your truth. You clothe and beautify me with the riches of forgiveness. Your forgiveness taught me the meaning of compassion for others. I recognize my self-proclaimed righteousness, and I ask for Your forgiveness. I forgive others freely; seven times seventy, just as you forgive me. Forgiveness requires me to change my old way of thinking, and I seek Your righteousness through the power of the Holy Spirit. I glorify, honor and praise You. Everything is cleansed with blood, and without the shedding of blood there is no forgiveness. Jesus' blood was the atonement, the living sacrifice, for the forgiveness of sins. You placed on my heart to spread the Good News of forgiveness to everyone that will hear; the poor at heart, to those who are captivated by the illusion of this world, the depressed, the hopeless, and those that have lost heart. In forgiveness, my spiritual eyes are open, and I receive the gift of the Holy Spirit according to Your riches and grace. Your forgiveness releases me from all guilt, shame, and condemnation. Your forgiveness makes me free indeed. I am ever so grateful for Your mercy, patience, love, acceptance, compassion, and forgiveness. Love is the goal of my life. I am alive in my life because of Your grace. You are my Father, find me where You want me to be. I am supremely happy with You, now and forever. I am ever so grateful. In You, I move, I live, and have my being. Thank You Father. Amen

15

FORGIVENESS AS A SPIRITUAL PRACTICE

Forgiveness. To pardon an offense or debt; absolve; to cancel an indebtedness or liability; peaceful approach after a disagreement. Akan symbol of reconciliation and peaceful-making.

Forgiveness means to 'let go' or to pardon. Forgiveness gives us an opportunity to be honest and responsible for our behavior. Anger and frustration are wasted energy and distracts us from our vision. Forgiveness does not give others the right to be emotionally or physically abusive. Examine your role in conflict and set boundaries. Unforgiveness reveals the heart's condition. Guard against selfishness, betrayal, rejection, anger, and carelessness. Watch over your heart with all diligence, for from it flow the springs of life (Proverbs 4:23 AMP). Forgiveness is a win-win; forgiving others is like forgiving self.

The beginning of wisdom is understanding, and with all you acquire, get understanding [actively seek spiritual discernment, mature comprehension, and logical interpretation] (Proverbs 4:7 AMP). To understand all is to forgive all (Evelyn Waugh). Jesus demonstrates understanding and forgiveness when He asked forgiveness from God – "Father, forgive them; for they do not know what they are doing" (Luke 23:34 AMP). Say silently to the other "You my brother or sister, have wronged me in the past. I now understand that it was because you were unaware and did not see clearly. I no longer feel anger toward you" (Hanh). Forgiveness and understanding are close partners. Forgiveness is for you, not the other person. Unforgiveness is not an option, the inner work of forgiveness strengthens the heart. Through forgiveness, we connect to the Holy Spirit.

If you are in the process of forgiving and you remain angry, you probably want revenge. Forgive yourself for believing things about yourself and others that are not true. Acknowledge when you are practicing ego-based conduct (judgment of others, needing to be right, discord). Allow *soul qualities* of love and compassion to replace unforgiveness. Jesus was questioned on the necessity of forgiveness, and His response was "not up to seven times, but seventy times seven" (Matthew 18:22 AMP). We ask God to forgive our debts, as we have forgiven our debtors [letting go of both the wrong and the resentment] (Matthew 6:12 AMP). Forgiveness is a requirement for inner peace.

When an unfortunate event happens to the person you forgave and you feel satisfaction, saying "serves them right" or "they got what they deserved" you did not forgive. The litmus test for forgiveness is compassion. Think forgiving thoughts and speak forgiving words. What do we 'give for' the other? Give love, joy, goodwill, and The Blessing. Wish for good health, happiness, and peace. Forgiveness is love in action. Forgiveness is a BIG thing.

Soul Inquiry

What does forgiveness look like?

What will it take to forgive others?

What prevents me from forgiving?

Am I aware when my actions and words offend others?

Are there things I cannot forgive myself for doing?

If my life depended on it, could I let it go? Can I drop the story of why and because?

How and what offends me?

Why is it necessary to forgive?

Is my need for revenge greater than my desire to forgive?

What needs to be forgiven, and am I willing to forgive?

D. A. Williams

Soul Practice

Affirmation: I take full responsibility for my actions and forgive myself for all that I have knowingly or unknowingly done to hurt myself and others. I AM cleansed of the toxin of un-forgiveness. I give thanks for this realization through the power of the Holy Spirit. I AM unconditional love, compassion, and forgiveness. You are free and I am free. All is well between us. (Beckwith).

The Forgiveness Diet: Forgiveness is a spiritual laxative which cleanses the mind, heart and spirit of impurities. Forgiveness opens us to the power of the Holy Spirit. You will need a notebook, 20 minutes in the morning, and 20 minutes at night. On a clear page, number every other line, 1 through 35. Write the following sentences 35 times:

I forgive myself totally and unconditionally for _____.

I forgive _____totally and unconditionally.

Do not pick and choose who you will or will not forgive. Do not think before you write. Write whatever name comes to mind. Try to write 35 different names, if one name is repeated, that is fine. When you have repeated the exercise, take a long deep breath and close the book.

Repeat this exercise twice a day, before noon and before midnight for 7 days. If you miss a day, start over. True forgiveness requires work. Missing a day reflects resistance. Be gentle with yourself and don't be alarmed if you see or hear from the person you are forgiving. When you need help, ask for the guidance of the Holy Spirit. The byproduct of forgiveness is peace and freedom (Vanzant).

What is your process of forgiving self and others? Develop your own spiritual practice?

Peace and Many Blessings

Prayer

Dear Father,

You called me to freedom and You renewed and empowered my mind, body, and soul. You gave me the freedom to love, and to serve others, asking for nothing in return. Your Holy Spirit gives me life, and I am free indeed. When I am in right order with You, I am safe. I guard my thoughts, and desire to live in perfect freedom. I receive what You promised. Your Holy Spirit guarantees life. When You direct my life, I produce the fruits of the Holy Spirit - love, joy, peace, patience, kindness, goodness, faithfulness, and I share the glorious freedom of Your presence. You are my Father and I am always in Your care. Help me to maintain my freedom. How wonderful are the good things you keep for those who honor You! Love is the goal of my life. I am alive in my life because of Your grace. You are my Father, find me where You want me to be. I am supremely happy with You, now and forever. I am ever so grateful. In You, I move, I live, and have my being. Thank You Father.

16

FREEDOM AS A SPIRITUAL PRACTICE

Freedom. The quality or state of being free; the absence of coercion or constraint in choice or action; liberty; the condition of acting without compulsion. Freedom is unlimited possibilities. Akan symbol of authority and greatness. Literal meaning: King of the Adinkra symbols.

The goal of a spiritual life is freedom; it was for this freedom that Christ set us free [completely liberating us]; therefore, keep standing firm and do not be subject again to a yoke of slavery [which you once removed] (Galatians 5:1 AMP). Freedom is awareness of how past experiences, societal expectations, and social conditioning distract us from becoming who we are created to be. Habitual reactions rob us of our freedom. When we live under the burden of the past, we are not free. When we are free, we can stop doing the same old thing and do a new thing.

Actions that are soul-inspired result in peace. Ego-based

responses result in division and drama. The thief comes only to steal, kill and destroy [peace of mind]. I [Spirit of God] came so that you may have and enjoy life, and have it in abundance [to the full, till it overflows] (John 10:10 AMP). We have the option to choose ego-based or soul inspired behavior. *Soul qualities* are the qualities of the Holy Spirit. Trust the Holy Spirit to be the primary driver in your life, and let the ego take a backseat.

What does freedom cost? When we are free, we take off the mask and reveal our authentic self, without apology. When we are free, we are independent of the good and bad opinions of others. When we are free, our responses are not based on past conditioning. When we are free, we release guilt, hate, anger, and shame. When we are free, we help others with no expectation of payment or reward. When we are free, we do not have ulterior motives, we are transparent. For we were called to freedom; only do not let freedom become an opportunity for the sinful nature (worldliness, selfishness), but through love, serve *and* seek the best for one another (Galatians 5:13 AMP). When we are free, we live the qualities of the Holy Spirit, transcending the self-importance of the ego.

Freedom is making the most of every experience by living fully in the present moment.

Soul Inquiry

Who do I think I am?

What does freedom look like?

Am I responsible for my feelings and actions?

How do I demonstrate the qualities of the Holy Spirit?

What past experiences have the most influence?

Am I free?

Do I serve without expectation of payment or reward?

Are my actions self-serving?

Is my service for me or do others benefit?

How do I create drama?

D. A. Williams

Soul Practice

Affirmation: I am totally independent of the good and bad opinions of others. I am beneath no one. I am fearless in the face of any and all challenges. I am emotionally free. (Chopra 2003).

Recapitulation: At the end of the day before you sleep, take a few moments to review or witness the day. Quiet your mind and relax, setting the intent. Watch yourself move through the day. Witness how you interact with yourself and how you respond to others. Examine your ego-based behaviors listed under *Awareness as a Spiritual Practice*, the fourth *soul quality*. Notice what triggered the behavior (habits, societal expectations, and social conditioning), your mind/body response, and the response of the people directly or indirectly involved. Were you aware of the behavior or was the behavior automatic? How could you behave differently? Think of the possibility of intentionally choosing soul-inspired behaviors in the future.

What is your daily process of attaining and maintaining freedom? Develop your own spiritual practice.

Peace and Many Blessings

Prayer

Dear Father,

Through Your grace, I am willing and able to practice Your gifts of love, joy, peace, patience, kindness, goodness, faithfulness, gentleness, and self-control. I use your special gifts for the good of others and I give grace to others by giving and forgiving. Your grace delivers, provides, and protects; Your grace is sufficient. You bless me with grace and truth and make it possible for me to know Your wisdom. I have a sacred festival in Your honor, walking and singing praises to You in my temple. When I quietly trust in You, I am strong and secure. You are compassionate and You provide sunshine and rain to all those that have breath. You are grace and mercy. I always give thanks to You because of the grace You have given. I am firmly established in You and receive all Your blessings. It is by Your grace that I have been saved through faith. Your grace is overabundance — pressed down, shaken together, with overflow. You provide me with every good thing and I offer myself as a living sacrifice to You, dedicated to Your service. You are merciful. Love is the goal of my life. I am alive in my life because of Your grace. You are my Father, find me where You want me to be. I am supremely happy with You, now and forever. I am ever so grateful. In You, I move, I live, and have my being. All glory, honor, and power belong to You forever and ever. Thank You Father. Amen.

17

GRACE AS A SPIRITUAL PRACTICE

Grace. Simple elegance or refinement; the free and unmerited favor of God; the bestowal of blessings; an act of kindness, courtesy, or mercy; service. By God's Grace we are here. God is my refuge and fortress. Akan symbol of faith and trust in God. Literal meaning: By God's Grace.

Grace is undeserved kindness and mercy. Grace is God's trump card – you win, not by your strategy, but by His grace. The act of being graceful denotes effortless ease. There is nothing we can do to receive grace – grace is free. Grace is in every breath we take, every thought we think, and every step we take. Thought is energy, and positive energy creates 'good' karma - the opposite occurs when our intentions are detrimental to others. Grace alleviates the severity of 'bad' karma, canceling the negative effects of our actions. Our thoughts affect others, even when we are unaware. Grace is not an excuse to practice ego-based behaviors. We all transgress and stray in our actions; all have sinned and continually fall short of the glory of God (Romans 3:23 AMP); there are no perfect people. Grace sees to it that we *do not* get exactly what we deserve.

Giving grace to others creates opportunities to receive grace. Give and it will be given to you in good measure— pressed down, shaken together, and running over [with no space left for more]. For with the standard of measurement you use [when you do good to others], it will be measured to you in return (Luke 6:38 AMP). Be selfless, giving with no expectation of nothing in return. Just as we received special gifts [a spiritual talent, an ability graciously given by God], use it in serving one another as good stewards of God's multi-faceted grace [faithfully using gifts and abilities granted by God's unmerited favor] (1 Peter 4:10 AMP). Give unconditionally - to have is to give.

Grace sustains, guides, and transforms. We receive grace in the form of a thought and a call to action. Your ears will hear a word behind you, "This is the way, walk in it," whenever you turn to the right or to the left. (Isaiah 30:21 AMP). Through the transformative power of the Holy Spirit, grace is the generous and loving part of the personality. His grace is sufficient for us [His lovingkindness and mercy are more than enough—always available—regardless of the situation] (2 Corinthians 12:9 AMP). There are no limits to God's grace - the Spirit gives freely. Give grace to others by giving and forgiving.

Soul Inquiry

How much thought/energy do I give in deciding if I will help someone?

Am I generous?

Do I forgive unconditionally?

Is my giving unconditional?

Am I willing and available to receive?

Am I grateful for all that I have in the present moment?

Do I have expectations of receiving a blessing or miracle?

If I had opportunity and resources, what would I do for others?

Who can I forgive?

How do I serve others?

What is my talent or gift?

How do I share my gifts and talents?

Soul Practice

Recapitulation: At the end of the day before you sleep, take a few moments to review or witness the day. Quiet your mind and relax, setting the intent. Watch yourself move through the day. Witness how you interact with yourself and how you respond to others. Were you unkind to yourself, and others? Did you miss an opportunity to show compassion? Were you willing and able to help others? Were you aware of the energy you created throughout the day? As you begin to fall asleep, think of behaviors you may want to intentionally change tomorrow.

Keep a journal and begin to recognize the energy you carry throughout the day and how it affects others. When you show grace to others you are more likely to recognize when you receive grace.

How do you demonstrate grace to others? Develop your own spiritual practice.

Peace and Many Blessings

Prayer

Dear Father,

As I rise up, I thank You for the opportunity to be on this earth. I thank You for my mind and body. I thank You for my life. Use my life for Your purpose. May I rise up strong today and my soul radiate with Your Love. May all impurities be cast out of my mind, my heart, my body, and every cell of my being be filled with Your Light for the sake of the world. I give you every praise, honor, glory, and worship for the rest of my days. There is nobody greater than You. I am grateful for all You have done for me — the victories of past, present and future. Thank You for Your grace, mercy, and kindness. Your works are magnificent. I never would have made it without Your grace, power, and presence. I am stronger, wiser, and better because You are my Father, Savior, Healer, and Protector. Love is the goal of my life. I am alive in my life because of Your grace. Your will be done. Find me where You want me to be. I am supremely happy with You, now and forever. I am ever so grateful. In You, I move, I live, and have my being. Thank You Father. Amen.

18

GRATITUDE AS A SPIRITUAL PRACTICE

Gratitude. The quality or feeling of being grateful; being thank-filled; appreciation. Sharing the overflow with others. Expressing gratitude by giving the gift of time and attention. Akan symbol of abundance, plenty, and unity.

Gratitude is giving thanks and appreciation for all that is and will be. Gratitude is an act of humility. The benefits of appreciation are intangible, raising the energy level of the giver and receiver. Decide today what and how much gratitude you want to experience by giving and receiving. Begin with giving. Give your talent, service, a great idea, a generous thought. Give wisdom, peace, harmony, a prayer. Give appreciation, joy, and a smile. Give extra effort and energy. Use your voice to create peace and love. You get back what you give, only multiplied; Give, and it will be given to you. They will pour into your lap a good measure—pressed down, shaken together, and running over [with no space left for more]. For with the standard of measurement you use [when you do good to others], it will be measured to you in return (Luke 6:38 AMP). Giving and receiving are one in the same.

Gratitude parallels several universal laws: Law of Compensation, Law of Sowing and Reaping, Law of Karma, Law of Attraction, Law of Service, Law of Cause and Effect, and the Law of Love. We receive in direct proportion to what we put out in the Universe. Research studies show that we respond to feelings of gratitude on a cellular level. When we experience elevated emotions such as joy, gratitude, love, peace, and kindness, the body releases a chemical called Immunoglobulin A (IgA), triggering genes to release proteins (building blocks) for cellular renewal. The opposite occurs when our thoughts are consumed with anger, guilt, shame, fear and resentment, releasing toxic chemicals that cause dis-ease cause (Dispenza). Thought is pure energy and cells are directly affected by our thoughts and feelings. Choose feelings of gratitude, and other elevated emotions such as peace, love, kindness, mindfulness, forgiveness, creativity, praise, and prayer. For as we think in our heart, we are (Proverbs 23:7 AMP).

Gratitude and well-being are connected. When we feel good, we align with our Source – God. Finally, believers, whatever is true, whatever is honorable and worthy of respect, whatever is right and confirmed by God's word, whatever is pure and wholesome, whatever is lovely and brings peace, whatever is admirable and of good repute; if there is any excellence, if there is anything worthy of praise, think continually on these things [center your mind on them, and implant them in your heart] (Philippians 4:8

AMP). We are not obligated to feel good about the negative energy of others. We have no control of what others feel, or how they feel, but we can control how we feel. Our primary goal is to feel good, to feel grateful and appreciative.

Notice your competing thoughts or double-mindedness - for such a person ought not to think or expect that he will receive anything [at all] from the Lord, being a double-minded man, unstable and restless in all his ways [in everything he thinks, feels, or decides] (James 1:7,8 AMP).

You cannot be grateful and resentful at the same time. Choose the qualities of the Holy Spirit to fuel the inner being – the soul, and teach others about the benefits of gratitude.

Soul Inquiry

What am I willing and able to give to others?
Can I receive what is given to me?
Have I been called to do something inspirational?
What is the value of gratitude?
What am I thankful for?
Am I a complainer?
What and who am I most grateful for?
Have I missed an opportunity to give?
How do I express gratitude?
Is my 'thank you' heartfelt or a reflex?
Is there anything more important to me than feeling good?

D. A. Williams

Soul Practice

Group/Family Appreciation: Celebrate family by supporting and recognizing successes. Focus less on mistakes and deficiencies by celebrating family achievements. Sit together with your family and express your appreciation for each other. You can do this in rounds. Start by saying *I really appreciate that you… I really appreciate how kind you were when you… I appreciate that you make sure we …* Allow all family members an opportunity to give appreciation to each other, then do a second round and a third, until everyone has appreciated everyone else in the family. Notice not only how it makes people feel to be appreciated, but how it feels to give appreciation.

Gratitude Journal: A Gratitude Journal supports physical and spiritual well-being. List every day at least three experiences that you are grateful for – person, place, or thing. In addition, list the good things that happened to you and others. Studies indicate that acknowledging your gratitude and appreciation impacts your level of happiness.

Elevated Emotions: Positive emotions such as gratitude, increase the level of proteins (building blocks) for cell renewal. Elevated emotions renew and increase our energy, and release chemicals that repair the body. Commit to practicing Elevated Emotions through Affirmations or Affirmative Prayer at least 10 minutes a day, three times a day. Emotions are energy in motion. For example, repeating the word 'GRATITUDE' swells the heart, or looking at pictures of babies evokes the feeling of awe. Think, write, and record the thoughts that give you a feeling of well-being.

How do you make gratitude an effortless practice? Develop your own spiritual practice.

Peace and Many Blessings

Prayer

Dear Father,

I am under Your mighty hand, and I cast my cares, on You because You affectionately love and care for me. You bring instruction and wisdom, and You reward the humble with riches, honor, and life. Humility comes before honor, and in due time, You exalt those You love. You lift me up and make my life significant. You set Yourself against the proud and haughty, but give grace continually to those who are humble enough to receive it. I reverently and worshipfully fear You. You know the desires of my heart. I do all things with an attitude of humility, and regard others as more important than myself. I clothe myself with the wisdom of humility toward others with good deeds, and You give me the grace to be humble. You are mindful of Your servants and place me under Your control. You are my Father, find me where you want me to be. In You, I move, I live, and have my being. Thank You God. Amen.

19

HUMILITY AS A SPIRITUAL PRACTICE

Humility. The absence of any feelings of being better than others; humbleness; meekness; modesty. Akan Proverb: The horns of a ram are not used for strength or force. The ram may bully, not with its horns but with his heart.

Humility is derived from the root word humus. The words humus, humble and human have similar meanings associated with earth - profitable and worth cultivating. Humility is how we act toward others. A humble spirit is willing and able to serve. When we humble ourselves, God can mold us into what He wants us to be when we are willing and able to listen and follow His direction. Clothe yourselves with humility toward one another [tie on the servant's apron], for God is opposed to the proud [the disdainful, the presumptuous, and He defeats them], but He gives grace to the humble (1 Peter 5:5 AMP).

We do not demonstrate humility when the ego is the

primary driver. The ego insists on being right and its only goal is to protect the false self. The ego flaunts cleverness, seeks competition for external power and prestige. The ego is without compassion, and is haughty, arrogant, prideful and judgmental. Ego is 'easing God out' with no recognition of God's grace, power, and mercy. We can do nothing without the grace of God. Allow the qualities of the Holy Spirit to drive your thoughts and actions and place ego in a subordinate position by challenging ideas that do not contribute to peaceful relationships with self and others. But the fruit of the Spirit [the result of His presence within us] is love [unselfish concern for others], joy, [inner] peace, patience [not the ability to wait, but how we act while waiting], kindness, goodness, faithfulness, gentleness, self-control. Against such things there is no law (Galatians 5:22-23 AMP). The qualities of Spirit suppress the ego.

True humility is the foundation for serving others. False humility is a self-righteous attitude of "I am better than you, but I will help you and take credit." True humility is helping others without expectation of payment or reward. We may be able to fool others, but God sees the heart. Humility and kindness are close partners; you cannot be unkind and humble. Jesus demonstrated the 'how to' of humility on countless occasions. As a humble servant, He washed the feet of His disciples (John 13:12 AMP); He recognized and demonstrated compassion toward children (Matthew 19:14 AMP; Matthew 21:16 AMP; Mark 10:14 AMP); He rode on a donkey (Matthew 21:5 AMP); and He relentlessly serviced everyone who received Him.

We are all on a base level of human-ness regardless of

gender, race, age, sex, ethnicity, and socio-economic status. Practice humility and live in the ideal by living and enjoying your best life in the present moment.

Soul Inquiry

Who am I and why am I here?
What are my lessons in humility?
How do I serve others with humility?
Do I judge others by what I see?
Does my right-ness discount other's opinions?
Am I the center, or do others exist?
How do my actions affect others?
Who do I value and why?

Soul Practice

The following are exercises in awareness and taming the ego:

LISTENING: Start with family by listening and valuing what children are saying. A child's opinion is equal when we are aware of who they are in Spirit (Matthew 19:14 AMP).

COMPASSION: Be willing to become all things to all people. Even though I am free of the demands and expectations of everyone, I have voluntarily become a servant to any and all in order to reach a wide range of people: religious, nonreligious, meticulous moralists, loose-living immoralists, the defeated, the demoralized—whoever. I didn't take on their way of life, but I entered their world and tried to experience things from their point of view. I've become just about every sort of servant there is in my attempts to lead those I meet into a God-centered life. I didn't just want to talk about it; I wanted to be about it (1 Corinthians 9:19-23 AMP).

NON-JUDGMENTAL: 'Right-ness' is the activity of the ego. Surrender the need to judge others by practicing non-judgment. Begin the day with the statement "Today I will judge nothing that occurs" and remind yourself throughout the day not to judge (Schucman).

How do you practice humility? Develop your own spiritual practice.

Peace and Many Blessings

Prayer

Dear Father,

You are here to be bring the Light in the world. You are not a secret to be kept. You made us Your light-bearers. You provide Your people with a glimpse of good living and of Your Grace. We carry Your Light with faith, love, and the hope of salvation. Our heart regulates our hands. Keep our hearts and intentions pure. You make all things right. You are a compassionate God. You know us far better than we know ourselves. You know our condition, and You keep us present before You. All things work together for the good of those who love You. Love is the goal of my life. I am alive in my life because of Your grace. You are my Father, find me where You want me to be. I am supremely happy with You, now and forever. I am ever so grateful. In You, I move, I live, and have my being. Thank You Father. Amen.

20

INTENTION AS A SPIRITUAL PRACTICE

Intention implies a deliberate action toward a specific outcome. God-centered intentions reflect love, truth, happiness, and peace. Let your light shine before men in such a way that they may see your good deeds and moral excellence, and [recognize and honor and] glorify your Father who is in heaven. (Matthew 5:16 AMP). Akan symbol of hope and inspiration.

Our intent to know God makes our life spiritual. We are responsible for setting our intention; our light. The Holy Spirit's intention is toward the best possible solution for everyone. The ego's intention is to create drama, strife, discord, and division. We can give our time and money to genuinely help others, or to receive recognition and reward. If we had forgotten the name of our God, or stretched out our hands to a strange god, would not God discover this? For He knows the secrets of the heart (Psalm 44:20-21 AMP). Others cannot determine our true intentions – only you and God know the intent of your actions. Intent comes from the heart, fueled by ego or Spirit.

Inner growth requires daily disciplines of prayer, affirmations, mindfulness, and service. These disciplines unmask false intentions that retard spiritual growth. It is possible that we are not aware of our own intentions. Quality of intention is manifested in how we think, feel, and behave. When intentions (thoughts, words, and actions) are ambiguous, our light cannot shine brightly. Come close to God [with a contrite and apologetic heart] and He will come close to you. Wash your hands and purify your [unfaithful] hearts, you double-minded [people] (James 4:8 AMP). The Light is always available. Clear intentions move us toward the Source of our Light – God.

Our intention affects our inner and outer world. Thought is energy, and our thoughts affect our physical body, mental state, and emotions. In addition, positive or negative intentions affect our environment, remaining long after we leave. Like gravity, intention is always in operation and manifests itself as an unseen present force. We have the ability to strengthen our intentions through association by choosing positive, like-minded people. For where two or three are gathered in My name [meeting together as My followers], I am there among them (Matthew 18:20 AMP).

Spiritual growth is setting the intention to allow the Light of the Holy Spirit to shine within.

Soul Inquiry

Am I aware of my intention for self and others?
How do I shine my light?

What is my intention for the day?
What is my intention for my family?
Am I aware of how I affect others?
When do I create drama, strife, discord, and division?
Am I guided by the ego or Holy Spirit?

Soul Practice

Write down your intentions for every area of your life - family, work, church, community, and world. State your intentions for your physical, spiritual, mental well-being. What do you want? Have a vision of you in the Light. Share your vision with others.

Master your intentions by giving a percentage of time daily to spiritual growth. Practice kindness, mindfulness, patience, affirmations, gratitude, and humility. In the presence of God's Light, all things are possible.

How do you intend to let your light shine? Develop your own spiritual practice.

Peace and Many Blessings

Prayer

Dear Father,

I justify and declare Your righteousness and You give me a right standing with You. Through Your Spirit and with Your help I anticipate and wait for Your blessing and goodness. Your will, purpose, thought, and actions, give hope. Your Spirit produces fruit in my life: love, joy, peace, patience, kindness, goodness, faithfulness, gentleness, and self-control. There is no law against these things! I give thanks to You, for You are good! Your faithful love endures forever. Who can list all of Your glorious miracles? Who can ever praise You enough? I am overjoyed with those who deal justly with others and always do what is right. I have not forgotten Your miraculous deeds and abundant acts of kindness. I believe Your promises and sing Your praises. My Father, You remember Your covenant with me and Your relentless and unfailing love. You cause my adversaries to treat me with kindness. You are everlasting to everlasting! Love is the goal of my life. I am alive in my life because of Your grace. You are my Father, find me where You want me to be. I am supremely happy with You, now and forever. I am ever so grateful. In You, I move, I live, and have my being. Thank You Father. Amen

21

KINDNESS AS A SPIRITUAL PRACTICE

Kindness. The quality of being kind; good and benevolent nature or disposition; considerate and helpful; humane; passionate affection for another person. A feeling of warm personal attachment or deep affection. The Akan symbol friendliness and interdependence. Literal meaning: the teeth and the tongue.

Kindness is intentionally creating peace for the benefit of others. Kindness is everyday moral and humane interactions with others. We demonstrate kindness by how we intentionally treat the people we know (family, friends and co-workers) and the strangers we do not know. Kindness is walking in love. We are given ample opportunities to exhibit kindness towards others. There is no greater act than kindness because kindness encompasses love, selflessness, compassion, forgiveness, generosity, gratitude, humility, service, patience, and mindfulness. Being kind to ourselves is a prerequisite to being kind to others. We cannot be authentically kind if our cup is not overflowing.

We are encouraged to show God's grace and mercy by demonstrating kindness. Regard others as valuable and overlook others when they are discourteous. See that no one repays another with evil for evil, but always seek that which is good for one another and for all people (1 Thessalonians 5:15 AMP). People who hurt others are hurting and may not be aware of their inconsiderate acts. Have compassion for others because you never know what they may be going through. Return kindness to those who cause conflict and confusion. If your actions do not create peace, it is not the right action.

Kindness increases positive social interactions with others. We might think that people mistake our kindness as weakness. Not so, kindness is an intentional act, given freely. Do good and bless those who are unkind. Do not focus on their imperfections. Instead, notice the good deeds that others do. But I say to you, love [that is, unselfishly seek the best or higher good for] your enemies and pray for those who persecute you, so that you may [show yourselves to] be the children of your Father who is in heaven; for He makes His sun rise on those who are evil and on those who are good, and makes the rain fall on the righteous [those who are morally upright] and the unrighteous [the unrepentant, those who oppose Him] (Matthew 5:44-45 AMP).

Choose not to be offended when others are unkind. Be the better person by practicing forgiveness. Your kindness will not go unnoticed and will be rewarded in due season. You will receive Blessings on Blessings for your acts of kindness when you move toward unity and peace. Above all, have fervent and unfailing love for one another, because love covers a multitude of sins [it overlooks unkindness and unselfishly seeks the best for others] (1 Peter 4:8 AMP).

If possible, communicate your grievances immediately. The ego is unwilling to communicate and thrives on conflict, division and separation. The Holy Spirit always promotes peace. When you have an option of being right or being kind, choose kindness; being right is over-rated when the outcome alienates others. The litmus test for kindness is peace. Your calling may be revealed in your acts of kindness. He refreshes and restores my soul (life); He leads me in the paths of righteousness for His name's sake (Psalm 23:3 AMP). Give without expectation, silently bless others, and look for the passion in your giving.

Make the difference in someone's day through an act kindness.

Soul Inquiry

Do I resist communicating with others?

How do I measure kindness?

What am I communicating to others through my thoughts and actions?

Am I unkind?

Do my thoughts and actions promote peace or conflict?

Are others happy to be in my presence?

What keeps me from being kind to myself and others?

How am I proactive in being kind to others?

Can I do more?

Soul Practice

Commit to a Day of Kindness; five or more acts of kindness per day. Or pledge at least one act of kindness for the next 30 days. Kindness begets kindness. Kindness is contagious, pay it forward:

Put money into an expired parking meter.

In a 24-hour time span, smile and greet everyone you encounter.

When standing in line at the grocery store, allow someone to go before you.

Give someone room to have a bad day by offering words of encouragement.

Volunteer to read books at a daycare for children or adults.

Donate books to a local library.

Bring gifts (flower, card, food item, love, peace, etc.) when visiting friends and relatives.

Package food provisions for a homeless person and carry it with you in your car (bottled water, apple, nuts, crackers, etc.).

Send flowers to uplift someone's day.

Bring gifts to a nursing home for residents to enjoy.

Leave an inspirational book on the seat in a public place (bus, train, doctor's office) with a note stating "Enjoy, pass it on".

Post an inspiring story on a bulletin board for others to read.

Donate items to an animal shelter (blankets, cat litter, etc.).

Volunteer at a homeless shelter, hospital, nursing home, or a place that is in need of assistance.

Anonymously send an item that you know is needed by someone you know.

Help plant/organize a community garden.

Write a letter of encouragement to someone who is incarcerated.

Plant flowers to beautify a neighborhood.

Donate a coat to a winter coat drive.

Donate infant clothing to a women's shelter.

Pick up a restaurant tab for someone you do not know.

Do someone else's dishes.

Hold the door open for a stranger.

Donate blood.

Visit a sick relative.

Help prepare meals for a program like Meals-on-Wheels.

Send a care package to someone in service overseas.

Leave a toy on a door step for a child.

Donate school and art supplies to a community center.

What are your acts of kindness practiced daily, weekly, and monthly? Develop your own spiritual practice.

Peace and Many Blessings

Prayer

Dear Father,

I love You; I know I am one with You. Guide and direct me to love myself enough to stay balanced and avoid extremes. I surrender my thoughts of judgment of Self and others to You. I appreciate the goodness in others. Teach me Your way of Love. Give me the wisdom to utilize my time and energy to serve others as I serve You. Give me new eyes to love myself and to let love flow to others. Teach me how to encourage myself and others and to be all that You created me to be. I am grateful for what I have and thankful for what I am becoming. Give me a glimpse of the beauty, peace, and Light that is You. You are Infinite Love, Compassion, and Total Perfection. You are the essence of Love. You are my Father. In You, I move, I live, and have my being. Thank You God, Amen.

22

LOVE AS A SPIRITUAL PRACTICE

Love. Unselfish loyal and compassionate concern for the good of another; God's concern for humankind; brotherly concern for others; goodwill. I Am my brother's keeper. Akan symbol of love, endurance, and consistency. Literal meaning: The heart.

You shall love the Lord your God with all your heart, and with all your soul and with all your mind. This is the first and greatest commandment. The second is like it, you shall love your neighbor as yourself [that is, unselfishly seek the best or higher good for others]. The whole Law and the [writings of the] Prophets depend on these two commandments (Matthew 22:37-40 AMP). All religions recognize the philosophy of love. We are challenged first to love God, to love ourselves, and then to love others as we love ourselves. Before we can truly love others, it's essential to find the courage to love Self. Love is what we have come to life to be and to give. Unconditional love is free from guilt, shame, and blame, which means loving the imperfect parts of Self in the present moment. Love and acceptance are close partners.

Does your self-talk affirm the best of who you are? How you treat Self is a direct correlation of your love of Self. We cannot love others if we do not love ourselves. Love endures with patience and serenity, love is kind and thoughtful, and is not jealous or envious; love does not brag and is not proud or arrogant. It is not rude; it is not self-seeking; it is not provoked [nor overly sensitive and easily angered]; it does not take into account a wrong endured. It does not rejoice at injustice, but rejoices with the truth [when right and truth prevail]. Love bears all things [regardless of what comes], believes all things [looking for the best in each one], hopes all things [remaining steadfast during difficult times], endures all things [without weakening]. Love never fails [it never fades nor ends] (1 Corinthians 13:4-8 AMP). When we love ourselves, we, are compassionate, gentle, kind, forgiving and nonjudgmental. We trust that what we do and say is in our best interest. We tell ourselves the truth about what we do and why. We take responsibility for all that we are and who we are becoming. Loving Self means we value and celebrate who we are; human and divine.

How we treat others (in thought, word, and deed) is a demonstration of love. The goal is to make others feel welcome and comfortable by demonstrating compassion, patience, mindfulness, kindness, and peace; the qualities of the Holy Spirit. You may be the only demonstration of love a person may see today, don't miss the opportunity to love.

The opposite of love is fear. Where there is fear, there is no love. Hate drains, hardens, and closes the heart. Love is the glue that holds everything together. Love is God; God is love. Where God is, there is no fear. Experience yourself as loving by being kind, gentle, compassionate, mindful, forgiving, and valuing who you are. You are worthy and complete. You are enough.

"I wish I woulda knowed more people. If I woulda knowed more, I woulda loved more" (Toni Morrison). Everyone is worthy of love; love is why we are here. Love sees beyond all divisions. Begin today to fill the gap and be the bridge; greet others with a smile, a nod, a gaze, a hello. Make it a daily practice to love and extend more of you, to more people. More love, less room for fear. Love is the fulfillment of the law. Make love the goal of your life.

Soul Inquiry

Can I love in spite of unpleasant memories from past experiences?

Did I miss an opportunity to love?

What does unconditional love look like?

Am I willing and able to love myself as I am?

How do I know when others love what they do?

How do I know when I love what I do?

What does it feel like when my heart is open? Or closed?

When have I endured pain and called it love?

Is my self-talk loving and kind? Critical or debasing?

How and why do I withhold my love?

What does withholding love look like?

Soul Practice

Activate internal love. Reduce the use of 'I'. Be interested versus interesting. Look for something to love in the other person by taking the focus off of Self. Show concern for the other through active listening.

Affirmation: Silently say "Namaste"; The Light of God in me salutes the Light of God in you.

Affirmation: Every morning for 30 days, look into your eyes, in the mirror, and say "I love you; I really love you." Your mind responds to what you say and believe, and within days your body will reflect what you affirm.

Look at pictures or imagine the face of a newborn baby. Feel the awe-ness and warmth as your heart opens. That's love in action.

Stand, Share, Honor. Stand in the truth of your authentic Self. Share the whys of your actions. Honor yourself and others enough to be fully present in your relationships. These are loving acts.

Appreciating the beauty of nature. Watch a breathtaking sunrise, sunset, the moonlight and stars, the ageless and magnificent mountains, the vibrant fall colors of spring and autumn, the vast life sustaining ocean, flowers in unlimited shapes, sizes, and colors, fresh crisp fruit and vegetables kissed by the sun, and the fresh air and water that sustains life. Appreciate nature's beauty through the five senses.

How do you demonstrate love for Self and others? Develop your own spiritual practice.

Peace and Many Blessings

Prayer

Dear Father,

I enter into the shadow of Your All Mighty Power to be nourished, and protected, I AM Your child. You are my safe and strong place, my Father, I trust You. You protect me from deception, and from sickness. Under Your wings and I AM safe. You are faithful and You cover me like a strong wall. I AM not afraid of trouble at night, or of the arrow that flies by day, or the sickness that walks in darkness, or the trouble that destroys at noon. A thousand may fall at my side, and ten thousand at my right hand, but it will not come near me. I make You, Lord, my safe place, and where I AM, nothing will hurt me and no trouble will come near me. For You will tell Your angels to care for me and keep me in all Your ways. They will hold me up in their hands and protect me from all bodily harm. I will walk among those who intend to harm me, and crush them under my feet because You are with me. You bring me out of trouble and set me in a safe place on High. I find the peace which strengthens; the peace which surpasses understanding. In the sanctuary of Your temple, my heart, I find You and love You, and understand how much You love me. I call upon You and You answer me. You are with me when I AM in need and You honor me. I AM Blessed with long life and Your saving power. Love is the goal of my life. I am alive in my life because of Your grace. You are my Father, find me where You want me to be. I am supremely happy with You, now and forever. I am ever so grateful. In You, I move, I live, and have my being. Thank You Father. Amen (Psalm 91 NLV).

23

MEDITATION AS A SPIRITUAL PRACTICE

Meditation. To engage in thought or contemplation; reflection; devout religious or spiritual introspection; to intend; silence within the mind, body, and spirit. Connecting to unlimited power, Supreme Being. Akan symbol of the omnipotence, omnipresence, and immortality of God. Literal meaning: Tis Only God or Except God.

Meditation is the art of listening and tuning in to the inner voice that enriches spiritual growth. Meditation is the purest level of awareness; the field of pure potentiality. The root word "medi" means to heal. Soul qualities of kindness, compassion, humility, responsibility, and love, involve interacting with others. Meditation is between you and God. Meditation is a relaxed, conscious and disciplined effort to still the mind/body. Optimally, build a meditation practice, 30 minutes in the morning (meeting the day) and 30 minutes in the evening (leaving the day). A morning meditation is like meeting the day before it begins, which means you are present for the day before it is born. You are not required to do anything; your presence is enough. Be still and know (recognize, understand) that I am God (Psalm 46:10 AMP). Meet the day with peace, love, creativity, and harmony; the qualities of the Holy Spirit. Meeting the day provides an opportunity to bless the day before it begins and to carry peace throughout the day.

Meditation has a number of benefits. Stillness prepares the mind to receive direction from God, produces calmness, relaxation, a sense of peace, increased coping skills, enhanced immune system, and an awakened consciousness. Meditation is an evolutionary process and eventually it will become as natural as breathing. Meditation is a practice but also a way of being with yourself and with life. The feeling of peace from the practice of meditation will flow into daily activities, providing a sense of timelessness.

There are numerous meditation techniques and spiritual unfolding is as unique as a thumb print. Keep your process as simple as possible and be patience, consistent, and disciplined. A two-year old does not struggle to become three; the process of development unfolds in its own time. Develop a meditation process that feels natural and fluid. How long does it take to communion with a Higher Power; God? It takes as long as it takes. Meditation is like repair work; it takes time. Be still while He works. God is present in stillness. The goal is to end with a feeling of newness, peace, harmony, love, and wholeness. Do not judge the sessions good or bad. Sometimes awareness is present and sometimes it is not.

Establish a clean and uncluttered space for meditating.

Take a few minutes to relax the body, speak to every part of the body by telling each part to relax. Listen to thoughts and let them flow. Start your meditation with a Psalm, sacred scripture, or hymn to settle the mind. Pray/Chant in preparation (5 minutes) and meditate (20 minutes). It may be necessary to settle the mind into silence just like Jesus spoke to the wind. "Hush, be still (muzzled)!" And the wind died down [as if it had grown weary] and there was [at once] a great calm [a perfect peacefulness]. (Mark 4:39 AMP). Attempt to meditate at the same time and place each day. Meditate as if every time is the first time. Keep your meditation practice fresh with no expectations and show up with an open heart/mind. When you find what works, be open to improvements. Meditation adapts to your level of awareness, and as awareness increases, your meditation practice changes. When we wait, the work is being done. God is as close as our breath – For in Him we live and move and exist [that is, in Him we actually have our being] (Acts17:28 AMP). God is sovereign and welcomes us into His secret place (Psalm 91 AMP).

The purpose of life is to develop the divinity within. With practice, meditation finds our point of contact with The Divine. And we know [with great confidence] that God [who is deeply concerned about us] causes all things to work together [as a plan] for good for those who love Him, to those who are called according to His plan and purpose (Romans 8:28 AMP) - and we cannot do better than all.

Soul Inquiry

What is my process of communion with God?

How often do I connect with God? Are their difficulties?

What physical, mental, and spiritual benefits have I experienced from practicing meditation?

In what way has my meditation practice changed my life?

Soul Practice

Our life begins and ends with the breath. The breath comes in and goes out almost a billion times in an average lifetime. The breath is a movement of energy, master it. First notice your breathing, then regulate your breathing and follow the breath during meditation. Just before the in-breath turns into the out-breath, notice the small gap. Be present in the gap and discover the true nature of silence.

Affirmation: Fulfill Your highest thought in me. I AM transformed and progressively changed by the renewing of my mind, and I live Your good, acceptable, perfect Will and Purpose for my life (Romans 12:2 AMP).

Affirmation: The Holy Spirit goes before me and shows me the way – Infinite Spirit shows me what to do. You abide in me now, from the center, to the circumference of my being. My answers are revealed in the stillness of my Spirit. What is the next step to take?

Affirmation: Your kingdom come, Your will be done on earth as it is in heaven (Matthew 6:10 AMP).

How do you awaken to your inherently Divine consciousness? Develop your own spiritual practice.

Peace and Many Blessings

Prayer

Dear Father,

I am mindful of Your covenant, and Your promises that You established a thousand generations. I will meditate upon all Your works and consider all Your enormous deeds. You are a forgiving God, and You are kind, full of mercy, patience and love. I remember Your glorious miracles and I search for You. I thirst for You as parched land thirsts for rain. Let me see Your kindness to me in the morning, for I am trusting You. Show me where to walk, for my prayer is sincere. Save me from my enemies, O God, and help me to do Your will. Lead me to good paths, for Your Spirit is good. You are my God, find me where you want me to be. I am ever so grateful for You, now and forever. In You, I move, I live, and have my being. Thank You Father. Amen.

24

MINDFULNESS AS A SPIRITUAL PRACTICE

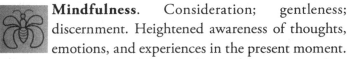 **Mindfulness**. Consideration; gentleness; discernment. Heightened awareness of thoughts, emotions, and experiences in the present moment. Akan Proverb: The butterfly may be fluttering around a pot of palm wine, but it will not drink it because it cannot afford to buy it. The butterfly is a symbol of honesty and gentleness.

Mindfulness means we are aware of what is happening in and around us, moment to moment. The scriptures are clear that God is mindful of His creation: What is man that You are mindful of him, and the son of [earthborn] man that You care for him? Yet You have made him a little lower than God, and You have crowned him with glory and honor (Psalm 8:4-5 AMP); The LORD has been mindful of us, He will bless [His people] (Psalm 115:12 AMP); What is man, that You are mindful of him, or the son of man, that you graciously care for him (Hebrews 2:6 AMP)? Mindfulness is also associated with Buddhist practices in relieving the suffering of others through loving speech and deep listening.

The outcome of mindfulness is compassion, kindness, intimacy, love, and understanding. We are encouraged to always be mindful of ourselves and others; Therefore see that you walk carefully [living life with honor, purpose, and courage; shunning those who tolerate and enable evil], not as the unwise, but as wise [sensible, intelligent, discerning people], making the very most of your time [on earth, recognizing and taking advantage of each opportunity and using it with wisdom and diligence], because the days are [filled with] evil (Ephesians 5:15-16 AMP).

In contrast, our actions are disastrous when we are negligent, rude, inattentive, and uncaring. The practice of mindfulness requires our full presence and attention and is the best gift we can give to ourselves and others.

Giving our full attention to one thing is challenging in a multi-tasking society when many of our actions are automated. The ancient recipe for staying in the present is 'Do what you are doing.' When you eat, eat. When you walk, walk. When you sit, sit. Whatever you do, do it with full attention. When we operate on autopilot, our actions are automated and we only see what we expect to find. Mindfulness is bringing our whole self to every experience. Mindfulness is living our best life.

Thich Nhat Hanh (2009), details numerous practices to honor and respect the life of self and others in *Happiness*. The five basic mindfulness practices or trainings for the purpose of relieving the suffering of self and others are:

- Practice compassion, kindness, and generosity

- Practice responsible behavior and respect for all life
- Protect ourselves and others from sexual abuse and unloving relationships
- Practice loving speech and deep listening
- Cultivate healthy habits in consuming products for the mind, body, and Spirit

Communing with the Holy Spirit is being mindful of the moment. We demonstrate the power of healing in our acts of kindness and compassion as demonstrated in the scriptures: Then a woman who had suffered from a hemorrhage for twelve years came up behind Him and touched the [tassel] fringe of His outer robe; for she had been saying to herself, "If I only touch His outer robe, I will be healed." But Jesus turning and seeing her said, "Take courage, daughter; your [personal trust and confident] faith [in Me] has made you well." And at once the woman was [completely] healed (Matthew 9:20-22 AMP). Mindfulness is tapping into the healing energies of the Holy Spirit – God's Energy to serve others.

Soul Inquiry

Am I mindful of how I speak to others?

Am I gentle with myself?

Do I take my time and enjoy what I am eating and drinking?

How do I stay in the moment?

What am I missing?

Did I miss an opportunity to serve?

Who did I serve today?

Am I kind? Or unkind?

Soul Practice

Ask others: Do you think I understand you and your difficulties? Please tell me so that I do not contribute to your dis-ease or dis-comfort. And I can love you in a way that you love (Hanh). Use kind and loving speech. Listen to the response without interpretation or judgment and do not interrupt others when they speak. Through deep listening and kind speech, mindfulness deepens understanding and is healing; like touching.

Mindfulness for a day: Eat vegetables, fruit, and drink water – just for today; Go for a walk – just for today; Refrain from judging others - just for today; Be kind, smile, and give a compliment to someone – just for today. Notice how you feel at the end of the day, and then decide the following morning if you want to continue for an additional day. 'A Journey of 100 miles begins with a single step' (Chinese Proverb). The key is to start the sacred Journey.

Mindfulness is living a God-realized life. Mindfulness can be adopted with any spiritual tradition or faith. Mindfulness is awareness of the energy of the Spirit in the present moment.

What is your daily process of tapping into the healing power of mindfulness? Develop your own spiritual practice.

Peace and Many Blessings

Prayer

Dear Father,

The standard I use in judging is the standard by which You will judge me. I will not judge by appearance or make decisions based on hearsay. Help me to be kind and compassionate to others, and create in me a pure heart. Let Your Spirit of wisdom, understanding, and knowledge rest in me— Help me to see the inadequacies in myself. My desire is to be understanding of the imperfections of others, for I will be treated as I treat others. When I have done all that You require, give me the wisdom and discretion to not waste what is sacred on people who are ungodly. The earth will shake at the force of Your word, and one breath from Your mouth will destroy the wicked. You are just, righteous, and compassionate to all who love You. I delight in You and all You have in store for me. The amount I give will determine the amount I get back. Your gift to me is pressed down, shaken together to make room for more. I humble myself before You, and You lift me up in honor. Love is the goal of my life. I am alive in my life because of Your grace. You are my Father, find me where You want me to be. I am supremely happy with You, now and forever. I am ever so grateful. In You, I move, I live, and have my being. Thank You Father. Amen

25

NON-JUDGMENT AS A SPIRITUAL PRACTICE

Non-judgment. The ability not to judge; not forming an opinion; discretion. The act of judging is unbecoming of good character. Jealousy, envy, gossip, and bullying reflect insecurity in one's self. Be more concerned about what God thinks, than what others think. Be kind. Akan symbol warns against jealousy and covetousness.

In today's culture, physical appearances supersede what we cannot see; if we look good, we are perceived to be good and if we don't look good, we are perceived to be lazy, unattractive, and dishonest. Judgment and criticism of others, says "If I am not right, then nothing can be right with you." Outer appearances are not a good gauge of a person. The scriptures counsel us: Do not judge and criticize and condemn [others unfairly with an attitude of self-righteous superiority as though assuming the office of a judge], so that you will not be judged [unfairly] (Matthew

7:1 AMP). When our judgments are "I don't like...; look at their hair...; they talk funny..." we create an atmosphere of discord, division, and conflict. We create a spiritual deficit when we are self-absorbed in judging others. Judgment closes the heart and is a spiritual dis-service.

The primary function of the ego is to keep us from a state of peace. The thief comes only in order to steal and kill and destroy. I came that they may have and enjoy life, and have it in abundance [to the full, till it overflows] (John 10:10 AMP). The ego always seeks validation by comparison, creating an illusion that success is measured in external acquisitions, such as appearances, credentials, accomplishments, status, position, and success by association. We measure success by the number of 'friends and followers' we acquire on social media (people we do not know). External acquisitions are tools to upgrade the self and do not create peace. The ego creates doubt regarding the importance of our inner-being. We are counseled: Do not become discouraged [spiritless, disappointed, or afraid]. Though our outer self is [progressively] wasting away, yet our inner self is being [progressively] renewed day by day. (2 Corinthians 4:16 AMP).

Judgment is a sign of perceived self-importance. Gain an understanding to what troubles you about others: Get [skillful and godly] wisdom [it is preeminent]! And with all your acquiring, get understanding [actively seek spiritual discernment, mature comprehension, and logical interpretation] (Proverbs 4:7 AMP). What irritates us about others leads us to understanding parts of ourselves that we deny, disavow, and negate. When we judge others, we are more likely to judge ourselves in the same way. Notice what you think and say about others (commentators, panhandlers, co-workers, relatives, etc.). There is always something we cannot see that is hidden. We don't have enough information to judge. Instead of judging, find a creative response by being aware of the needs of others. The absence of judgment and the ability to forgive leads to freedom. The 49th Verse of the Tao Te Ching states: Be kind to the kind and kind to the unkind, because the nature of being is kindness (Dyer). Judging is habitual and compulsive; challenge the impulse to judge.

Do not judge or reject the past, but identify the lesson from past experiences and make a personal agreement to not repeat the lesson. The first step to change is awareness. We cannot change what we do not see. Give up the attitude of 'that's just the way I am' and have the courage to change. Shift your mind to, whatever is true, whatever is honorable and worthy of respect, whatever is right and confirmed by God's word, whatever is pure and wholesome, whatever is lovely and brings peace, whatever is admirable and of good repute; if there is any excellence, if there is anything worthy of praise, think continually on these things [center your mind on them, and implant them in your heart] (Philippians 4:8 AMP). Remind yourself to replace judging with love, and view the past as seeing your life unfold. You are spirit, having a human experience, every experience is valuable for growth.

Soul Inquiry

Do I judge others based on what I see or hear?
Am I aware of the judgments I have of self and others?

How do I feel when I judge others?

What stereotypes do I place on others based on their appearance?

How will I make the shift to going beyond appearances to awareness?

When am I cynical and critical?

What excuse do I give for a critical spirit (i.e. that's just the way I am; my parents are that way; I can't help the way I am)?

What unresolved issues am I not allowing myself to see about myself?

What are the lessons learned from past experience? How many times did I repeat the lesson?

How can I live life fully?

Soul Practice

Make a commitment to silently witness the goodness in all things. When meeting someone, get to know something about the person that is non-superficial. Replace the habit to judge by affirming: "Namaste" – I honor the place in you where we are one.

Develop trigger points when you notice that you notice when you are judgmental. For example, before you open a door and enter a room, or when you pick up a phone affirm silently, "Today I will judge nothing that occurs. And throughout the day I will remind myself not to judge" (Schucman).

Affirmation: I am totally independent of the good and bad opinions of others; I am beneath no one. I am fearless in the face of any and all challenges (Chopra).

Who am I? Who am I not? Who do I serve? Who am I independent of my five senses? Remove the labels that you attach to yourself. Describe yourself in 150 words or less by omitting your age, possessions, accomplishments, experiences, or heritage.

The path of ego is earthly and evolving as we practice non-judgment. Your kingdom come, Your will be done on earth as it is in heaven (Matthew 6:10 AMP). A healthy mind thinks about enjoying life, family, work, and friends. You get to know people and have fun - not judging, just enjoying. Make living beyond judgment a preference. Replace judgment with compassion and kindness.

How do you create an atmosphere free of judgment? Develop your own spiritual practice.

Peace and Many Blessings

Prayer

Dear Father,

You are a God of order. The Universe is order, the planets in orbit, day to night, and the seasons. You set the sun, moon, and morning star in the sky. I am wonderfully made with a natural order built into my cells and body. My cells know what it means to be timeless. I operate on various time clocks and am wonderfully made from birth. Help me develop a process and live as if I have all the time in the world. You care enough to provide a system of sowing and reaping, and at the appointed time I will reap. You began a good work in me. Help me continue developing that good work, bringing it to full completion in You. I remain faithful and committed to Your Word, and nothing is impossible with You. You make Your ways of righteousness and justice known to Your servants. When I walk in all the ways You command, I live a long and prosperous life. My peace and prosperity are like a flowing river. Your presence is life-ward and heals my flesh, and You establish all my ways. I hold on to the things that I have learned, and I am convinced that Your Truth is the Light of my life. You are my Father, and You teach me the way I should go. I profit from Your counsel. Love is the goal of my life. Find me where You want me to be. I am supremely happy with You, now and forever. I am ever so grateful. In You, I move, I live, and have my being. Thank You Father. Amen.

26

ORDER AS A SPIRITUAL PRACTICE

Order. To put in order; arrange; order suggests a straightening out so as to eliminate confusion. The first law of the universe is the Law of Order – 1st God, 2nd You, 3rd Family and Friends, and 4th Work. Akan symbol of supreme authority and justice.

God has an operating system to order our spiritual and material life. The essence of spirituality is creation and God's rule of creation is order: "I will never again destroy every living thing, as I have done. While the earth remains, seedtime and harvest, cold and heat, winter and summer, and day and night shall not cease" (Genesis 8:21-22 AMP). The Creator of the universe established order in the creative process.

Words are things, words are seeds, and seeds reproduce after their kind – love produces love; hate produces hate; corn produces corn. As we think in our heart, so we are (Proverbs 23:7 AMP). In God's operating system we reap what we sow. Scripture counsels: We are snared with the words of our lips, and trapped by the speech of our mouth. Do not be deceived, God is not mocked [He will not allow Himself to be ridiculed, nor treated with contempt nor allow His precepts to be scornfully set aside]; for whatever a man sows, this *and* this only is what he will reap. For the one who sows to his flesh [his sinful capacity, his worldliness, his disgraceful impulses] will reap from the flesh ruin and destruction, but the one who sows to the Spirit will from the Spirit reap eternal life (Proverbs 6:2; Galatians 6:7-8 AMP).

Words of faith or fear are planted through the ears, eyes, and mouth. Our seeds (positive or negative) cultivate and fertilize the soil of the heart. The objective of planting seeds is to prepare the soil of the heart to accept what we believe through what we think, say, and hear. We water faith seeds through prayer, worship, praise, affirmation, and meditation. In contrast, we water our fears through worry, guilt, unforgiveness, anger, doubt, and shame. Faith or fear – we choose.

God gave us the easy part – planting, sowing, and keeping out the weed of doubt and disbelief. The harvest is governed by persistence and belief, but the Creator is responsible for the manifestation: "Because of your little faith [your lack of trust and confidence in the power of God]; for I assure you and most solemnly say to you, if you have [living] faith the size of a mustard seed, you will say to this mountain, 'Move from here to there,' and [if it is God's will] it will move; and nothing will be impossible for you (Matthew 17:20 AMP). Nothing is impossible for a person who has a solid belief system that includes faith, commitment, discipline, patience, and perseverance.

God's presence in our life will show us how to move from point A to point B. Answers come when there is order. One word from God can change everything. God has something to say and He instructs and teaches us if we allow Him. We are encouraged to, come close to God [with a contrite heart] and He will come close to us (James 4:8 AMP). God becomes personal when:

- Events in life reflect our thoughts
- People in our life are present for a reason
- Attention creates our reality
- Nothing is random, all things are in order

Soul Inquiry

Are spiritual principles working in my life?

How much time do I commit to spiritual principles (prayer, mindfulness, affirmations, praise)?

Am I aware of God's operating system?

When I sow seeds, what happens to my seed?

What are my faith seeds? How do I fertilize and cultivate?

What are my fears and doubts?

What is my process in maintaining order in my life?

How is my prayer life or seed planting?

Soul Practice

Develop a prayer life. Commune with God as your first contact of the day. Meet the day in silent unity with God and set a subtle intention on the day's activities. Affirm, "Find me where you want me to be" and "Your will be done". Be alert, authentic and pray what you feel, not what you think. God is concerned with your heart, not intellect. The Master taught us how to construct a simplistic form of prayer that includes recognition of God, requesting daily provisions, forgiveness, and protection (Matthew 6:9-13 AMP). You can never pray too much.

Develop an orderly process for living. Retuning the body creates order. Start with a few simple things. Develop a daily regimen for the next ten days to put order in your daily life: everyday clean your house, make your bed every morning, eat breakfast, and arrive at work 15 minutes early. Address the simple things to bring the body back in order.

Maintain order in the mind and body by developing a daily pattern for eating, sleeping, prayer and meditation, physical activity, order your work environment, limit drama, don't rush through undertakings, and be mindful in all activities. Limit confusion, chatter, and drama to create peace and serenity.

God's operating system is word to heart. What we speak, see, hear and do is planted in the heart and produces peace or chaos. Watch over your heart with all diligence, for from it flow the springs of life (Proverbs 4:23 AMP). Plant faith seeds in the fertile ground of the heart.

How do you practice God's operating system of order? Develop your own spiritual practice.

Peace and Many Blessings

Prayer

Dear Father,

I am confident and acknowledge that the trials and proving of my faith bring out endurance, dedication and patience so that I may be perfectly and fully developed; lacking in nothing. I am like a seed in the good soil. I hear Your Word, and bring forth fruit with patience. Your kindness and patience are intended to lead me to repent and to prompt me to accept Your will. I am in need of patience and perseverance so that I may fully accomplish Your Will. The fruit of Your Spirit is love, joy, peace, patience, kindness, goodness, and faithfulness. I enjoy to the full Your promises. I am supremely happy with You, now and forever. I am ever so grateful for the wealth of Your kindness, mercy, long-suffering and patience. You are my Father, find me where you want me to be. In You, I move, I live, and have my being. Thank You Father, Amen.

27

PATIENCE AS A SPIRITUAL PRACTICE

Patience. Steady perseverance without complaint; an ability or willingness to suppress restlessness or annoyance when confronted with delay; even-tempered; diligence. Akan Proverb: It takes the moon sometime to go around the nation.

Patience is waiting with anticipation, and being open to what will come next. Patience is knowing that a delay is not a denial. As God's own chosen people, who are holy [set apart, sanctified for His purpose] and well-beloved [by God Himself], put on a heart of compassion, kindness, humility, gentleness, and patience [which has the power to endure whatever injustice or unpleasantness comes, with good temper]; bearing graciously with one another, and willingly forgiving each other if one has a cause for complaint against another; just as the Lord has forgiven you, so should you forgive (Colossians 3:12-13 AMP). Patience requires acceptance, awareness, and perseverance. Impatience is anticipation of a future event, with limited restraint. Impatience is being offended, and in fear of not getting what you want. Beneath all our agitation, restlessness, and boredom is patience waiting to calm the mind.

Can you hurry the growth of a seed? Our thoughts, words, desires, and actions are like seeds. We don't see the roots growing underground and if we are impatient, we miss the first sprout above ground. Let us not grow weary or become discouraged in doing good, for at the proper time we will reap, if we do not give in (Galatians 6:9 AMP). It takes less than twenty-four hours for a mushroom to grow, compared to decades for an oak tree. Our thoughts, words, and actions are like seeds, and with patience and faith, all things come to full maturity. And we know [with great confidence] that God [who is deeply concerned about us] causes all things to work together [as a plan] for good for those who love Him, to those who are called according to His plan and purpose (Romans 8:28 AMP).

Patience strengthens us for what comes next. Exercising patience is an opportunity for growth. We will not be asked to do more than we are able to do. The scriptures are clear on the purpose of patience. Consider it nothing but joy, my brothers and sisters, whenever you fall into various trials. Be assured that the testing of your faith [through experience] produces endurance [leading to spiritual maturity, and inner peace]. And let endurance have its perfect result and do a thorough work, so that you may be perfect and completely developed [in your faith], lacking in nothing (James 1:2-4 AMP). Be patient, real change takes time. During your transitional period of growth, old patterns take time to dissolve.

Kindness and patience are close partners. The more we hurry, the less time we take to help others. The concept of time differs between cultures, locations, and families. Fast and slow rhythms in cultures are neither good nor bad. What is important is to be kind and respect the other's rhythm (fast or slow) with patience.

Soul Inquiry

When am I the most impatient?
What are my thoughts and feelings when I am impatient?
How do I experience time? Am I hurried?
Do I wait in doubt and fear? Or with patience and love?
What does my waiting look like?
When do I experience timeless awareness?
How is my faith tested?

Soul Practice

Waiting as a meditative state. Utilize meditation as a tool to slow your pace – sit and wait. Practice waiting, doing nothing but sitting and waiting like a cat or bird; be available for further instruction.

Time as an illusion. Think of a time when you experienced timeless awareness. Time passed by quickly and you lost track of time. Where did the time go? Or you experienced a 'long' day where time moved slowly. Be aware of your perception of time and events.

Breathing. Practice body awareness by being conscious of your breath (inhale and exhale). Focus on your breathing, not on your thoughts.

The process of making tea; waiting from the beginning to the end and doing nothing in between.

Soul Practice. Do not delay your spiritual work because you are hurried. Enjoy what is now by practicing the qualities of the Holy Spirit - patience, kindness, humility, mindfulness, and include all forty *Soul Qualities*.

How do you demonstrate patience with Self and others? Develop your own spiritual practice.

Peace and Many Blessings

Prayer

Dear Father,

Your ways are pleasant, and all Your paths are peace. You bless the peacemakers, and give them the discipline to practice the fruits of the Spirit: love, joy, peace, and mercy. Keep my tongue from evil and my lips from telling lies. Help me to do good and to seek peace. Give me the discernment to know when I am not welcome, and grant me peace wherever I go. Satisfy me with all that is good. You give me strength and You bless me. You are righteous and faithful, and You grant me Your salvation. I enjoy peace and prosperity when I listen to Your promises and nothing can make me stumble. Let me live to see the peace of my children's children. You prolong my life and provide my heart with peace, joy, and love; giving life to my body. You take pleasure in me and cause my enemies to make peace with me. Guard my heart and mind. Your peace transcends all understanding. I do the thing that You command, and am willing and able to endure in peace. Your will be done. Love and peace are the goal of my life. I am alive in my life because of Your grace. You are my Father, find me where You want me to be. I am supremely happy with You, now and forever. I am ever so grateful. In You, I move, I live, and have my being. Thank You Father. Amen.

28

PEACE AS A SPIRITUAL PRACTICE

 Peace. A state of mutual harmony between people or groups, especially in personal relations; the mind free from annoyance, distraction, anxiety, an obsession; a state of tranquility or serenity; silence; stillness; refrain from creating a disturbance. The Akan symbol represents a knot of hope and reconciliation, and forming a tight bond after a disagreement.

If your heart and a feather were placed on the scales of justice, would the scales be balanced? Or would your heart be heavier than the feather? The ancient Egyptian concept of Ma'at was practiced in 2375 BCE, and determined the place where individuals would spend their next phase of life. The principles of Ma'at (truth, justice, righteousness, harmony, order, balance, and reciprocity) are principles that create peace in the present moment. A clean and weightless heart, free from anger, unforgiveness, hate, guilt, and shame creates peace. As the saying goes, keep your heart as light as a feather. The scriptures counsel us to guard our heart: Watch over your heart with all diligence, for from it flow the springs of life. (Proverbs 4:23 AMP). Is your heart as light as a feather? Are you at peace? If not – why not? If we sow peace, we reap peace. Peace is a quality of the Holy Spirit.

Peace and compassion are close partners. Observe how you relate to others. You can be educated or uneducated and be ignorant and unaware. A condescending attitude, bullying, being argumentative and unkind, are opportunities to self-correct, for the sake of peace. When thoughts are scattered, the mind is not peaceful. For such a person ought not to think or expect that he will receive anything [at all] from the Lord, being a double-minded man, unstable and restless in all his ways [in everything he thinks, feels, or decides] (James 1:7-8 AMP). Shame, dishonesty, hate, judgment, discontent, competition, contentiousness, and drama create non-peace.

Move from duality to unity. Awareness creates peace of mind. And the peace of God [that peace which reassures the heart, that peace] which transcends all understanding, [that peace which] stands guard over your hearts and your minds in Christ Jesus [is yours] (Philippians 4:7 AMP). The more awareness, the more peace we experience.

Soul Inquiry

What is my model of peace?
Do I ask the question "What's in it for me?"
Do I have a 'need to be right' attitude?
Am I unkind or rude?
Do I rank others as important or unimportant?

What tilts the scale and prevents peace in my life experiences?

What are my requirements to live a peace-filled life?

What beliefs cause non-peace?

Can I reflect on a period of time when I was in a state of peace?

How do I quiet the mind?

Is my heart as light as a feather?

Soul Practice

With family, friends, associates, and others, stop 'pulling rank' based on age, status, and gender. Remove status by not saying "I'm older, educated, etc." Treat adults as adults – everyone has the right to their opinion. Allow others to have opinions and beliefs without debate, even if you feel you are right. Being right is over-rated when it causes conflict.

Decrease the atmosphere of competition where there are winners and losers. Strive for an atmosphere of cooperation, collaboration, mutual recognition, and respect.

Keep the lines of communication open with yourself and others. Notice when you avoid others and 'shut down' communication. Strive to keep your heart open and allow all feelings/emotions, good and not so good to pass through you.

Commit to one day of peace – free from drama, worry, shame, jealousy, obsessiveness, and judgment. Decide the following day, if you would like to practice peace for the next 24 hours.

Become teachable. No one has knowledge and expertise about everything. Create a space for peace by admitting you don't know – not knowing is okay. Not knowing is a space for newness. There is no pretense, embarrassment or shame in not knowing. Don't hide or camouflage who you are. Be authentic.

To create peace, apply the principles of forgiveness. Offer peace in the present moment, and seek to know who you are on a deeper level. Self-knowledge is the beginning of wisdom and peace.

What is your process for creating internal and external peace for Self, family, community, and world? Develop your own spiritual practice.

Peace and Many Blessings

Prayer

Dear Father,

I continue to endure, persevere, and have faith. You will save me. I am waiting patiently with perseverance, joy, and hope for something I do not have yet. When suffering and tribulation come, I pray that You will hear and help. I pursue righteousness and a godly life, along with faith, love, gentleness and kindness. Endurance develops strength of character, and good character strengthens me. I have been made right in Your sight by faith, I have peace with You, and I confidently and joyfully look forward to sharing Your glory. Your people demonstrate what endurance means, let me run the race that is before me and never give up. I cast aside anything that hinders, entangles and holds me back from receiving Your grace. Your grace is sufficient. I rejoice, when I run into problems and trials, because I know that challenges help me develop endurance, faith, and patience. I rejoice in my relationship with You and I fight the good fight of faith. I hold tightly to the eternal life to which You called me, and I guard what You entrusted to me. I avoid godless, foolish discussions with those who oppose You. I depend on the Spirit at all times, asking for everything I need. Love is the goal of my life. I am alive in my life because of Your grace. You are my Father, find me where You want me to be. I am supremely happy with You, now and forever. I am ever so grateful. In You, I move, I live, and have my being. Thank You Father. Amen.

29

PERSEVERANCE AS A SPIRITUAL PRACTICE

Perseverance. Steady persistence in a course of action in spite of difficulties, obstacles, or discouragement; continuance in a state of grace to the end. Akan symbol of a wawa nut, the hardwood of the tree is used for carving. Akan saying: He is tough as the seed of the wawa tree.

Webster defines perseverance as a continued effort to do or achieve something despite difficulties, failure, or opposition; steadfastness. Combine perseverance with industry, diligence, a positive attitude, determination, and flexibility. Let us not grow weary or become discouraged in doing good, for at the proper time we will reap, if we do not give in (Galatians 6:9 AMP). The right time is God's perfect timing - the appointed time.

Is there a benefit to hard times? Challenge brings out our greatest assets. When all is well, we are at our peak, but every peak is prefaced by a valley. God uses situations and people to refine us. When faced with challenges, do all you can do to the best of your ability, and expect the best possible outcome. Trust that you will reap the benefits of your efforts. Perseverance tests the quality of our character, heart condition, and faith. The good news about perseverance is that it provides an opportunity to correct the areas that are brought to our awareness. Repeat challenges are indications that we missed a previous lesson; similar challenges occur until we work through our issues. For we are His workmanship [His own master work, a work of art], created in Christ Jesus [reborn from above— spiritually transformed, renewed, ready to be used] for good works, which God prepared [for us] beforehand [taking paths which He set], so that we would walk in them [living the good life which He prearranged and made ready for us] (Ephesians 2:10 AMP). We are clay in the Potter's Hand.

While waiting for your desires to come to manifest, believe and expect that what you ask for is attainable. The scriptures counsel on perseverance: In this you rejoice greatly, even though now for a little while, if necessary, you have been distressed by various trials, so that the genuineness of your faith, which is much more precious than gold which is perishable, even though tested and purified by fire, may be found to result in [your] praise and glory and honor on the day of his return (1 Peter 1:6-7 AMP). Water your seeds with prayer, affirmations, and praise, and remain cheerful with a positive attitude. Delight yourself in the LORD, And He will give you the desires and petitions of your heart (Psalm 37:4 AMP). Remove frustration, complaining, and impatience and rise to a new level, be the person God created you to be.

Soul Inquiry

Is God in the midst of what I am doing?

How do I demonstrate my impatience and frustration when I am required to wait?

What attitudes and behaviors do I need to change?

Am I aware of my intent and motives?

How do I react when things don't go my way?

Whose life inspires me and why?

What did I do today to advance me toward my goals?

How long will I be faithful to my desire?

Do I believe I can have what I want?

When was I tested and how did I handle the test?

D. A. Williams

Soul Practice

Affirmation: God is in control of my life; working out His plan for my life.

Prayer and meditation. God knows the end, middle, and beginning. Spending time with God will increase perseverance and commitment.

Service. Help others that are less fortunate, without expectation, recognition, or reward - volunteer.

Do one thing daily that advances you toward your goals.

Encourage yourself. Read, listen, and watch how others are inspired. Success stories contain failures, perseverance, struggle, and character building. Use the experiences of others as teaching tools, and encourage yourself through positive self-talk. Feed yourself a daily spiritual diet of reading and studying, prayer, affirmations, praise and worship music, listening and watching faith ministries, and fellowship.

Trust God's timing and use trials as teaching tools. Enjoy your life while you are waiting with expectation.

How do you persevere when people and life challenges become difficult? Develop your own spiritual practice.

Peace and Much Blessings

Prayer

Dear Father,

Let everything that has breath and every breath of life praise You! You are Great; past, present, and future. You are Power and Abundance. I praise You with song and dance. Your energy and Your presence are my strength and stronghold. You are gracious, compassionate, merciful, and full of loving kindness. You deserve All worship, praise, and glory. Guide and direct me to spread well-being to all and I give You the Glory. I will give thanks and sing praise to You with all my heart according to Your righteousness and justice. I will tell about all Your wonders and marvelous deeds. You are my strength and my shield; I trust in You and I rejoice with song and dance. You lift me up and protect me from my enemies. I will bless You at all times. I place my hope in You and I wait expectantly for You, and praise You to the ends of the earth. Your right hand is full of righteousness, and I offer myself as a sacrifice of praise and thanksgiving. Love is the goal of my life. I am alive in my life because of Your grace. You are my Father, find me where You want me to be. I am supremely happy with You, now and forever. I am ever so grateful. In You, I move, I live, and have my being. Thank You Father. Amen.

30

PRAISE AS A SPIRITUAL PRACTICE

Praise. To proclaim the glory of God; to bless; celebrate; exalt; glorify; magnify; worship; to declare enthusiastic approval. The Akan symbol of the drum represents goodwill and elation, and its literal meaning is, 'the tension talking drum.' The sound of the drum intensifies the art of praise and worship.

Praise is service, devotion, and reverence to God. Praise is a celebration of the goodness of God. Praise and worship are an intentional act. Thinking of God's goodness produces feelings of joy, gratitude, and thankfulness. Joy and praise are inseparable. Joy is the energy that converts to praise. The scriptures affirm that a time is coming and is already here when the true worshipers will worship the Father in spirit [from the heart, the inner self] and in truth; for the Father seeks such people to be His worshipers. God is spirit [the Source of life, yet invisible to mankind], and those who worship Him must worship in spirit and truth (John

4:23-24 AMP). If you have something to be thankful for, you have cause to praise God.

There are numerous practices and rituals for praise and worship. Some cultures offer animal sacrifices as a demonstration of reverence and worship. During the season of Lent, Christians make personal sacrifices as a religious practice. The key element of praise and worship is that it is practiced with heart; You are our letter [of recommendation], written in our hearts, recognized and read by everyone. You show that you are a letter from Christ, delivered by us, written not with ink but with the Spirit of the living God, not on tablets of stone but on tablets of human hearts (2 Corinthians 3:2-3 AMP). Life is sacred, cultivate praise and worship as a lifestyle.

A friendly countenance gives God praise. Share a genuine gift of friendliness, and bring the Light of the Holy Spirit wherever you go. Praise is living with enthusiasm. Rejoice, brighten-up, and put on a smile. You have loved righteousness [integrity, virtue, uprightness in purpose] and have hated lawlessness [injustice, sin]. Therefore God, your God, has anointed you with the oil of gladness above your companions (Hebrews 1:9 AMP). When we praise God, we open ourselves up to the grace and goodness of the Holy Spirit.

Soul Inquiry

What does my countenance reveal about me?
What experiences bring me joy?
Do I have a grateful heart?
Am I happy to serve?

Am I joyful?

Why am I unhappy?

How and why do I stop being joyful?

What is my praise practice?

What does God require for praise and worship?

D. A. Williams

Soul Practice

Cultivate a feeling of thank-feel-ness as you wake, and carry it with you throughout the day. Take time to give God the praise and credit for everything. Be thankful for the simple things.

Give God the glory by always doing your best.

Demonstrate radical kindness to everyone you encounter.

Dance with the Divine – The art of dance and music is a practice of worship and devotion.

Smile – reset your attitude.

Be humble.

The purpose of life is to awaken, share your gift, celebrate life, and do what brings you joy. Joy is our natural state of communion with God. What if wherever we went, we brought joy to the present moment, and people felt happy, joyous, and peaceful in our presence. Make a difference in someone's day and feel the joy return to you.

How do you praise God? Develop your own spiritual practice.

Peace and Many Blessings

Prayer

Dear Father,

You are all knowing, the Source of all good, and the giver of all gifts. You are the essence of Wisdom, Intelligence, and Power. You are Love. You made the heavens and the Earth, and I am ever so grateful. I pray for my family and friends in need of Your Divine healing. With faith and Your power, all things are possible. Thank you for daily provisions, Keep us safe from ourselves and others. Forgive me when I fall from glory and remind me of the importance to forgive others. Give me peace above my understanding so that I can encourage others. You do great works through me, continue to guide and direct my path. Love is the goal of my life. I am alive in my life because of Your grace. You are my Father, find me where You want me to be. I am supremely happy with You, now and forever. I am ever so grateful. In You, I move, I live, and have my being. Thank You Father. Amen.

31

PRAYER AS A SPIRITUAL PRACTICE

Prayer. An earnest petition or spiritual communion with God; thanksgiving; the act or practice of praying to God; a religious observance, either public or private. The Akan symbol of strength, seat of power, fortress, and magnificence.

Prayer is our connection with God, and belief and expectation are key components. Prayer, belief, and expectation are close partners. Prayers are delayed by doubt, disbelief, and covetousness. You are jealous and covet [what others have] and your lust goes unfulfilled. You are envious and cannot obtain [the object of your envy]. You do not have because you do not ask [it of God] (James 4:2 AMP). Prayers are like seeds, only plant what you want to harvest. Would you expect to grow corn while planting cabbage? Have a clear idea of the harvest and water the seed with earnest prayer. Believe, affirm, expect the best, and see the end at the beginning. Everything we think, say, and do either enhances or weakens our prayers (seeds). Again, I say to you, that if two believers on earth agree [that is, are of one mind, in harmony] about anything that they ask [within the will of God], it will be done for them by My Father in heaven (Matthew 18:19 AMP).

Consider your prayer request in relation to your state of awareness. A high level of awareness is focused on a specific request. A low level of awareness pleads for help. Do not be anxious or worried about anything, but in everything [every circumstance and situation] by prayer and petition with thanksgiving, continue to make your [specific] requests known to God (Philippians 4:16 AMP). Monitor thoughts of fear, worry, and anxiety, that create feelings of desperation and fear. For my groaning comes at the sight of my food, and my cries [of despair] are poured out like water. "For the thing which I greatly fear comes upon me, and that of which I am afraid has come upon me (Job 3:24-25 AMP). Remove the fear and affirm your belief that all things are possible for the one who believes and trusts [in God] (Mark 9:23 AMP).

Affirming, asking, and believing, is prayer. An authentic pray is saying what you feel, not what you think – God is concerned with the heart, not the intellect. Reciting long prayers are unnecessary and pretentious (Luke 20:47 AMP). The Master taught us how to construct a simplistic form of prayer that includes recognition of God, requesting daily provisions, and forgiveness. When we do not know the words to pray, the Holy Spirit [comes to us and] helps us in our weakness. We do not know what prayer to offer or how to offer it as we should, but the Holy Spirit Himself [knows our need and at the right time] intercedes on our behalf with sighs and groanings too deep for words (Romans 8:26 AMP).

Prayer is talking with God, and we can never pray too much. With all prayer and petition, pray [with specific requests] at all times [on every occasion and in every season] in the Spirit, and with this in view, stay alert with all perseverance and petition [interceding in prayer] for all God's people (Ephesians 6:18 AMP). Pray for love, pray for strength, pray for purpose, pray for the sick, the homeless, the jobless, the addicted, pray for peace, pray for protection, pray for the grieving and lost; pray for family and friends. The Lord restored the fortunes of Job when he prayed for his friends, and the LORD gave Job twice as much as he had before (Job 42:10 AMP).

God is omnipotent, omniscience and omnipresent and knows what we want and need. Why pray for it? Ask and keep on asking and it will be given to you; seek and keep on seeking and you will find; knock and keep on knocking and the door will be opened to you. For everyone who keeps on asking receives, and he who keeps on seeking finds, and to him who keeps on knocking, it will be opened. Or what man is there among you who, if his son asks for bread, will [instead] give him a stone (Mathew 7:8 AMP)? And be persistent and devoted to prayer, being alert and focused in your prayer life with an attitude of thanksgiving (Colossians 4:12 AMP). Make prayer a part of your spiritual practice, and above all, be thankful.

Soul Inquiry

Am I intimate or separated from God?

How do I know God?

Can I expect God to fulfill my desires and not know Him?

Do I know the promises of God?

Am I aware?

Who am I?

Who is God?

Am I aware of my connection to God?

Do I pray from a state of gratitude or fear?

Who needs prayer?

Do I want God's help and guidance?

Soul Practice

Make your first contact of the day in communion with God. Meet the day in silent unity with God. Meeting the day is an opportunity to be present for a new day, welcoming the possibilities and good intentions on the day's activities. This [day in which God has saved me] is the day which the LORD has made; Let us rejoice and be glad in it (Psalm 118:24 AMP).

BELIEVE! All things are possible for the one who believes and trusts [in Me] (Mark 9:23 AMP).

What is your daily process of communicating with the Creator of the Universe; God? Develop your own spiritual practice.

Peace and Many Blessings

Prayer

Dear Father,

You will instruct me and teach me the way to go and You counsel me with Your Eye upon me. Create in me a clean heart, and renew a right, persevering, and steadfast spirit. My desire is to live in a way that honors You. My purpose is to bring peace to every person and place, and to help others grow stronger in faith. My purpose is to love—the kind of love demonstrated by kindness, mercy and compassion. Love that promotes what I know is right; my faith in You is real. Your Purpose is to help me know I am one with You. Use me for Your purposes, and protect me from all evil. You brought me here for a purpose and You make known the hidden places in my heart. I am willing and able to stand and to help others know that You are love, grace, and mercy. Your will be done. Love is the goal of my life. I am alive in my life because of Your grace. You are my Father, find me where You want me to be. I am supremely happy with You, now and forever. I am ever so grateful. In You, I move, I live, and have my being. Thank You Father. Amen

32

PURPOSE AS A SPIRITUAL PRACTICE

Purpose. The reason for which something exists or is done; an intended or desired result; the point at issue; resoluteness; intention, or goal for oneself. Akan symbol for greatness, affluence, power, and good character.

Who am I? Why am I here? How can I help? How can I serve? These critical questions are tied to purpose. The purpose of life experiences is to heighten awareness. Our purpose is to demonstrate the qualities of the Holy Spirit – peace, love, compassion, wisdom, and grace – right here, right now. We are here to fulfill a purpose with our gifts and talents. Purpose is mastered through practice. Since we have gifts that differ according to the grace given to us, each of us is to use them accordingly: if [someone has the gift of] prophecy, [let him speak a new message from God to His people] in proportion to the faith possessed; if service, in the act of serving; or he who teaches, in the act of teaching;

or he who encourages, in the act of encouragement; he who gives, with generosity; he who leads, with diligence; he who shows mercy [in caring for others], with cheerfulness (Romans 12:6-8 AMP). Be interested in the assignment you were called to do – and do it. Our purpose is to bring forth and manifest the best of who we are and to create peace. If you are at peace and have a sense of well-being, you are on purpose.

Who are you? Your true self is your inner being. Therefore, do not become discouraged [spiritless, disappointed, or afraid]. Though our outer self is [progressively] wasting away, yet our inner self is being [progressively] renewed day by day (2 Corinthians 4:16 AMP). To know God is to develop God-like qualities - *Soul Qualities*. The spirit (conscience) of man is the lamp of the LORD, Searching and examining all the innermost parts of his being (Proverbs 20:27 AMP). We are both human and divine, and the Divine takes human form to fulfill a purpose. Our purpose is to have the courage to develop the divinity within. When we know our mission and purpose, we utilize our resources efficiently and effectively. Find your purpose, and live it, knowing that you will be supported.

Develop a life purpose statement (LPS). A life purpose statement is not a goal. Goals are temporary, but God's purpose for His people is eternal. The LORD nullifies the counsel of the nations; He makes the thoughts and plans of the people ineffective. The counsel of the LORD stands forever, the thoughts and plans of His heart through all generations. Blessed [fortunate, prosperous, and favored by God] is the nation whose God is the LORD, the people whom He has chosen as His own inheritance (Psalm 33:10-12 AMP). God's purpose is generational.

An LPS provides a sense of direction. We are counseled: Consider well and watch carefully the path of your feet, and all your ways will be steadfast and sure (Proverbs 4:26 AMP). LPS places us on a path of moving in a direction that feels right. We are not required to know the end result, but we are required to plant the seed, and start the journey. LPS plants the seed. Prayer, affirmation, and praise, waters the seed. And God - the Source, will bring the harvest. And we know [with great confidence] that God [who is deeply concerned about us] causes all things to work together [as a plan] for good for those who love God, to those who are called according to His plan and purpose (Romans 8:28 AMP). *All* means unlimited possibilities and leaves nothing out.

Develop a process that feels right, and trust that you will be supported. But those who wait for the LORD [who expect, look for, and hope in Him] will gain new strength and renew their power; they will lift up their wings [and rise up close to God] like eagles [rising toward the sun]; they will run and not become weary, they will walk and not grow tired (Isaiah 40:31 AMP). God's plans and purposes are eternal and limitless.

Our core purpose in life is to serve others with our unique talents and gifts. Your gift could be singing, encouraging others, dancing, writing, cooking, painting, etc. Purpose is using your gift to serve others effortlessly and easily. Your talents bring others joy and also brings joy to your soul. Explore your interests and ask for guidance. The Creator instructs us and teaches us the way we should go, and guides us with His eye upon us (Psalm 32:8 AMP).

D. A. Williams

Soul Inquiry

What are my natural gifts and talents?

What do I do better than anyone?

How and when am I in touch with my inner being?

If money and time were not a concern, what would I do?

What activity gives me a sense of timeless awareness and places me in the zone?

What stirs my passion?

What is my life purpose?

Do I know what I want?

What and who am I building my life around?

Is God the center of my life? If not, why not?

Do I know what God wants me to do?

Soul Practice

Life Purpose Statement. What have you come to life to do? Develop a clear and articulate Life Purpose Statement. Write it down and post it where you can review it daily. Then, live it.

Being and Doing: Be aware of what you think, say, feel, and do, and work to bring them in alignment. Avoid double-mindedness – For such a person ought not to think or expect that he will receive anything [at all] from the Lord, being double-minded, unstable and restless in all his ways [in everything he thinks, feels, or decides] (James 1:7-8 AMP).

Affirmation: Why am I here? I am here to serve, inspire, love, and live the truth of who I am, and to do what brings me joy.

How do you live a conscious and meaningful life with purpose? Develop your own spiritual practice.

Peace and Many Blessings

Prayer

Dear Father,

You love righteousness and justice; the Earth is full of Your loving-kindness. Your loving-kindness is sweet and comforting; according to Your abundant mercy and love. Have mercy on me and show Your loving-kindness to Your people. For You are a God of justice. Blessed, happy, and fortunate are those who wait with Great expectation for You. You are kind and Your love endure forever. You instruct us to love our enemies and be kind and do well to and for others, expecting nothing. Our reward from You will be great, rich, strong, and abundant. You are the Most High, for You are charitable and good to the ungrateful, selfish, and wicked. You are my God, find me where you want me to be. I am supremely happy with You, now and forever. I am ever so grateful. In You, I move, I live, and have my being. Thank You God. Amen.

33

RELATIONSHIPS AS A SPIRITUAL PRACTICE

Relationship. The way in which two or more people or things are connected; the state of being related or interrelated; linkage; connection. Create relationships based on authenticity, love, and compassion. Akan symbol of brotherhood, safety, and solidarity.

Family is our greatest asset, and our best is achieved through relationships. Too often, relationships bring out the worst in us. At the level of the ego (easing God out), conditions are placed on how we love others. Loving others is based on our level of awareness. Unconditional love, transforms human love to Divine Love. The gap between human and Divine Love is an opportunity for change.

Relationships cause anxiety, pain, and uneasiness for a reason. The purpose of relationships is to heighten awareness – not make us happy. Being aware of how we respond to others, exposes core issues and provides opportunity to self-correct. We cannot love others if our cup is not full. We cannot give what we do not possess. When we are full-filled we give the overflow to others. Like a pebble thrown in a lake, the effects of our love ripple outward like waves, affecting all of our relationships. Divine Love is life giving nourishment, like the sunshine and the rain.

Human love is earned through reciprocity, and the person closest to us receives our attention. Human love is based on survival – survival of the ego. To protect the ego's position, we accuse, defend, attack, need to be right, argue, become angry and jealous; and have temper tantrums or refuse to communicate. Our demands to receive attention are in the name of love – human love. The more we identify with the ego – the more drama, discontent, discord and dysfunction we experience in relationships. These patterns of behavior are the ego's defense to get its needs met.

Divine Love is unearned. Love your neighbor and love your enemies. You have heard that it was said, 'You shall love your neighbor (fellow man) and hate your enemy.' But I say to you, love [that is, unselfishly seek the best or higher good for] your enemies and pray for those who persecute you, so that you may [show yourselves to] be the children of your Father who is in heaven; for He makes His sun rise on those who are evil and on those who are good, and makes the rain fall on the righteous [those who are morally upright] and the unrighteous [the unrepentant, those who oppose Him] (Matthew 5:43-45 AMP). To love on this level is a love between souls. To love your enemy requires a Higher Awareness; a God-Consciousness. Divine Love radiates, compassion, forgiveness, peace, humility, cooperation, and the fruits of the Spirit. But the fruit of the Spirit [the result of His presence within us] is love [unselfish concern for others], joy, [inner] peace, patience [not the ability to wait, but how we act while waiting], kindness, goodness, faithfulness, gentleness, self-control. Against such things there is no law (Galatians 5:22-23 AMP). Divine Love identifies with the heart and soul. The Holy Spirit is all about helping us to develop great relationships with self, family, and others.

How many people does it take to make your life a spiritual practice? You only need you – you make the change to transform self and others. You make the difference, 'You are the world' - you matter. You are one out of many.

Soul Inquiry

Who am I and why am I here?

Where are my relationships located on a continuum of human love and Divine Love?

Will my relationships survive without Divine Love?

Who receives the best of who I am?

Do I treat others with love, kindness, and respect?

Does my family find time to relate to one another?

Do I bribe my children or others with material objects to get what I want?

Am I able and willing to bring 100% of who I am to a relationship?

Who makes me a better person?

How can I impact the world?

Are my relationships based on material gain?

Can I give without expectation?

Do I know what I want and am I willing to ask for it?

D. A. Williams

Soul Practice

Affirmation: Namaste – I honor the place in you where we are One.

Envision positive interactions and encourage creativity in your relationships with self, family, friends, and coworkers. Guard against boredom and repetition. Journal the best possible scenario and live it.

Take 5 minutes and reflect on each of your relationships. What is unique about the relationship, and learn to appreciate that goodness. Take note of others who drain your energy and decide a course of action; limit, increase, or modify contact.

Affirmation: Through the mirror of relationship, I discover myself. I see the other in myself and myself in others (Chopra).

How do you demonstrate Divine Love in your relationships? Develop your own spiritual practice.

Peace and Many Blessings

Prayer

Dear Father,

Teach me how to reach out to those who are in need, and share their burdens. I live creatively and am created to do good works. I search for good, and find Your favor. I am not here to be served, but to help others. Teach me Your laws and show me the way in which I must walk and the work that I must do. I am glad for all Your planning for me and am patient and prayerful always. I explore who I am and the work you have given me, and I embrace it, not comparing myself with others. I take responsibility for doing the creative best I can with my life. You trained me to do all the good things that I have experienced. You are Blessed and You deliver me out of the hands of the enemy and into Your grace. You are Omnipotent, Omniscience, and Omnipresent – you are GREAT! You listen to me, advise me, and You are with me. The things that I am not able to do by myself, You send help. I am capable for the task ahead, hating dishonest gain. I am my brother's keeper and I help to bear their burdens – I am my brother. I do the thing that You command, and am willing and able to endure in peace. Your will be done. I am alive in my life because of Your grace. You are my Father, find me where You want me to be. I am supremely happy with You, now and forever. I am ever so grateful. In You, I move, I live, and have my being. Thank You Father, Amen.

34

RESPONSIBILITY AS A SPIRITUAL PRACTICE

Responsibility. Being accountable for something within one's power; having the power to control or manage. Akan symbol of unity, responsibility, brotherhood, and cooperation. Akan saying: We are linked in both life and death. Literal meaning: A chain, or a link.

Responsibility is one of the seven principles of Kwanzaa, a celebration of family, and community in the African American culture. Responsibility is to make our brother's and sister's problems our problems and to solve them together. I am my brother's keeper - I am my brother. No man is an island No man stands alone. Each man's joy is joy to me. Each man's grief is my own. We need one another, so I will defend each man as my brother. Each man as my friend (Joan Baez). We accomplish nothing by ourselves, someone helped us along the way.

The following short essay by William M. Elder, titled

Responsibility (Montapert) is succinct and eloquent in our responsibility to God, self, and others:

"I am responsible for the 24 hours of every day. How I use them and whether I abuse them concerns others as well as myself. Time is God given; I cannot do with it as I please. It belongs to all and I must share time with others. I am responsible for property, for money and for those things bought and sold, used and enjoyed, given and received. I did not create them; others have helped me to obtain them. I cannot use them alone; others are concerned. I am responsible for the development of my mental powers. My mind is my kingdom of opportunities. I am responsible for my religious development. I am spirit as well as flesh. Into me God breathed the breath of life; I am His breath. In Him I live and move and have my being. I am responsible for others. I cannot live in a vacuum. I must live among people my own age, among those who are younger, in the presence of those who are older. We live together; therefore, we have responsibilities toward one another. I am responsible for seeking to help to find my way through life. My help is friends, in literature, in the Bible, in communion with the Divine. All these will help me and I shall help others. I am a responsible human being."

We are responsible for our mental, physical, emotional and spiritual development. In addition, we contribute to the development of others. We are responsible for building and destroying others. For we [believers will be called to account and] must all appear before the judgment seat of Christ, so that each one may be repaid for what has been done in the body, whether good or bad [that is, each will be held responsible for his actions, purposes, goals, motives—the use or misuse of his time, opportunities and abilities] (2 Corinthians 5:10 AMP). Responsibility provides us an opportunity to leave every person, place, and thing in a restored condition. Did others experience joy, peace and love for knowing us? Or did we create sadness, anxiety and hate. Take responsibility, own your inappropriate behavior, and self-correct.

We do not live in a vacuum. We are measured by how we affect others. For every person will have to bear [with patience] his own burden [of faults and shortcomings for which he alone is responsible] (Galatians 6:5 AMP). Own your actions. Holding others responsible, is like giving your power away. All experiences are useful, use them as teachable moments. You may be the only goodness a person encounters today. Be responsible, shine your light, and make a difference. You know what you know to help someone else; be responsible for that.

Soul Inquiry

Who am I and why am I here?
Who did I encourage today?
Who did I serve today?
How did I create negativity? Or peace?
What were my negative and unkind thoughts, today?
How did I show kindness to others today?
How did I demonstrate love, compassion, and humility?
Do I claim responsibility only when I get caught?
Am I responsible human being?

D. A. Williams

Soul Practice

Affirmation: I will clean up after myself.

Journal the good and the not-so-good you participated in today (joy, sorrow, hate, love). Find ways to self-correct, going forward. Be aware how you affect the environment. As adults, we should clean up after ourselves, and teach those who come after us (children and youth). People learn by observing what we do, not what we say.

Be responsible for your intentions – why you do what you do. Intentions link to sowing and reaping; karma. If someone is causing pain to another, they are in pain. People can only respond at their level of awareness. When we know better, we do better. The key is to want to know and do better. Be a responsible human being.

How do you demonstrate responsible choice? Develop your own spiritual practice.

Peace and Many Blessings

Prayer

Dear Father,

I thank You for Your Divine Love, Light, Grace, Guidance, Mercy, and Protection. I am thankful for my life through which I am able to serve You. Use my mind, eyes, ears, hands and feet as an instrument of peace. Give me strength, patience, peace, and love that I may serve those in need. My desire is to serve others through You — Your will be done through me, today. You gave me spiritual gifts to serve You by serving others; the ability to give wise advice, special knowledge, the gift of great faith, the gift of healing, the gift to perform miracles, the ability to prophesy, the gift of discernment, and the ability to speak and interpret languages. I am ever so grateful for what You have given to me. I give and receive freely and I desire to live my highest potential. Love is the goal of my life. I am alive in my life because of Your grace. You are my Father, find me where You want me to be. I am supremely happy with You, now and forever. I am ever so grateful. In You, I move, I live, and have my being. Thank You Father. Amen

35

SERVICE AS A SPIRITUAL PRACTICE

Service. The action of helping or doing work for someone; contribution to the welfare of others; to provide someone with something that is needed or wanted; a helpful or useful act. The Akan symbol represents adaptability, toughness and selfless devotion to service. Changing one's self and playing many roles. Literal meaning: Twisting.

Service is the act of doing. Our highest honor to God is to live our best life and to serve others. In essence, we serve God by serving others. Service is giving more to life than what we take; leaving people, places, and situations better than we found them. The most powerful form of giving is nonmaterial (caring, compassion, attention, affection, appreciation, blessings, happiness, joy, laughter, compliments, prayer, smile, and love).

The term servant is perceived as low-ranking and unimportant. But service is the greatest gift we can offer.

Service and humility are partners. Let us not grow weary or become discouraged in doing good, for at the proper time we will reap, if we do not give in (Galatians 6:9 AMP). Serve others by being present for those in need. For by the grace [of God] given to me I say to every one of you not to think more highly of himself [and of his importance and ability] than he ought to think; but to think so as to have sound judgment, as God has apportioned to each a degree of faith [and a purpose designed for service] (Romans12:3 AMP). Quality service includes compassion, clarity, kindness, mindfulness, purpose, acceptance, nonjudgment, forgiveness, and authenticity – *soul qualities*. Service is communication between the heart and mind. Ask your Higher Self "What will you have me to do and say to create peace?"

Examine your life. Are you taking care of your physical body? Are you serving yourself to the best of your ability? Are you eating healthy, live food, drinking fresh water, breathing clean air, getting adequate movement and sleep? With service comes responsibility. Take care of you before attempting to take care of others. As a safety precaution, a flight attendant's instruction is apropos to serving others. If your energy is diminished, your service is detrimental – "put your oxygen mask on first before assisting others." We do our best service from a place of overflow.

What is your gift? What is your unique talent? What brings you joy? What is your passion? What activity creates a sense of timeless awareness? What do you do that places others in a state of joy and appreciation? Be dressed and ready for active service, and keep your lamps continuously burning. Be like men who are waiting for their master when he returns from the wedding feast, so that when he comes and knocks, they may immediately open the door for him. (Luke 12:34-36 AMP). Serve others with satisfaction, excellence, reverence, and creativity. Service is living your highest potential.

Soul Inquiry

Am I willing and able to serve others?

Am I willing and able to encourage others?

What is quality service?

When am I available to serve?

How can I do what I love and serve others?

What inhibits me from providing service to others?

Do my experiences serve my highest good?

What is my ideal vision of service?

What does my highest potential look like?

Am I my brother's keeper?

D. A. Williams

Soul Practice

Be a lighthouse by servicing others in need. Protect a child. Service elders by spending time reading, cooking a meal, running errands, and listening with compassion.

Shift your career to a calling. You are here to serve.

Give a gift to everyone you contact, today. The most powerful form of giving is nonmaterial (caring, compassion, attention, affection, appreciation, blessings, happiness, joy, laughter, compliments, prayer, smile, and love).

Write your obituary. Examine your life. Does your life serve you, God, and others? What do you want others to say about you when you transition? Going forward, live a life of excellence.

What is your process of living your highest potential and serving others? Develop your own spiritual practice.

Peace and Many Blessings

Prayer

Dear Father,

You are worthy of praise for Your power-filled acts and Your magnificent greatness. You set the mountaintops, sun, moon, and the morning star in place. The heavens praise You from all time to eternity. You are magnificent! Your radiance exceeds anything in the Earth and sky; You are GREAT, with limitless strength; Let every living, breathing creature praise You. Let my words be few, and Your power be revealed through Your Spirit. I take delight in You. You are All Mighty and Powerful and I look to You with joy. You hear my prayers and You help me do what I promised. Love is the goal of my life; I am alive because of Your Grace. You are my Father, find me where You want me to be. I am supremely happy with You, now and forever. I am ever so grateful. In You, I move, I live, and have my being. Thank You Father. Amen.

36

SIMPLICITY AS A SPIRITUAL PRACTICE

Simplicity. The quality of being easy to understand or use; the state or quality of being plain; not fancy or complicated; clearness in speaking or writing; sincerity. God is revealed in His creation – simplistic and beautiful. Akan symbol of providence and the divinity of Mother Earth.

The simplicity of nature supports and nourishes life. All creation has an invisible connection with the sun, moon, stars, earth and sky. God saw everything that He had made, and behold, it was very good and He validated it completely. And there was evening and there was morning, a sixth day (Genesis 1:31 AMP). The simplicity of love is compassion, patience, mindfulness and a peaceful approach to all things. Fellowship with God through nature by taking time to appreciate the sunrise, sunset, flowers, ocean, moon, mountain, air; God is in His Creation. Naturalness is simple and easy.

Simplicity is being clear and direct in communication with others. But I say to you, do not make an oath at all, either by heaven, for it is the throne of God; or by the earth, for it is the footstool of His feet; or by Jerusalem, for it is the City of the Great King. Nor shall you make an oath by your head, for you are not able to make a single hair white or black. But let your statement be, 'Yes, yes' or 'No, no' [a firm yes or no]; anything more than that comes from the evil one (Matthew 5:34-37 AMP). All of nature is simple and direct - except humans. We say one thing and mean another. Simplicity is living with purpose, asking and answering questions free of deception.

Practice doing your best; practice makes mastery a reality. Study and do your best to present yourself to God approved, a workman [tested by trial] who has no reason to be ashamed, accurately handling and skillfully teaching the word of truth (2 Timothy 2:15 AMP). Giving your best is simple because your best depends on how you feel in the present moment. If you were asked to do fifty pushups in five minutes, the best you may be able to do is ten. Overtime, your best will improve with practice - practice makes the master.

Soul Inquiry

Do I express myself clearly and directly?

What are the simple requests that would make life more enjoyable?

What inspires me?

How much of my life is mine?

What consumes my day?

List five things that would simplify my life.

What distracts me from what's important?

How much time do I spend doing the things I like to do?

How much time daily do I spend with God?

Am I in tune with natural cycle?

Soul Practice

Discover the things that you like that make you happy, and find and make time to do them. Allow at least one hour per day to do what pleases you.

Make God a priority. For 90 days, fellowship with God twenty minutes in the morning and twenty minutes in the evening. Imagine how life will change when you give God a percentage of your time.

Simplify your life; what are the top five things that would provide you with peace and serenity.

Take a digital holiday, no cellphone, emails, or social media. In a multi-tasking society, it's rare to have a conversation uninterrupted by a cellphone. When we give our undivided attention, it shows the other that they matter, and we 'see' them.

Evaluate what is meaningful in your daily life. Family, close friends, love, and laughter are the simple things that matter. The simple things are easy to do, and easy not to do. Cook and eat at least one healthy meal with your family; pray; get up early to meet the day and see the sunrise; take a walk and admire nature (God is in His Creation); read an inspiring book; show a child a new skill; write a letter; visit a friend.

How do you live a simple, meaningful life? Develop your own spiritual practice.

Peace and Blessings

Prayer

Dear Father,

Your grace transforms my thinking and restores my mind. I am becoming the person You created me to be and I am grateful for Your patience and love. I move toward what I dwell on, and I become what I think about; I am victorious. My thoughts are on whatever is true, whatever is worthy of reverence and is honorable and right, whatever is just, whatever is pure, whatever is lovely and lovable, whatever is kind and pleasant and gracious. My thoughts are on virtue and excellence, I praise You. When I dwell upon Your goodness, I become good and right. You are encouragement and oxygen to my soul. I put into practice what I learn, and my desire is to know what is good and pleasing to You. Love is the goal of my life. I am alive in my life because of Your grace. You are my Father, find me where You want me to be. I am supremely happy with You, now and forever. I am ever so grateful. In You, I move, I live, and have my being. Thank You Father. Amen.

37

THOUGHT AS A SPIRITUAL PRACTICE

Thought. An idea, plan, opinion, or picture, that is formed in the mind; the act of carefully thinking about the details of something. Thought is energy. Think on good things. You become what you think about repeatedly. Akan symbol of wisdom, knowledge and forethought. Literal meaning: What I hear, I keep, I understand.

Be conscious of your thoughts, because thinking identifies core issues. We become what we think about. For as we think in our heart, so we are [in behavior] (Proverbs 23:7 AMP). The condition of our heart is determined by our thoughts and emotions. We can change our heart by changing our thinking.

The mind is like a garden; thoughts are seeds planted in the heart that manifest in our life. The creation process begins with thought, and seeds produce according to their kind. The earth sprouted and abundantly produced vegetation, plants yielding seed according to their kind, and trees bearing fruit with seed in them, according to their kind; and God saw that it was good and He affirmed and sustained it (Genesis 1:12 AMP). What kind of seeds are you planting?

We fertilize our thought seeds, by thinking on good things. Finally believers, whatever is true, whatever is honorable and worthy of respect, whatever is right and confirmed by God's word, whatever is pure and wholesome, whatever is lovely and brings peace, whatever is admirable and of good repute; if there is any excellence, if there is anything worthy of praise, think continually on these things [center your mind on them, and implant them in your heart] (Philippians 4:8 AMP). Thinking on good things encourages us and is oxygen to the soul. Thought and awareness are close partners, and we can only change what is in the scope of our awareness. Thought causes the invisible to become visible – from nowhere to now here. We delay our good with doubt, fear, and double-mindedness. Master your thought life.

Deceptive intelligence is the negative mental chatter of the mind. Thoughts of anger, jealousy, division, shame, blame, and guilt are the cause of stress and dis-ease in the mind and body. Deceptive intelligence is the activity of the ego whose purpose is to keep us from peace. The thief comes only in order to steal and kill and destroy. I came that you may have and enjoy life, and have it in abundance [to the full, till it overflows] (John 10:10 AMP). We can choose not to interact with mental chatter and focus on thoughts that create a positive future vision. Think about the things you want to see. Be transformed and progressively changed [as you mature spiritually] by the renewing of your mind [focusing on godly values and ethical attitudes], so that you may prove [for yourselves] what the will of God is, that which is good and acceptable and perfect [in His plan and purpose for you] (Romans 12:2 AMP).

In *The Spontaneous Fulfillment of Desire*, Chopra's third principle of synchro-destiny is mastering your inner dialogue. First step to mastery is awareness. We are what we think all day long. Think on good things such as: Wisdom, Joy, Peace, Freedom, Kindness, Goodness, Faithfulness, Gentleness, Self-Control, Virtue, Knowledge, Trust, Courage, Balance, Right Action, Simplicity, Bliss, Oneness, Willingness, Reciprocity, Truth, Faith, Hope, Heaven, Understanding, Goodwill, Vitality, Empathy, Compassion, Wholeness, Serenity, Divinity, Creativity, Beauty, Strength, Energy, Wholeness, Service, Authenticity, Acceptance, Confidence, Inspiration, Encouragement, Gratitude, Mindfulness, Abundance, Peace, Justice, Happiness, Praise, Honor, Kindness, Harmony, Compassion, Cooperation, Honesty, Prayer, Victory, Purpose, Discipline, Order, Balance. Grace, Liberty, Enlightenment, Intelligence, Patience, Prosperity, Honesty, Integrity, Excellence, and Above All - Love. Love is the fulfillment of the Law; God is LOVE.

Soul Inquiry

What do I think of myself?
Who am I and why am I here?
Am I aware of the mental chatter in the mind?
What do I think about where I am?
What am I thinking and is it to my benefit?
Are my thoughts habitual?
What is the cause of my inner disturbances?

Soul Practice

Mental Health Plan. Thought is energy. Clear the mind of daily debris from past experiences and future fears, with affirmations and deep breathing exercises. Decide what you want and act as if you have it by bringing thoughts, speech, and actions into alignment. Journal your Ideal Scene or create a vision board and review it often. Renewing the mind is a process, and it takes time to reprogram.

Affirmation: My thoughts decide my destiny. I move toward what I dwell on, and I become what I think about. I am victorious. The way I think determines how I live. I am as great as my highest thought. My life is lived from the inside out.

Affirmation: I am totally independent of the good and bad opinions of others. I am beneath no one. I am fearless in the face of any and all challenges.

Affirmation: I AM GREAT – Integrity, All Manifesting, Graciously, Rising, Evolving, All Together. I Am Great both human and Divine, Thank You for aspiration.

How do you harness the power of your thoughts? Develop your own spiritual practice.

Peace and Many Blessings

Prayer

Dear Father,

You are my Rock, my Fortress, and my Deliverer, I will not be afraid. What can man do to me? You are my God, my Strength and my protection. I rely on You and I put my trust in You. I lean on, trust in, and am confident in You. In all my ways I know, recognize, and acknowledge You. Your way is perfect and has been tested and tried. Guide, direct, and make straight and plain my path. I trust You from the bottom of my heart and I listen for Your voice in everything I do, and everywhere I go. You are the One who will keep me on track. I know Your mercy and have experienced Your kindness. I lean on and confidently put my trust in You, for You have not abandoned me. I seek and inquire of You out of necessity. You are my Father and I am supremely happy with You now and forever. I am ever so grateful. In You, I move, I live, and have my being. Thank You Father, Amen.

38

TRUST AS A SPIRITUAL PRACTICE

 Trust. A belief that someone or something is reliable, good, honest, and effective; assured reliance on the character, ability, strength, or truth of someone or something. The two-headed crocodile is the Akan symbol for unity and oneness.

Trust is a positive assumption that what you believe and expect will happen, with no evidence you will be supported. Trust is taking a risk, and believing what you cannot see with the physical eyes. To trust is to know and to feel.

Self-trust is the foundation of all trust. If we do not trust ourselves, we will not trust others. Self-trust is paramount in identifying and practicing our gifts and talents. Our purpose is to share our gift with humanity. The scriptures identify the gifts given by the Holy Spirit : To one is given through the [Holy] Spirit [the power to speak] the message of wisdom, and to another [the power to express] the word of knowledge and understanding according to the same

Spirit; to another [wonder-working] faith [is given] by the same [Holy] Spirit, and to another the [extraordinary] gifts of healings by the one Spirit; and to another the working of miracles, and to another prophecy [foretelling the future, speaking a new message from God to the people], and to another discernment of spirits [the ability to distinguish sound, godly doctrine from the deceptive doctrine of man-made religions and cults], to another various kinds of [unknown] tongues, and to another interpretation of tongues (1 Corinthians 12:8-10 AMP). There are many variations of gifts, and our gift is as unique as our thumbprint. Our gift/talent is our soul's calling to serve God, others, and Self. What does a gift look like and how will you know it is a gift?

- Your activities are gratifying
- Your desire is to help and serve others
- Your unique talent satisfies a need
- You experience timeless awareness
- You experience joy
- You are not burdened by your task
- You share your awareness with others

Trusting Self is the segue into trusting God. Trust in and rely confidently on the LORD with all your heart and do not rely on your own insight or understanding. In all your ways know and acknowledge and recognize Him and He will make your paths straight and smooth [removing obstacles that block your way] (Proverbs 3:5-6 AMP). We trust ourselves to know that God is our Source and He supplies all our needs, according to His riches and glory.

Trust the process of life. Put a process together and trust

that it will work. Ask for the guidance of the Holy Spirit, listen for directions. He will most certainly be gracious to you at the sound of your cry for help; when He hears it, He will answer you. Your ears will hear a word behind you, "This is the way, walk in it," whenever you turn to the right or to the left (Isaiah 30:19, 21 AMP).

Trust that God is in control and wants to give you the desires of your heart.

Explore your interests and visualize the things you love to do and do them. You know the things that you do better than anyone else. Develop self-trust, trust God, and trust the process of life.

Soul Inquiry

Who do I trust and why?
Do I trust myself?
Do I trust God?
Can God trust me?
What are my gifts and talents?

Soul Practice

Trust your process. Here is a simple process in developing trust in yourself and God. Does it feel right? Do your best, and have good intentions:

- Have a good thought about yourself
- Believe it (no fear, doubt, or negative dialogue)
- Develop a plan that includes your gift /talent
- Give the plan to God
- Ask for guidance from God
- Put forth a disciplined effort
- Be thankful

When in doubt, repeat the process.

God Jar (Vanzant): You will need a mason jar (if you choose, decorate it). After you've done all you can do about a concern, write the concern on a small piece of paper, fold the paper, and place the paper in the God Jar. Surrender your request to God. When you are anxious, affirm: "God is taking care of it. The LORD will accomplish that which concerns me; Your [unwavering] lovingkindness, O LORD, endures forever" (Psalm 138:8 AMP). Don't forget to thank God when your desires and requests manifest.

How do you trust the process of life? How do you share your unique talents and gifts with others? Develop your own spiritual practice.

Peace and Many Blessings

Prayer

Dear Father,

With Your guidance, I can accomplish all You have in store for me. Where there is no wise guidance, I fall from grace, and when I listen and heed Your counsel, I am safe. What will You have me to do? I follow all Your directions. I love and worship You with all my heart and soul. Remember, O God, Your tender mercy and loving-kindness; for they are everlasting. All Your paths are merciful and steadfast, and Your truth and faithfulness are for those who keep Your covenant. You are reverently feared and worshiped. You teach me the way I should choose. Show me Your ways, and teach me Your paths. Guide me in Your truth and faithfulness for You are the God of my salvation; I wait on You expectantly all the day long. I am supremely happy with You, now and forever. I am ever so grateful. You are my Father, find me where you want me to be. In You, I move, I live, and have my being. Thank You Father. Amen.

39

VISION AS A SPIRITUAL PRACTICE

Vision. An image created by the imagination, having no objective reality; discernment, insight, perceptiveness; wisdom; preparation and readiness for the future. Akan symbol of fortitude and preparedness to face the changes of life.

Where there is no vision, the people perish (Proverbs 29:18 AMP).

Vision is a deeper awareness – not a five-sensory experience. We are advised that: It shall come about after this that I shall pour out My Spirit on all mankind; and your sons and your daughters will prophesy, your old men will dream dreams, your young men will see visions (Joel 2:28 AMP). Prophetic visions are messages sanctioned by God and serve a Divine purpose. The Holy Spirit continues to reveal future events to us for guidance, protection, and revelation.

We are blessed with the ability to think, create,

commune with the Holy Spirit, and endowed with a Higher vision. God's promise is to give us the desires of our heart when we seek (aim at, strive after) His kingdom and His righteousness [His way of doing and being right—the attitude and character of God], and all things will be given to us (Matthew 6:33 AMP).

The visioning process begins with the mind. God communes with us, through our mind; from thought to heart to soul. You will instruct us and teach us in the way we should go; and You will counsel us [who are willing to learn] with Your eye upon us (Psalm 32:8 AMP). In addition, we connect to God in nature, through others, and through spiritual practice. The Holy Spirit is always available, and is as close to us as our breath.

We create our best life through a vision. Have a vision of peace, patience, love, kindness, and mindfulness – practice *Soul Qualities* until you reach your ideal, and be passionate about the future. Do not allow others to create your vision – create your own. Choose a positive future vision, devoid of egotistical, self-centered goals. Ego's only concern is the 'I'; make choices for the good of all. Do not reduce the scope of your vision because others don't understand. Your vision is between you and God. The vision God has for you is more than you can imagine.

Our present actions link to our future. God's Kingdom manifests in the present, through what we think, say, and do. But first and most importantly seek (aim at, strive after) His kingdom and His righteousness [His way of doing and being right—the attitude and character of God], and all these things will be given to you also (Matthew 6:33 AMP). All things are possible for the one who believes and trusts [in

God] (Mark 9:23 AMP). Have a great expectation, and keep your vision in the forefront of your mind. The Kingdom of God is the promise of an ideal future – the Highest vision for mankind.

Soul Inquiry

What is my vision for self, family, community, and world?

Are there others who benefit from my vision?

Do I sense a Divine design for my life?

Can I imagine achieving all that I desire and more?

Does my vision involve God's Divine purpose?

What are the promises of God?

Do I live as if God really matters?

What percentage of my attention per day do I give to my vision?

Where am I on my spiritual journey?

What do I want to achieve spiritually in the next six months?

What is my ideal scene and can I trust that my vision is reachable?

Soul Practice

Family Vision: In weekly or monthly family meetings, take the opportunity to discuss a family vision. Select a specific theme, and encourage full participation. A family vision manifests when all members are viewed as stakeholders. Family visioning creates a sense of oneness and cohesiveness within the family.

Enlarge your vision. Create a vision board and review it daily. Spend ten minutes in the morning and ten minutes at night on visioning. Visioning is seeing all possibilities of your ideal life. Develop a natural sense of passion and love for your vision.

What does your vision look like for yourself and family, and does it include God? Develop your own spiritual practice.

Peace and Many Blessings

Prayer

Dear Father,

Give me wisdom. Your every word is a treasure of knowledge and understanding. You are my protection and You guard my pathway. You show me how to distinguish right from wrong, and how to find the right decision every time. Wisdom and truth enter the center of my being, filling my life with joy. I desire my actions to be aligned with Your Divine will for my life. Help me to stay on course so that whatever Your will is for me, I am willing and able to accomplish it with knowingness and ease. Give me the wisdom to follow my heart, examine the quality of my intent, and act with love. Give me the wisdom and discipline to set a routine, and to live to honor You. Balance my physical, mental, emotional, and spiritual Self to glorify You. Your will be done. I am supremely happy with You, now and forever. I am ever so grateful. You are my Father, find me where you want me to be. In You, I move, I live, and have my being. Thank You Father. Amen.

40

WISDOM AS A
SPIRITUAL PRACTICE

Wisdom. The quality or state of being wise; knowledge of what is true or right coupled with right action; understanding; discernment and insight; wise sayings or teachings. Akan symbol of wisdom, ingenuity, intelligence, and patience. Akan saying – A knot made with wisdom can only be undone by the wise and not the fool.

Wisdom is discernment, comprehension, intuition, and interpretation. Through study, experience, and wisdom, there are four areas that increase the quality of life. When these areas are aligned, we experience oneness and wholeness. Alignment is being in harmony with what we think, say, and do. Mental, emotional, physical, and spiritual alignment creates total well-being. If we focus our attention on one area, the other areas atrophy. Wisdom is living on all levels and striking a balance. Wisdom and balance are close partners.

Physical level of awareness consists of the five senses; it is the base level of our experience. We are more knowledgeable and less wise in this area. The basics for optimal health in this area: eat fresh vegetables, drink clean water, breathe fresh air; get adequate sleep and physical activity. Daily Suggestions: 30 minutes of conscious deep breathing of fresh air; consume plain water; eat 6-8 fresh fruits/vegetables; 30 minutes of conscious exercise (walk, bike, jog, swim).

Mental level of awareness consists of our internal thoughts. Thoughts are things and create our experiences. Listen to your internal dialogue and filter out thoughts that you know are not true about you. Replace negative thoughts by affirming your good and the good you expect. Affirmations change your mental programming. Study and do your best to present yourself to God approved, a workman [tested by trial] who has no reason to be ashamed, accurately handling and skillfully teaching the word of truth (2 Timothy 2:15 AMP). Recurring thoughts and ideas may be the activity of the Holy Spirit.

Emotional level of awareness consists of an internal energy system. The heart is part of that energy system - not the physical heart, but the feeling heart. The scripture counsels: Watch over your heart with all diligence, for from it flow the springs of life (Proverbs 4:23 AMP). Masking emotions with food, sleep, drugs, shopping, and nonessential activity is unwise. Keep the heart open and acknowledge what you feel when you feel. Emotions are messages from the soul.

Spiritual level of awareness consists of our connection with God; our Source. Develop a personal relationship with God through daily practice of prayer, meditation, acts of faith, kindness, and living spiritual principles – *soul qualities*. Wisdom is the principal and most important thing. The beginning of wisdom is: Get [skillful and godly] wisdom [it is preeminent]! And with all your acquiring, get understanding [actively seek spiritual discernment, mature comprehension, and logical interpretation] (Proverbs 4:7 AMP).

Soul Inquiry

Did I honor my agreements with myself and others?
Did I honor my feelings throughout the day?
What things did I do today that I could do better?
Who did I share my knowledge with today?
Who did I serve today?
What were the things I did well?
Did I celebrate my successes?
What am I willing to work on tomorrow?
Did I ask for guidance and follow it?
Did I give thanks for the guidance I received?

Soul Practice

Develop a regimen and live on all levels (physical, mental, emotional, and spiritual) for optimal wellness. You will need a journal to record your progress. Establish a baseline for the next 30 days, then set goals. You cannot change behavior if you are unaware. Chart your progress and adjust your activities. It takes disciplined obedience to live your best life. Change takes time. Be gentle with yourself.

How do you demonstrate wisdom in every area of your life? Develop your own spiritual practice.

Peace and Many Blessings

ADINKRA SYMBOLS

Adinkra is an art form that originated with the Akan people in Ghana, one of the largest ethnic groups in West Africa. The Adinkra symbols reflect traditions, proverbs, philosophy and values of the Akan people and have multiple meanings or translations. Adinkra cloth is traditionally hand painted and stamped, however, through social change and modern technology, the textile industry has popularized Adinkra cloth. Today the cloth may be seen on furniture, home, décor, clothing, jewelry, cards, and body art. Many are fascinated by the bold geometric design of the art form, and unaware of the spiritual and cultural meanings of the symbols.

Symbols are powerful. An Adinkra symbol was selected to coincide with a *Soul Quality* to demonstrate the timeless, spiritual meaning of each of the principles in *Soul Qualities: The Art of Becoming.*

SOUL. The Adinkra symbol Sunsum (soon-soom) An immaterial force that gives the body life, energy, and power; spirit; life; vitality; being; essence. The Akan symbol of the Soul. The symbol of spirituality, spiritual purity, and the cleanliness of the soul.

ACCEPTANCE as a Spiritual Practice. The Adinkra symbol Akoma Ntoaso- (ah-ko-mah n-to-as-so) – favorable reception; agreement and togetherness in thought and deed. Akan symbol of joined and united hearts.

AFFIRMATION as a Spiritual Practice. The Adinkra symbol Akoben (ah-ko-ben) – call to action, readiness; the assertion that something exists or is true. The Akan symbol represents a War Horn.

AUTHENTICITY as a Spiritual Practice. The Adinkra symbol Nsaa (n-sah) – real and genuine; not copied or false; fully trustworthy. Akan saying: He who does not know the real design will turn to an imitation.

AWARENESS as a Spiritual Practice. The Adinkra symbol Nyame Dua (n-yah-may doo-ah) – the state or condition of being aware; having knowledge; informed and alert. Awareness of and connection to God. Akan symbol of the presence of God and of God's protection.

BALANCE as a Spiritual Practice. The Adinkra symbol Krapa (khe-rap-ah) – a state of equilibrium; equal distribution of weight. Akan symbol of spiritual balance, good fortune, and spiritual strength.

CHOICE as a Spiritual Practice. The Adinkra symbol Mate Masie (mah-tee mah-see-uh) – being obedient; taking care of Self and making good choices. Akan symbol of wisdom, knowledge, and forethought.

CLARITY as a Spiritual Practice. The Adinkra symbol Mframadan (m-fra-mah-dan) – the quality of being easily understood in an exact way; being clear. Akan symbol of fortitude preparedness and readiness to face challenges and weather the storm.

COMMITMENT as a Spiritual Practice. The Adinkra symbol Fi-Hankra (fee-han-krah) – a promise to give or do something; to be loyal. Akan symbol of brotherhood, completeness, and solidarity; commitment to family and community.

COURAGE as a Spiritual Practice. The Adinkra symbol Akofena (ah-ko-fe-nah) – the ability to face difficulty, danger, and pain without fear; bravery; fearlessness. Akan symbol represents legitimized authority, heroic deeds, and courageous acts.

CREATIVITY as a Spiritual Practice. The Adinkra symbol Ananse Ntontan (ah-nan-se n-to-n-tan) – craftiness; the use of the imagination; original ideas; vision and inspiration. Akan symbol represents a spider demonstrating its resourcefulness and creativity by weaving an intricate and elaborate web for survival.

DETACHMENT as a Spiritual Practice. The Adinkra symbol Bi-nka-bi (bee-in-ka-bee) – freedom, peace, and avoidance of conflict. Akan saying: Bite not one another.

DISCIPLINE as a Spiritual Practice. The Adinkra symbol Ani bre a gya (auh-ne bree ah jah) – self-containment; self-discipline; and self-sensory. Self-mastery requires discipline – and discipline comes from doing. Akan saying: Seriousness of one's deeds is demonstrated by one's actions, not appearance.

EVOLUTION as a Spiritual Practice. The Adinkra symbol Nyame Nwu Na mawu (n-yah-may n-woo nah mah-woo) – a process of gradual growth, progressive change, and development. Spiritual evolution is living the qualities of the soul. Akan symbol represents the perpetual existence of man's spirit.

FAITH as a Spiritual Practice. The Adinkra symbol Nsoroma (n-soar-row-mah) – having confidence and trust; the belief and dependency on a Supreme Being. Akan saying: I AM a child of the Supreme Being; I do not depend on myself. My illumination is only a reflection of His.

FORGIVENESS as a Spiritual Practice. The Adinkra symbol Mpatapo (m-pah-tah-poh) – to pardon an offense or debt; to cease resentment. Akan symbol represents a knot of reconciliation, peace-making, and hope.

FREEDOM as a Spiritual Practice. The Adinkra symbol Adinkrahene (ah-dink-kra-hen-knee) – the absence of coercion or constraint in choice or action; liberty. Akan symbol represents authority and greatness.

GRACE as a Spiritual Practice. The Adinkra symbol Nyame Nti (n-yah-may n-tee) – simple elegance; the free and unmerited favor of God; the unexpected bestowal of Blessings. Literal meaning: By God's Grace.

GRATITUDE as a Spiritual Practice. The Adinkra symbol Bese Saka (bes-e sah-ka) – being thankful; appreciation; sharing the overflow with others. The cola nut represents power, abundance, affluence, and expresses admiration and good will. Akan symbol of affluence, power, and abundance.

HUMILITY as a Spiritual Practice. The Adinkra symbol Dwennimmen (djwin-knee-mann) – humbleness; meekness; and modesty. Akan proverb: The ram may bully, not with its horns but with its heart.

INTENTION as a Spiritual Practice. The Adinkra symbol Nyame Biribi Wo Soro (n-yah-may Bear-ree-bee who soh-row – an aim or purpose; the thing you plan to do or achieve. Intention implies action. Literal meaning: God there is something in the heavens!

KINDNESS as a Spiritual Practice. The Adinkra symbol S E Ne Tekrama (s-e knee teh-kra-mah) – considerate and helpful; humane; passionate affection for Self and others. Akan symbol for the need for friendliness, like the teeth and the tongue.

LOVE as a Spiritual Practice. The Adinkra symbol Akoma (ah-ko-mah) – unselfish, loyal, and compassionate concern for the good of another; good will, patience, faithfulness, and fondness. Literal meaning: The Heart.

MEDITATION as a Spiritual Practice. The Adinkra symbol Gye Nyame (jeh N-yah-mee) - to engage in thought; reflection; devout religious contemplation or spiritual introspection; to intend; silence within the mind, body, and spirit. Akan symbol for Supreme Being, meaning 'Tis God Only.'

MINDFULNESS as a Spiritual Practice. The Adinkra symbol Fafanto (fa-fan-taw) – gentleness; discernment; consideration; and awareness of the present moment. The butterfly is the Akan symbol of tenderness, gentleness, honesty, and fragileness.

NONJUDGMENT as a Spiritual Practice. The Adinkra symbol Fofo (foo-foo) – not forming an opinion; the ability not to judge. The Akan symbol is a warning against jealousy and covetousness, which is unbecoming of good citizenship.

ORDER as a Spiritual Practice. The Adinkra symbol Mmara Krado (m-mah-rah crar-dough) – order suggests a straightening out so as to eliminate confusion; to arrange. order is the first law of the Universe.

PATIENCE as a Spiritual Practice. The Adinkra symbol Osram (o-srahm) – an ability or willingness to suppress restlessness or annoyance when confronted with delay. Akan proverb: It takes the moon sometime to go around the nation.

PEACE as a Spiritual Practice. The Adinkra symbol Mpatapo (m-pah-tah-poh) – a state of mutual harmony between people or groups; the mind free from annoyance, distraction, and anxiety. Akan symbol represents a knot of reconciliation forming a tight bond after a disagreement.

PERSEVERANCE as a Spiritual Practice. The Adinkra symbol Wawa Aba (wah-wah ah-ba) – persistence in a course of action in spite of difficulties; hardiness; and toughness. The Akan symbol represents the hard seed of the wawa tree that is used for carving.

PRAISE as a Spiritual Practice. The Adinkra symbol Dono (dough-no) – celebration, praise, goodwill, and rhythm. The Akan symbol represents the tension talking drum. The sound of the drum intensifies the art of praise and worship.

PRAYER as a Spiritual Practice. The Adinkra symbol Aban (ah-ban) - spiritual communion with God; thanksgiving. Akan symbol represents strength, seat of power, authority and magnificence; Great Fortress.

PURPOSE as a Spiritual Practice. The Adinkra symbol Nkurumah Kesee (n-kroo-mah Keh-see) – the reason for which something exists; an intended or desired result. Akan symbol represents greatness of purpose and good character.

RELATIONSHIPS as a Spiritual Practice. The Adinkra symbol Fi-Hankra (fee-han-krah) – the way in which two or more people or things are connected; linkage; connection. Akan symbol represents brotherhood, safety, security, and solidarity.

RESPONSIBILITY as a Spiritual Practice. The Adinkra symbol Nkon Osnk Nkon Osnk (corn-song-corn-song) – the way in which two or more people or things are connected; linkage. Akan saying: We are linked in both life and death. Those who share common blood never break apart.

SERVICE as a Spiritual Practice. The Adinkra symbol Nkyinkyin (n-chin-chin) – the action of helping or doing work for someone; contributing to the welfare of others. Akan symbol represents selfless devotion to service and ability to withstand hardships.

SIMPLICITY as a Spiritual Practice. The Adinkra symbol Asase Ye Duru (Ah-sa-see yeah doo-roo) – the quality of being easy to understand; plain, not fancy. The Akan symbol represents divinity of the Earth; nature.

THOUGHT as a Spiritual Practice. The Adinkra symbol Mate Masie (mah-tee mah-see-uh) – an idea, plan, opinion, or picture that is formed in the mind. Akan symbol represents wisdom and knowledge. Akan saying: What I hear, I keep, I understand.

TRUST as a Spiritual Practice. The Adinkra symbol Funtummireku (fun-tum-me-rek-koo) – a belief that someone or something is reliable, good, honest; assured reliance on character and strength of someone or something. The Akan symbol of oneness, unity, and cooperation represented by a two-headed crocodile.

VISION as a Spiritual Practice. The Adinkra symbol Mframadan (m-fra-mah-dan) – a conception or image created by the imagination having no objective reality; discernment and insight. Akan symbol of fortitude, excellence, and preparedness to face life's challenges.

WISDOM as a Spiritual Practice. The Adinkra symbol Nyansapo (n-yahn-sah-poh) – the quality or state of being wise; knowledge of what is true coupled with right action. The Akan symbol represents the wisdom Knot; the wisdom of intelligence, ingenuity, and patience.

SOUL INQUIRY. The Adinkra symbol Hwehwemudua (scheweb-scheweb-meu-doo-ah) - The Akan symbol of a measuring rod indicates excellence, quality, and critical examination. Test and evaluate yourselves to see whether you are in the faith and living your lives as committed believers (2 Corinthians 13:5 AMP).

FAQ'S: SOUL MATTERS

How do you remain authentic and not drift back into pretense?

Stay in the moment, forgive yourself, and forgive others. See others as an extension of your true self. Namaste – I honor the place in you where we are one.

How are we connected to God?

We are connected to God via our soul. God is the Source and our soul is connected to God. We can allow God to lead us to Higher Awareness – the soul. Through the soul, the Higher Self, we have the ability to *see* unlimited possibilities available to us by incorporating *soul qualities* into daily life through the Power of the Holy Spirit.

How can we allow God qualities to take precedence in our life?

A spiritual discipline or principle can assist in where to start your practice. Choose a principle that feels right for you. Contemplate the principle and think of activities that demonstrate the principle. Ask for guidance from the Holy Spirit and when received, do/be the principle without expectation, reward, or acknowledgement from others. Repeat the practice, and be consistent for at least 5-7 days. Ask the question, "What will you have me to do?" Then, follow the energy of the principle.

Why do I attract drama and discontent in my life?

No one intentionally chooses drama, jealousy, revenge, anger, and unkindness. We default to lower level emotions/vibrations from past conditioning and ego-driven attitudes of needing to be right and perceived power over others. Drama is the instrument of the ego. Imagine what would happen if we stopped the drama? Drama would cease to exist. We don't let go of drama because we are not aware of the hold the ego has on our thoughts of past conditioning and our addiction to drama. When we become aware, we watch how our past conditioning affects our present emotions. We can decide to react to drama or we can choose an alternative that is soul-driven – compassion, kindness, love, mercy, acceptance, and non-judgment. Our conscious choices move us closer to the ego or the soul. Track your patterns of behavior and be willing and able to make better choices by being aware and open to change.

What is the goal of a spiritual life?

The goal of a spiritual life is peace, forgiveness, love and freedom. With peace comes many soul qualities; compassion, love, mercy, humility, and a connection with the Divine – God. You remember why you have come to the planet; to do what makes you happy - to serve – to love and to do what brings you joy. To be who you were created to be.

Who are you at the soul level, at your core?

At the soul level we are peace, compassion, humility, kind, mindful, and an array of *soul qualities*. Occasionally we experience *soul qualities* when we engage with people that we like and accept. To be kind and compassionate to a select few is not a true demonstration of kindness. To be an authentically kind and compassionate person means you are kind to the unkind and compassionate to all. When we are selective in our kindness behavior, what we are really saying is, "You are unimportant and there is nothing you can do for me, therefore I do not see you. You don't matter." Self-importance is a demonstration of the ego. We come to this realization when our level of awareness is heightened. Affirm, *Namaste, I honor the place in you where we are one.*

What is the connection between relationships, forgiveness, and boundaries?

The purpose of relationships is not to make us happy, but to assist our spiritual growth and move us to awareness of our core issues. We all have core issues. Relationships are mirrors – they reveal who we are by how we respond to people and situations. If we continue to forgive others and have the same experiences with them, it may be an indication that we need to set boundaries. Proverbs 27:17 AMP counsels, as iron sharpens iron, so one person sharpens another. Relationships show us the work that we need to do in order to allow the soul to manifest our true Self. We are counseled to forgive seven times seventy (Mathew 18:22 AMP), and also not to cast our pearls to swine (Matthew 7:6 AMP). You are not required to continue to accept bad behavior from others. Your level of awareness and discernment will keep you in a state of forgiveness. Limit your level of involvement with those who are callous, careless, and unkind. Pray for those who persecute you (Matthew 5:44 AMP), and forgive them for they no not what they do (Luke 23:34 AMP). A higher level of awareness is lacking in others when they knowingly or unknowingly hurt others. People hurt others when they are hurting. It's never about you, but about how others feel about themselves. Forgive Self and forgive others - Forgiveness is a BIG thing.

Is there a benefit to hard times?

Hard times (situations and people) are a test of character. Hard times are meant to strengthen us, to grow us. No experience is wasted. Our challenges with family, friends, co-workers, and strangers are meant to reveal our core issues. We can miss the message if we do not pay attention to our feelings and reactions. The goal of a spiritual life is a life of peace. The experiences that we encounter equip us for future victories. Be willing and able to do what is required to move beyond challenging circumstances and difficult people. Believe that God is working on your behalf. We know [with great confidence] that God [who is deeply concerned about us] causes all things to work together [as a plan] for good for those who love God, to those who are called according to His plan *and* purpose (Romans 8:28 AMP). Affirm – *I can hardly wait to see what will come from this*. And be thank-filled. Trust, perseverance, and faith allots us the time to make a course correction. Be glad of your trials to trust your faith (1 Peter 1:6; James 1:3 AMP) and know that patience and faith are close partners.

What is the significance of our thoughts and what we say to Self and others?

Our thoughts are the source of how we feel at the present moment. What is your best thought at this moment? Does it evoke a good feeling? You are the only one who can think your thoughts. Thoughts are things. Words are things. Thoughts create emotions. Our thoughts are our *Emotional Guidance System* (Hicks, 2004). Words are like seeds – what are you planting in your life and in the lives of others? The scripture counsels: As I have observed, those who plow evil and those who sow trouble reap it (Job 4:8 AMP). Thoughts/seeds that are loving and compassionate will produce love and compassion. Thoughts/seeds of hate and jealousy will produce negativity. Train the mind to think on good things. Fix your thoughts on what is true, and honorable, and right, and pure, and lovely, and admirable. Think about things that are excellent and worthy of praise (Philippians 4:8 AMP).

SOUL TO SOUL: ADDITIONAL SOUL INQUIRIES

Soul Inquiry. The Adinkra symbol Hwehwemudua (scheweb-scheweb-meu-doo-ah) - The Akan symbol of a measuring rod indicates excellence, quality, and critical examination. Test and evaluate yourselves to see whether you are in the faith and living your lives as committed believers (2 Corinthians 13:5 AMP). Live your best life!

What is my model of spiritual activism?
What do I believe about myself?
Who do I admire and why?
How do I respond to criticism from others?
How does my behavior support what I have been told?
Am I interested in others beyond what they can do for me?
Do I feel anger, resentment, and stress?
How do I promote my self-interest?
Why do I subject myself to negative and degrading treatment?
How do I measure my worthiness?

What does my heart require to open and stay open?

Do I judge others based on what I see or hear?

Do I always want what others have; creating my relationships on what I can get from others?

How do I demonstrate my authentic Self?

When do I look for opportunities to give to others?

Do I always have my hand out to receive?

What is the truth of my story? Am I a victim or overcomer?

How do I share my story/my gift with others?

What are my requirements to give and receive love?

How do I shine my light?

How do I demonstrate humility?

How do I deceive others in hopes of not being alone?

Am I only interested in myself and what others can do for me?

Do I hate those who hate me?

What is my process of forgiving others?

How do I standup for wrongdoing?

How do I respond to other people's negative feelings?

Am I over sensitive – taking things personal?

Who do I blame for my misfortune?

Do I say "I can't help what I think"?

What is it that I refuse to admit about myself?

What do I do (behavior pattern) to avoid pain/inner disturbance/fear?

What do I do with my pain (behavior patterns)?

How do I demonstrate what I believe about myself and others?

What do the tapes running in my mind say to support my responses to difficulties or opportunities?

What are the things I cannot forgive myself for doing?

What things have I done in response to fear?

What things have I done in moments of weakness?

What things do I do for money or revenge that demean myself and others?

What are the root causes of my feelings?

How do I articulate what I feel (anger, resentment, and stress)?

What is the payoff for my emotional disturbances?

What am I willing to do to get what I say I want?

What is it that I believe is wrong with me or about me?

Why am I so angry with myself that I would subject myself to unkind and unloving treatment from myself and others?

What is God's will for my life?

What does God say about me and do I believe it?

What is the cause of my inner disturbances?

What is my model of peace?

Is it possible that my perceptions are an illusion?

Could I let go of the stories I tell myself and others that keep me from peace?

What are my avoidance behaviors?

How do I suppress my emotions?

What is my relationship with my inner being?

How does silence benefit me?

What is ego?

How do I entertain the ego?

Where do I find my peace and happiness?

What does it mean to be free?

How do I compare myself with others?

How do I imitate others?

What part of personal history restricts me from moving forward?

What does my appearance say about me, and is it the truth of who I am?

What are the desires of my heart? Are they achievable?

What is my Life Vision?

Who am I, why am I here and where did I come from?

What do I tell myself about my Life Vision?

Do I sense a Divine design for my life?

Is there another part of me other than my physical body?

How am I connected with others? (physical, mental, and spiritual)?

What do my patterns reveal about my life lessons?

What does my best Self look like?

Am I willing and able to be the best of who I am in every situation?

Am I self-directed?

What is my daily practice of stillness/meditation?

What is my personal truth?

What do I know for sure?

What do I believe and why?

How do I demonstrate self-doubt?

What is the difference between what I know and what I believe (direct experience)?

What are my self-imposed limitations?

What are my current activities that harm my mind and body?

What are my current activities that demonstrate love for Self?

How does my life make a difference?

How do I react to setbacks?

How or what do I turn to when things do not go the way I planned?

Who enables me?

Who do I enable?

How do I encourage others?

Who encourages me?

How do I encourage myself?

Who are my spiritual teachers?

What are my spiritual practices?

What are God's promises, blessings, and benefits?

Do I accept responsibility for what happens to me?

Do I pray?

Why don't I follow through with my thoughts, and what causes my stagnation?

Am I truthful to myself and others?

What am I lacking?

What do I stand for? What do I fall for?

What's on your heart?

What is peace of mind?

What is my God-given talent?

What is my purpose?

Can I trust God? Why do I believe God can trust me?

Who supports me?

How do I support others?

How am I supported?

How do I pay attention without judging others?

Am I awake?

Who sees when I see?

What does it look like when I am aware?

Who hears what I hear?

Who looks at the image in the mirror?

How do I live stress free – without fear or drama?

How do I promote peace?

How do I promote confusion, turmoil and division?

How separate am I from others?

How important is it for me to be noticed by others?

Whose attention am I trying to get?

How do I convince myself that I am better than others?

How and why do I distract myself with busy-ness and things to do?

What do I have to prove?

What things are more important than people?

Do I find happiness in the suffering of others? (gossip, other's humiliation)

Where do I feel tension in my body?

How do I demonstrate a keep up with the Jones' attitude?

How important is it for me to be first?

How am I confrontational with others?

Why do I constantly judge others, what they wear, how they speak, where they live?

Would I rather be right or kind?

How do I successfully communicate my feelings with others and self?

How do I avoid communicating with others?

How do I avoid listening to my inner voice?

How do I divert my feelings/emotions? (eat, sleep, drugs, shop, etc.)

What are the root causes of my emotions?

What is the condition of my heart – is it open?

What is my purpose?

Am I aware of the mental dialogue in my head? How does the "voice" (the narrator) affect the mind and body?

How much time do I spend thinking about myself?

How do I know that I am aware?

Do I struggle with my thoughts?

How do I demonstrate compassion?

When am I most compassionate?

What qualities do I dislike in others?

When am I preoccupied with what people say about me and how does it make me feel?

How do I live in the past?

What are my short comings, likes, dislikes, etc.?

What principles and standards do I live by?

How do I cling to the past?

What recurring or fixed thoughts do I have?

What personality have I created based on my thoughts, societal norms, etc.?

How do I influence the behavior of others?

Why do I cling to my self-concept?

How do I defend my self-concept?

Am I willing to watch and become aware and let go of my self-concept?

Could I abandon my position, even when I think I am right?

What will it take to forgive the grievances of others?

What do I do to avoid pain?

How do I process emotional pain/emotional disturbance?

How do I respond to rejection?

What do I remember being told about myself?

What do the tapes running in my mind say to support my responses to challenges?

What are the things I cannot forgive myself for doing?

Is the way I feel getting me what I want?

How and when do I demonstrate unkind behavior?

How does it feel when my thoughts, words, and actions are in harmony?

What is the connection between my inner world and outer world?

Are all my conversations about me?
Do others exist?
What is the reality that I want to experience?
What motivates me?
What drains my energy, and why?

BLESSING THE ENERGY CENTERS

Today's focus is Blessing the energy centers – there are seven chakras or energy centers that are connected to core areas of our physical anatomy. Keeping it simple, each of the energy centers have specific hormones, glands, cells, and tissues, designed to regulate the entire body system.

The energy centers are aligned with the spinal column:

Root – base of the spine.
Sacral – lower abdomen, about 2" below the naval.
Solar Plexus – upper abdomen, in the stomach.
Heart – center of the chest, above the heart.
Throat – Throat
Third Eye – Forehead, between the eye.
Crown – top of the head.

The purpose of Blessing the energy centers is healing.

In *Meditation as a Spiritual Practice*, 'medi' means to heal. All energy carries information, and the Blessing of the energy centers sends healing energies to specific parts of the body. The Blessing combines meditation with prayer, and affirmations. Thought is pure energy - where we place our attention and intention is where we place our energy. The Blessing of the energy centers, balances, renews, and heals the mindbody.

During meditation, the body receives healing energy when we focus on each center; moving energy upward. Think on good things (Philippians 4:8 AMP) – think gratitude, love, peace, and wholeness as you move energy upward through each center. Creating real change in the mindbody, requires thinking greater than we feel - this is the core purpose of the practice of Blessing the energy centers. We start the Blessing from the base of the spine and end at the crown of the head.

Root - The root chakra is the base of the energy center; the foundation where we connect with the physical body. The root chakra is the source of expansion in our life - **Pure Wisdom**.

Clarity. The Adinkra symbol Mframadan (m-fra-mah-dan) – preparedness and readiness to face challenges and weather the storm. The quality of being easily understood in a very exact way; state of being clear, facing changes with faith and assuredness, knowing that you have what it takes to stand.

Wisdom. The Adinkra symbol Nyansapo (n-yahn-sah-poh) – Wisdom Knot; the wisdom of intelligence, ingenuity, and patience. The quality or state of being wise; knowledge of what is true coupled with right action; understanding; discernment and insight. *Wisdom is the principal thing; therefore, get wisdom: and with all your getting, get understanding* (Proverbs 4:7 AMP).

Pure Wisdom

Simple, pure, untainted goodness – this is the wisdom of The Divine. The Divine is pure Spirit, and our spiritual nature is pure wisdom. Awareness is the key ingredient to our Spiritual nature; our inner Being. We are Divine Energy and Light flows through, in, and around us. We are human and Divine. Wisdom and awareness are close partners.

The things on Earth are a pattern of the celestial realm – a pattern of wholeness. In essence, there is a spiritual prototype that coincides with the physical Universe – on Earth as it is in Heaven (Matthew 6:10 AMP); natural and spiritual laws overlay. The deeper meaning of life is revealed in our spiritual nature. The celestial realm is our foundation, our dwelling place of peace – a peace surpassing understanding. Spiritual communication is not intellectual, but communication of a deeper nature.

If you could ask God for anything, what would you ask for? King Solomon had opportunity to ask God for many things, but he recognized the value of wisdom (1 Kings 3:9-13 AMP), and Solomon's request for wisdom made God happy. It's refreshing to know that The Presence wants to give us the desires of our heart (Psalm 37:4 AMP). Wisdom

257

is a valuable asset. Wisdom is having knowledge of what is true, coupled with the ability to make right decisions. Wisdom is the principal thing (Proverbs 4:7 AMP). The many benefits of Pure Wisdom include peace, joy, and long life (Proverbs 3:17-18 AMP), when combined with careful planning. Self-Knowledge is the beginning of wisdom.

Self-Inquiry: What is the Source of wisdom? What are the desires of my heart? What things did I do today that I could do better? Who did I share my knowledge with today? Who did I serve today?

Affirm: The Spirit of Pure Wisdom and truth enters the center of my being, filling my life with joy. I encourage and support myself and others. Pure Wisdom flows in through and as me. I have the wisdom and knowledge to express my feelings clearly and directly. I Trust my inner wisdom and use my wisdom to serve others. My purpose is to demonstrate Divine wisdom – right here, right now. Godly wisdom from the sacred scriptures makes me wise (2 Timothy 3:15 AMP). I study and do my own independent investigation of the Truth (2 Corinthians 13:5 AMP).

Trust your inner wisdom and give the best of who you are by living your best life. To Have is to Give is the wisdom of the Divine.

Peace and Blessings

Sacral - The energy of the sacral chakra is associated with creativity and sensuality. The sacral chakra links the powerful energy between male and female; the sun and the moon; the moon and water. The power of birthing a vision – **Life Visioning**.

Thought. The Adinkra symbol Mate Masie (mah-tee mah-see-uh) – wisdom and knowledge. An idea, plan, opinion, or picture that is formed in the mind; the act of carefully thinking about the details of something. Thought is energy. Think on good things. You become what you think about repeatedly.

Vision. The Adinkra symbol Mframadan (m-fra-mah-dan) – elegance, preparedness, and ready to face the changes of life. A concept or image created by the imagination; discernment, insight, perceptiveness; wisdom; preparation and readiness for the future. Where there is no vision, the people perish (Proverbs 29:18 AMP).

Life Visioning

A common question in reference to the mind is, where do our thoughts come from? Our thoughts don't originate from a particular area of our brain, our thoughts are retrieved from a database of past programming – similar to a computer program. That's a simple explanation, but what's important is that we can choose to override programming that doesn't contribute to our well-being.

Think about the reality you want to create. Michael Bernard Beckwith's book, *Life Visioning,* is an essential guide on the 'how to' of the Life Visioning process. We can enlarge our vision when we see the end at the beginning. Write about your ideal scene, create a vision board, and review it often. Breathe life into your vision. Visioning creates a sense of wholeness, harmony, and purpose. Think big – we are created for greatness. Have a vision of you in the light. You are so sacred.

Self-Inquiry: What is my Life Vision? Who benefits from my vision? What do I currently have to contribute to my vision? What do I need to manifest my vision? Does my vision have a Divine purpose? What percentage of my attention per day do I give to my vision?

Affirm: I AM inspired by my Life Vision. Universal Intelligence supports, guides, and encourages me and I encourage others. I AM loved. I envision the unlimited possibilities for love of Self and others. Faith keeps me true to my vision. Reveal to me Your Highest vision for my life – my Highest Potential. I see the end at the beginning and my vision includes peace and prosperity. I envision the things I love to do and do them.

Treat your life as if you are weaving a tapestry - create your best life now.

Peace and Blessings

Solar Plexus - City of Jewels or Seat of Gems. The solar plexus chakra is the seat of momentum and forward movement, playing a fundamental role in the development of personal power, desire and intention – **Affirmative Prayer**.

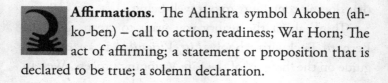

Affirmations. The Adinkra symbol Akoben (ah-ko-ben) – call to action, readiness; War Horn; The act of affirming; a statement or proposition that is declared to be true; a solemn declaration.

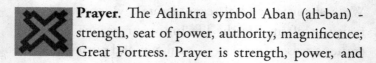

Prayer. The Adinkra symbol Aban (ah-ban) - strength, seat of power, authority, magnificence; Great Fortress. Prayer is strength, power, and

260

authority. Prayer is expressing gratitude and thanksgiving. Prayer is communion with the Divine.

Affirmative Prayer

The sacred scriptures affirm: One puts to flight a thousand, and two can put ten thousand to flight (Joshua 23:10 AMP; Deuteronomy 32:30 AMP). The one-pointed intention and desire of many can accomplish much. Consider the collective consciousness of the Affirmative Prayer of 1000+ people for the common purpose of demonstrating the power of the Ever-Loving Presence – God. If God be with you, who can be against you (Joshua 1:17,18 AMP) – you and The Divine are a majority. Affirmative Prayer is spiritual power that amplifies spiritual awareness. Affirmative Prayer is the right use of the mind.

Communication is a key component in all great relationships and Affirmative Prayer is communication with the Divine. Our relationship with The Divine is the most important relationship in our life. Think about the reality you intend to create for yourself and others. Reading, speaking, and listening is how we incorporate Affirmative Prayers into our inner being - our Spirit. Pray without ceasing by recording and listening to Affirmative Prayers in the first person - faith comes by hearing (Romans 10:17 AMP). Master your inner dialogue through Affirmative Prayer.

Self-Inquiry: Who am I? Why am I here? What do I want?

Affirm: Divine Energy strengthens and guides me to greatness and goodness I AM fruitful, prosperous, and nourished by Divine Energy. I live an abundant life – my best life, and all my needs are met. Thank You for every good intention I ever had for myself and others. I AM grateful for inspiration, guidance, courage, and love that supports my good intentions. Reveal to me my true intentions, and create in me a clean heart. There is life and death in the power of the tongue. Your Presence strengthens me, lifts me up to my Highest potential – I have access to more than I can see, say, and imagine. In You I move, I live, and have my being. Words have power.

Affirmative Prayer cancels the 25,000 plus hours of negative conditioning from childhood and adulthood that does not serve or benefit you and others. Intend to energize the mindbody through Affirmative Prayer.

Peace and Blessings

Heart - The sound of the celestial realm; balance, peace, and serenity – **Loving Forgiveness**.

Forgiveness. The Adinkra symbol Mpatapo (m-pah-tah-poh) - a knot of reconciliation, peace-making, and hope. To grant pardon for or remission of an offense or debt; absolve; to cease to feel resentment against; to cancel an indebtedness or liability; renewed connection.

Love. The Adinkra symbol Akoma (ah-ko-mah) – the heart; love, good will, patience, faithfulness, and fondness. Unselfish, loyal and compassionate concern for the good of another; God's concern for humankind; goodwill. I am my brother's keeper; I am my brother.

Loving Forgiveness

Love the Ever-Loving Presence -The Divine, with your entire Being, and love others as you love yourself. Loving the Divine is innate – Loving Self is a learned behavior. We are at a deficit when we attempt to give love to others and our cup is empty. We cannot give what we don't have. Lack of love results in dis-ease.

The heart is the center of our emotions, actions, and intentions. Be diligent in guarding your heart (Proverbs 4:23 AMP). The heart is the wellspring of life. Wellspring is defined as source and supply, storehouse, bank, and treasury. The Ever-Loving Presence, the Divine, Creator of the Universe is our Source and Supply.

Forgiveness demonstrates perfect love. The only way to have forgiveness is to offer it to others – To Have is to Give. When we forgive, we change our minds – transformation occurs. Just as the physical body requires regular elimination of waste for optimal health, the heart also has a need to eliminate waste; anger, resentment, hatred, and jealousy. Forgiveness is a spiritual laxative. Forgiveness is love in action.

Self-Inquiry: Who have I not forgiven? And what is the story around my unforgiveness? Can I imagine forgiving the same person 490 times (Matthew 18:22 AMP)? What does it feel like when my heart is open?

Affirm: I must have decided wrongly, because I am not at peace, I made the decision myself, but I can also decide otherwise. I want to decide otherwise, because I want to be at peace (Schucman). I choose to understand the lesson. All experiences are beneficial to me and others. I decide to practice Loving Forgiveness through the power of The Divine, The Miraculous, The Ever-Loving Presence in me.

Love is all there is – Love is all we need. Love is enough, be love in action, make practicing love the goal in life.

Peace and Blessings

Throat – The throat chakra is related to sound; speech. Sound vibrates through the throat and the entire body. The throat is the energy center of communication and expression. Be **Authentically Courageous**.

Authenticity. The Adinkra symbol Nsaa (n-sah) – Akan saying: He who does not know the real design will turn to an imitation. Real or genuine; not copied or false; true and accurate; excellence. Authentic implies being fully trustworthy. Akan saying: He who does not know the real design will turn to an imitation.

Courage. The Adinkra symbol Akofena (ah-ko-fe-nah) – legitimized authority, heroic deeds, and courageous acts. The quality of mind or spirit that enables a person to face difficulty, danger, and pain, without fear; bravery; fearlessness; to act in accordance with one's beliefs, especially in spite of criticism. Courage is required in becoming who we are created to be.

Authentically Courageous

Authenticity is to know your truth, live from the heart, and to have the courage to show up with integrity, substance, and honesty. Being Authentically Courageous is meeting challenges and oppositions based on who you are – no pretense, transparent, and vigilant for right-ness.

Courage is a test of character. Have the courage to grow without question, hesitation, or complaint. Becoming your true self is becoming authentic. Find the courage to live an authentic life. Reveal your authentic self to yourself and others, without apology. Being Authentically Courageous produces a high vibration.

Authenticity + Courage = Right Action. Thoughts, beliefs, and affirmations are powerful. Right Action requires courage. Fear not (Matthew 10:31 AMP) – know that you have what it takes to stand and act in accordance with your beliefs. The key to an abundant and peace-filled life is Right Action. Stand firm and be diligent in your spiritual practice (Ephesians 6:14 AMP).

Authentically Courageous is being more concerned about what the Creator of the Universe thinks of you than what others think of you. Be Authentically Courageous by sharing your gifts and talents. Use your talents and gifts to encourage others – be bold and vigilant.

Self-Inquiry: Am I double-minded? Do I create relationships based on authenticity? How do I overcome fear with courage? How do I develop the courage to be authentic in a culture that encourages me to fit in? What distracts me from being authentic?

Affirm: I am courageous. I stand in the truth of my authentic Self. In all things I demonstrate a pattern of good works, I demonstrate Integrity in thought, speech, and action. I AM Authentically Courageous and I express my feelings clearly and directly with kindness. I stand strong and walk in The Presence. I AM compassion, mindful, joyous, and jubilant. My vibration is high, and I AM grateful.

Have the courage to live your best life now.

Peace and Blessings

Third Eye - The Third eye chakra is associated with the pineal gland. The pineal gland regulates sleep patterns, biorhythms, perception, altered states of consciousness and **Creative Intention**.

 Creativity. The Adinkra symbol Ananse Ntontan (ah-nan-se n-to-n-tan) – craftiness; the use of the imagination; original ideas; vision and inspiration. A spider demonstrates its resourcefulness, creativity, and wisdom by weaving an intricate and elaborate web for survival.

Intention. The Adinkra symbol Nyame Biribi Wo Soro (n-yah-may Bear-ree-bee who soh-row) – God there is something in the heavens; hope and inspiration; direction during adversity. God-centered intentions reflect love, truth, happiness, and peace.

Creative Intention

Everything that takes up space is classified as matter, and all matter consists of carbon, nitrogen, and oxygen. In the Spirit, we are energy and information. We are endowed by the Creator of the Universe with gifts and talents. Our spirit (energy and information) radiates on a higher or lower frequency based on our thoughts. We create by what we think, say and do. With Creative Intention, our gifts and talents are amplified with light energy (Ephesians 5:13 AMP). How bright is your light?

Creative Intention is an evolutionary process. A quantum leap occurs, and something new is created. Thought coupled with emotions is a powerful creative tool. Creative Intention sets high standards for all areas of life (right livlihood, family, home, work life, relationships). Demonstrate Creative Intention by being aware of the needs of others. Words are things – intentionally create a life worthy of living; create your best life.

Self-Inquiry: What is the Divine Design for my life? Am I intentional in my creative process? Do my intentions benefit the Greater Good? What do I intend for every area of my life? What do I want? What are the desires of my heart?

Affirm: I AM intentionally creating my best life. My thoughts and speech reflect the creative power of The Miraculous, and I use my thoughts for right thinking and right seeing. The purpose of thought and speech is to create. Thought is Infinite, creative, and Divine. I treat the people I know, and the strangers I do not know with kindness, patience, and love. My heart is the center of my emotions, actions, and intentions. I am mindful in all activities and my intention is to create peace.

Live your best life now by setting Creative Intentions on how to live.

Peace and Blessings

Crown - The crown chakra is the energy center of Spirit and Universal Knowledge that links to the Divine, always creating a **Purposeful Response** in every situation.

Purpose. The Adinkra symbol Nkurumah Kesee (n-kroo-mah Keh-see) – greatness of purpose; good character; supemacy; and superioity. The reason for which something exists or is done; an intended or desired result; the point at issue; resoluteness.

Responsibility. The Adinkra symbol Nkon Osnk Nkon Osnk (corn-song-corn-song) — unity, responsibility, and cooperation; a chain link. Accountability as in having the power to control or manage. Akan saying: We are linked in both life and death. Those who share common blood never break apart.

Purposeful Response

Responsibility is being willing and able to respond to everyone and everything with love, kindness, and compassion. Being responsible means to choose the experience you want to create — create with purpose. Purposeful Responsibility is the opportunity to leave every person, place, and thing better than we found them. Thoughts create vibrations that affect people, places, and things — think on good things (Philippians 4:8 AMP). We are responsible for all that we are and who we are becoming.

Purpose is eternal. Greatness is finding and living our purpose. Have an intention to demonstrate a Purposeful Response to every experience. A Purposeful Response originates with a Life Purpose Statement (LPS). LPS provides a sense of direction. When we are clear about our purpose, our energy is limitless. If you are at peace and have a sense of well-being, you are on purpose. Spiritual principles are like renewable energy, fueling our purpose.

Self-Inquiry: Who am I? Why am I here? How can I help? How can I serve? What is my life purpose? Am I willing and able to respond based on my life purpose? Do I accept responsibility for what happens to me? Does my vision involve a Divine purpose?

Affirm: I am responsible for the development of my mental powers. My heart is open and receptive to Divine Energy. I know who I am and why I am here and I embrace it. My mind is my kingdom of opportunities. My purpose is to awaken to my soul's desire, celebrate life, share my gifts, and to do what brings me joy. My life purpose is my driver and motivator and I demonstrate love, compassion, wisdom, intelligence, and grace – right here, right now.

Live your best life now – Master purpose - make your Life Purpose your Life Practice.

Peace and Blessings

STUDY GUIDE

Soul Journey: The Practice

Welcome to *Soul Journey and Thank You for your Willingness.*

Are you willing and able to take the next step? Have you considered selecting a spiritual principle or *soul quality* as a life practice? Awareness, intention and attention creates transformation, growth, and change. Practicing *soul qualities* are easy to do and easy not to do,

Soul Journey: The Practice is a fast-paced, forty-day course (approximately six weeks - no weekend breaks) in practicing the qualities of the Holy Spirit, the fruits of the Spirit; there is no law against these things (Galatians 5:23 AMP). During the forty-day practice, fast from negativity (people, places, and things), and develop your thought life through affirmations and Affirmative Prayers (1 Thessalonians 5:17-18 AMP; Romans 12:12 AMP; Philippians 4:6 AMP). Do your own independent investigation of the scriptures listed in the entries – search the scriptures and know God's Will for yourself. Then, share your insights with others with love and kindness. Overtime, you will know yourself as The Presence, Jehovah, The Creator of the Universe, knows you. Every relationship mirrors our relationship with God – in essence, there is only you and God – 'Gye Nyame' Tis God Only; 'Namaste', the God in me recognizes the God in you; For in Him we live and move and have our being (Acts 17:28 AMP).

Make your Soul *Journey* a continuous practice by sharing your journey with others. Practice *soul qualities* four times a year: January 1st (winter), Lent (spring), July (summer), and October (fall).

The course can be practiced in alphabetical order or by randomly selecting a principle. We begin our forty-day journey with PRAYER:

Day 1

PRAYER as a Spiritual Practice (*Soul Qualities: The Art of Becoming, Chapter 31*)

The Adinkra symbol Aban (ah-ban) - strength, seat of power, authority, magnificence; Great Fortress.

PRAYER. A spiritual relationship with God; the act or practice of PRAYING to God; a public or private religious observance. PRAYER is strength, power, and authority. PRAYER is expressing gratitude, petitioning, and affirming. The Presence is as close to us as our breath. PRAYER is communion with The Divine.

Our relationship with God is the most important relationship in our lives – relationship is not religion. In essence, PRAYER is talking with God. When we do not have the words, God knows our hearts (Psalm 139). Faith, PRAYER, and gratitude are inseparable. PRAYER is the medium to receiving a revelation and miracle. A Gratitude Journal is like a love letter to The Divine, expressing appreciation for the greatness and goodness of life – we have much to be thankful for.

Everything we think, say, and do is a PRAYER. Negative PRAYERS contain thoughts of worry and doubt - complaints are like PRAYERS to the devil. Fear, worry, doubt, and anxiety are distractions - stealing, killing, and destroying, our joy (John 10:10 AMP). Jesus, the Master of humanity and Divinity, reveals the close relationship between PRAYER and Faith - Whatever things you ask for in PRAYER (in accordance with God's will), believe that you have received them, and they will be given to you (Mark 11:24 AMP). The Master taught us how to construct a simplistic PRAYER that includes grateful recognition of God, requesting daily provisions, and forgiveness (Matthew 6:9-13 AMP).

How can a united PRAYER affect our families, communities, and world? Collective PRAYER is a powerful spiritual practice when two or more people come together in agreement with God (Matthew 18:20 AMP). Consider the collective consciousness of an Affirmative PRAYER for the express purpose of demonstrating the power of The Ever-Loving Presence, The Divine – God. If God be with you, who can be against you (Romans 8:31 AMP). PRAYER is powerful – You and God are a majority.

Make your first contact of the day with The Divine - say an Affirmative PRAYER - affirming good intentions - bless the day. When we meet the day with expectations of love, knowingness, and bliss, there are unlimited possibilities in store. This is the day the Lord has made; we rejoice with gladness (Psalm 118:24 AMP).

Affirmative thought and Affirmative PRAYER are

partners. Each spiritual principle in *Soul Qualities: The Art of Becoming* contains an Affirmative PRAYER. Affirmative PRAYER is the right use of the Mind.

Here is an Affirmative PRAYER created from Psalm 8 AMP:

O Lord, my God, how great is Your Name in all the Earth. You have set Your shining-greatness above the heavens. Out of the mouth of babes, You are strengthened, because of those who hate You. You silence those who fight against You. When I look up and think about Your heavens, the work of Your fingers, the moon and the stars, that You set in place, who am I? You think of me and You care for me. You made me a little less than the angels and gave me a crown of Greatness and Honor. You made me to rule over the works of Your hands. You put all things under my feet: All sheep and cattle, all the wild animals, the birds of the air, and the fish of the sea, and all that pass through the sea. O Lord, my God, how great is Your name in all the Earth!

Thoughts are PRAYERS and we can choose to think and live affirmatively. See the best of life, the best of love, and the very best of everything.

What is your daily process of communication with your Higher Power - God? Be creative, personalize your Affirmative Prayers. Record and listen to your Affirmative Prayers throughout the day – make your spiritual practice personal.

Peace and Blessings

Day 2

GRATITUDE as a Spiritual Practice (*Soul Qualities: The Art of Becoming, Chapter 18*)

The Adinkra symbol Bese Saka (bes-e sah-ka) – the cola nut represents power, abundance, and affluence; expression of admiration and good will.

GRATITUDE. The quality or feeling of being GRATEFUL; being thankful; appreciation; GRATEFULNESS. Sharing the overflow with others. Expressing GRATITUDE by giving the gift of time and attention.

Thanksgiving, praise, appreciation - in everything give thanks, for this is the will of God in Christ Jesus concerning you (1 Thessalonians 5:18 AMP). Take a moment and feel your heart energy increase by repeatedly thinking and/or speaking the word GRATITUDE. Words are things and GRATITUDE is a powerful spiritual principle.

GRATITUDE in action is giving. Decide today the level of GRATITUDE you want to experience by giving a smile, extra effort, and service. Give your talent, wisdom, a prayer. Give peace and a Blessing. Give appreciation, joy, and love. Give and it will be given to you. A good measure, pressed down, shaken together, and running over, will be poured into your lap. For with the measure you use, it will be measured to you (Luke 6:38 AMP). In essence, be cognizant of what you are giving because the energy you give will return to you.

A GRATITUDE Journal is a powerful tool, shifting our focus from lack and limitation to a feeling of goodness in the mindbody, and spirit. A GRATITUDE Journal is like writing love letters to The Ever-Loving Presence - The Holy Spirit. Studies show that a feeling of GRATITUDE has a therapeutic affect at the cellular level. The vibrational frequency of GRATITUIDE results in total well-being; wholeness. This concept coincides with the biblical principle of thought: As we think in our hearts, that is who we are (Proverbs 23:7 AMP). In your journal, list at least three experiences that you are GRATEFUL for, today. Include the good things that happen to you and others. Make feeling good the number one goal in your life, and shift your awareness to thinking on good things (Philippians 4:8 AMP). GRATITUDE is a game changer and we have much to be thankful for.

What three things are you GRATEFUL for at this present moment? Share that feeling with others. To Have is to Give. Practice GRATITUDE – make your spiritual practice personal.

Peace and Blessings

Day 3

FORGIVENESS as a Spiritual Practice (*Soul Qualities: The Art of Becoming, Chapter 15*)

The Adinkra symbol Mpatapo (m-pah-tah-poh) - a knot of reconciliation, peace-making, and hope.

FORGIVENESS. To grant pardon for an offense; freedom; no feeling of resentment; to cancel an indebtedness or liability. Reconciliation and peaceful approach; a renewed connection.

Can you imagine FORGIVING the same person 490 times for the same or similar infraction? Jesus, our example of the highest level of spiritual practice tells us to FORGIVE seven times seventy (Matthew 18:22 AMP); FORGIVE us our trespasses as we FORGIVE those who trespass against us (Matthew 6:12 AMP); FORGIVE them for they know not what they do (Luke 23:34 AMP). FOREGIVENESS is a learning aide to demonstrating perfect love. The only way to have FORGIVENESS is to offer it to others – To Have is to Give.

When we FORGIVE, we change our minds. Transformation and the renewal of the mind occurs when we FORGIVE (Romans 12: 2 AMP). David, a man after God's heart, pleads: Create in me a clean heart and renew a right persevering and steadfast spirit in me (Psalm 51:10 AMP). It's crucial that we examine our heart of hearts because out of the heart are the issues of life (Proverbs 4:23 AMP). The Spiritual practice of FORGIVENESS cleanses the mind and heart of impurities, creating a flow of love, joy, and peace. The most powerful thing we can do is change our minds. As soon as possible, FORGIVE silently and choose a different response. Ask for help, if needed from the Holy Spirit, The Divine. The Holy Spirit is the resolution to conflict and only knows peace, love, joy, patience, and FORGIVENESS; *soul qualities.*

Who have you not FORGIVEN? And what is the story around your UNFORGIVENESS. Let go of your story, and create a new story. FORGIVENESS is for you, not the other person. FORGIVENESS is a big thing. Just as our physical body requires regular elimination of waste for optimal health, our heart also has a need to release anger, resentment, hatred, and jealousy. FORGIVENESS is a spiritual laxative. FORGIVENESS is love in action. God is love.

Affirm: I must have decided wrongly, because I am not at peace, I made the decision myself, but I can also decide otherwise. I want to decide otherwise, because I want to be at peace. I choose to understand the lesson (Schucman). All experiences are beneficial to me and others. I decide to FORGIVE through the power of the Holy Spirit, The Redeemer, The Comforter, The Holy One of God.

Make your Spiritual practice personal by replacing UNFORGIVENESS with Peace, Love, Kindness, Prayer, Service, Humility – *soul qualities*.

Peace and Much Blessings

Day 4

FAITH as a Spiritual Practice (*Soul Qualities: The Art of Becoming, Chapter14*)

The Adinkra symbol Nsoroma (n-soar-row-mah) – FAITH and the belief and dependency on a Supreme Being. FAITH is seeing the invisible and hearing the inaudible.

FAITH. Confidence or trust in a person or thing; belief in God or in the doctrines or teachings of religion. Akan saying: A child of the Supreme Being, I do not depend on myself. My illumination is only a reflection of His.

FAITH coupled with logic and reason is our base level of FAITH. We have FAITH in the natural laws of order, cause and effect, and the law of probability. We are confident that the sun will rise and set, and the law of gravity will remain stable. FAITH in what we do not see, from no where to now here, requires FAITH the size of a mustard seed (Matthew

17:20 AMP; Luke 17:6 AMP). Spiritual power is released through FAITH when we believe that all things are possible (Matthew 8:13 AMP; Matthew 9:29 AMP; Philippians 4:13 AMP). FAITH is a big thing.

Self-Inquiry is a powerful teaching aide when we ask who, what, when, where, how, and why of our FAITH. What do I have FAITH in? Can I see my FAITH? What does my FAITH look like? What are my core beliefs? What do I believe and why do I believe it? How big or small is my FAITH? Is my FAITH working? What does my FAITH demonstrate to others? Carefully scrutinize and examine your FAITH (actions, attitudes, and behavior). Test and evaluate yourself to see whether you are in the FAITH (Galatians 6:4 AMP; 2 Corinthians 13:5 AMP). Our FAITH is evident by what we think, say, and do - The Ever-Loving Presence, The Divine, The Holy One of God, sees our FAITH (Luke 5:20 AMP; Mark 2:5 AMP).

We are responsible for our FAITH – our belief system. Our FAITH is tested by our actions and reactions to life situations. We are always demonstrating what we believe – consciously or unconsciously. Our beliefs are manifested through thoughts, feelings/emotions, speech, and actions. FAITH without works is nonexistent (James 2:17 AMP). We demonstrate FAITH through practice. Love, peace, kindness, humility, forgiveness, courage, and acceptance are demonstrations of positive FAITH. Worry, anxiety, impatience, hate, fear, criticism, jealousy, and judgment demonstrates negative FAITH; the qualities of the ego (easing God out). Choose to demonstrate the Fruits of the Spirit - love, joy, peace, patience, kindness, goodness, faithfulness, gentleness, and self-control (Galatians 5:22-23 AMP) – the

Soul Qualities of The Divine. The Holy Spirit brings to our awareness all things that are good and beneficial (John 14:26 AMP). FAITH can be reactivated through hearing The Word of God (Romans 10:17 AMP). FAITH, thought and belief are inseparable.

FAITH requires us to develop the courage to stand firm (Galatians 5:1 AMP). Fight a good fight and remain free from conflict, anger, jealousy, contention - from the influence of deceptive intelligence and evil influences (1 Timothy 6:12 AMP). What does the good fight of FAITH look like? The good fight of FAITH is practicing spiritual principles of integrity, courage, righteousness, peace, prayer, and perserverence (Ephesians 6:10-18 AMP).

The process of our FAITH is strengthened and tested through life challenges. Pay attention to the details in your life. Whatever happens in life, there is a spiritual practice that is apropos to every life experience. We know that our FAITH is working when we walk by FAITH in the Spirit, and submit to God (Deuteronomy 28: 1 AMP; James 4:7 AMP). Our spiritual practice is renewable energy that fuels our FAITH.

Affirm: FAITH is the most important thing in my life. My inner Self is strengthened by FAITH. I hold life supporting core beliefs of love, acceptance, mindfulness, peace, gratitude, and forgiveness. My FAITH is renewed by the guidance of the Holy Spirit. I see my FAITH and out of my heart flows rivers of Living Water. I thoughtfully consider the Loving Kindness of the Ever-Loving Presence, and I receive unlimited pleasures and Blessings. FAITH comes by hearing and my prayer of FAITH corresponds to what I believe. I examine and test my FAITH.

Gratitude and FAITH are inseparable. As you move through the day, be willing to be guided by the Holy Spirit and put your acts of FAITH to practice.

Peace and Blessings

Day 5

Welcome to day five of *Soul Journey*. Today we will delve into the process of THOUGHT in relation to fasting from negativity, practicing spiritual disciplines, and prayer.

A common question in reference to the mind is, where do our THOUGHTS come from? Our THOUGHTS don't originate from a particular area of our brain, our THOUGHTS are retrieved from a database of past programming – similar to a computer program. Negative THOUGHTS come from past conditioning – something someone has said to us or something we've told ourselves, our experiences and perceptions, other people's experiences and perceptions, or negative images in the media. That's a simple explanation, but what's important is that we can override present programming that doesn't contribute to our well-being. Spiritual principles are renewable energy, transforming our minds through the activity of the Holy Spirit, which is the perfect will of God. Spiritual principles of gratitude, forgiveness, courage, clarity, patience, intention, and discipline assist in creating a beneficial THOUGHT program.

Are you aware of your dominant and passive THOUGHTS throughout the day? What are you THINKING this present moment? Take inventory of your THOUGHT life. We have the ability to program

THOUGHTS that are beneficial to the mindbody. Our cells are intelligent and have special functions. Every cell knows what every other cell is doing. We are wonderfully made (Psalm 139:14 AMP). THOUGHTS trigger the release of chemicals in the brain. Stressful THOUGHTS release cortisol and adrenaline in the body resulting in inflammation and dis-ease. In contrast, laughter, happiness, meditation, stillness, and exercise, release endorphins that improves the function of the immune system, creating a euphoric state of mind; a natural high. On a cellular level, stress causes chronic inflammation in the body and research studies indicate that low level inflammation is the cause of many ailments that can go undetected – such as heart disease, cancer, chronic lower respiratory disease, stroke, Alzheimer's disease, and diabetes. Our THOUGHTS directly affect the mindbody and it's crucial that we master our inner dialogue, and fast from negativity for total well-being.

Today's *soul quality* is THOUGHT:

THOUGHT as a Spiritual Practice (*Soul Qualities: The Art of Becoming, Chapter 37*)

The Adinkra symbol Mate Masie (mah-tee mah-see-uh) – wisdom and knowledge; What I hear, I keep, I understand.

THOUGHT. An idea, plan, opinion, or picture, that is formed in the mind; the act of carefully THINKING about the details of something. You become what you THINK about repeatedly. Pay attention to the THOUGHTS that trigger emotions – you don't have to do anything other than be aware.

What is the linkage between our THOUGHTS and the heart? The heart is the center of our emotions, actions, and intentions. Jesus, the Master Teacher forewarned: Out of the heart comes evil THOUGHTS, and plans, murders, adulteries, sexual immoralities, thefts, false testimonies, slander, and verbal abuse (Matthew 15:19 AMP). The correlation between our THOUGHTS and our heart is - What we THINK – we become (Proverbs 23:7 AMP).

We strengthen our mindbody internally and externally by practicing love, peace, discipline, patience, courage, kindness, and prayer. THINK about the reality you want to create. Daily affirmations, Affirmative Prayer, meditation, gratitude, and praise, clear the mind of debris from adverse past experiences and future fears. The wisdom of The Divine is, THINK on good things (Philippians 4:8 AMP).

Affirmative Prayer/Thought Programming:

My Affirmative THOUGHTS and speech create wholeness and well-being. Every day and everyway my mindbody is healthier, younger, and I am transformed into my younger self. I look and feel healthy; my essential nature is wholeness. The energy of The Ever-Loving Presence rejuvenates and enlivens every aspect of my THOUGHTS, speech, and actions. I open myself to the nourishment and energy in food that supports the mindbody. My THOUGHTS and speech reflect the Creative power of The Miraculous, The Divine, The Holy One of God and I use my THOUGHTS for right THINKING and right seeing. The Purpose of THOUGHT and speech is to create. I co-create my THOUGHT patterns with The Divine, and my good is multiplied. In Him I move, I live, and I have my being (Acts 17:28 AMP).

THOUGHT Programming is essential to a spiritual practice. We create through our THOUGHTS, words, and actions. What are you THINKING, saying and doing? What are you creating through your THOUGHT processes? The Spirit is always teaching and speaking. Are you available and receptive to the guidance of the Holy Spirit?

As you continue with your day, ask the question:

What is my process for creating goodness and greatness in my THOUGHT life? Develop a THOUGHT life that benefits the Greater good – The Kingdom, and make your practice personal.

Peace and Many Blessings

Day 6

PEACE as a Spiritual Practice (*Soul Qualities: The Art of Becoming, Chapter 28*)

The Adinkra symbol Mpatapo (m-pah-tah-poh) – A knot of reconciliation and hope; peace-making; bonding.

PEACE. A state of mutual harmony between people or groups; the mind free from annoyance, distraction, anxiety, and obsession; a state of tranquility or serenity; silence.

PEACE is the spiritual well-being that comes from walking with God. Picture placing your heart on one side of the scales of justice and a feather on the opposite side. Would the scales be balanced? How would your heart weigh in? What tilts the scales, causing a heavy heart? The wisdom of the ancient Egyptian principles of MAAT - truth, justice, righteousness, harmony, order, balance, and reciprocity - are principles that create PEACE. Is your heart as light as a feather? Are you at PEACE? Blessed are the makers and maintainers of PEACE, for they will be called the sons of God (Matthew 5:9 AMP). We experience PEACE when we surrender confusion, jealousy, conflict, and confrontation. PEACE and forgiveness are close partners.

Listed below are five practices that create PEACE:

(1) Allow others to have opinions and beliefs without debate, even if you feel you are right. Being right is over-rated when it causes conflict and discord.

(2) Decrease the atmosphere of competition where there are winners and losers, and replace with cooperation, collaboration, and mutual recognition.

(3) Keep the lines of communication open with Self and others. Keep your heart open by allowing all feelings and emotions, good and not so good, to pass through you.

(4) Become teachable. Create a space for PEACE by admitting you don't know - not knowing is a space for newness.

(5) Commit to a Day of PEACE, free from drama, worry, shame, impatience, and judgment.

Decide the following day if you want to commit to PEACE for an additional 24 hours. If possible, as far as it depends on you, live at PEACE with everyone (Romans 12:18 AMP).

Ask the question – Am I in a place of PEACE? We progress from worry, confusion, struggle and arrive at PEACE - a PEACE that surpasses understanding (Philippians 4:7 AMP). Prayer, forgiveness, and gratitude brings us to a place of PEACE. Make your practice a pathway to PEACE.

May the God of PEACE be with you.

Day 7

GRACE as a Spiritual Practice (*Soul Qualities: The Art of Becoming, Chapter 17*)

The Adinkra symbol Nyame Nti (n-yah-may n-tee) symbolizes an olive branch, representing peace – GRACE and peace are close partners. By God's Grace; faith and trust in God.

GRACE. Simple elegance or refinement; the free and unmerited favor of God; the bestowal of blessings; an act of instant kindness, courtesy, or mercy; service. We see the presence of GRACE everywhere when we seek opportunities to receive and give GRACE. Undeserved kindness and GRACE prevent us from getting exactly what we deserve. God is so merciful, He gives us a pass, and the opportunity to correct our behaviors. We can choose to continue our Journey in a state of GRACE, in spite of difficulties, obstacles, or discouragement. We all fall short in acts of kindness and compassion towards self and others (Romans 3:23 AMP), but God provides unmerited GRACE and favor - with gifts of GRACE (1 Corinthians 12:7-11 AMP).

We can do nothing without the GRACE of God. Ego is easing God out, with no recognition of God's GRACE, power, or mercy. Ego will have you believe that your accomplishments are a result of your efforts. You set yourself against the proud and haughty, but give GRACE continually to those who are humble enough to receive it (James 4:6 AMP). Challenge ideas that do not contribute to a true relationship with your Higher Power, Creator, God.

We are encouraged to show God's GRACE and mercy by demonstrating kindness. Regard others as valuable and overlook imperfections (Ephesians 2:8-9 AMP). See that none of you repays another with evil for evil, but always aim to show kindness (1 Thessalonians 5:15 AMP). The power of the Holy Spirit connects us to the energy of God's personal GRACE. A Course in Miracles states: Spirit is in a state of GRACE forever – our reality is Spirit – therefore we are in a state of GRACE forever. GRACE is the Givingness of God.

Share God's message of GRACE with others, and pass on to others what you learn – To Have is To Give. Experiencing God's GRACE increases our responsibility to others. Every experience is an opportunity to tell others about God's GRACE, power, and glory. Share your knowledge and bless others with your insight God (2 Timothy 2:15 AMP). You are a witness to the GRACE and greatness of God.

Self-inquiry brings God's GRACE to our awareness - ask the questions? Am I friendly and approachable? Am I joyful and enthusiastic? Do I recognize God's GRACE in all of my daily activities? How do I demonstrate GRACE to others? Am I open and available to the GRACE and guidance of the Holy Spirit? God's GRACE is simple, pure, and free (2 Corinthians 1:12 AMP). GRACE transforms and renews the mind. When we recognize The Divine, we open ourselves up to more of God's GRACE. Set an Intention to give GRACE to others and be thankful for the GRACE received. GRACE gives us an opportunity for a do over. His GRACE is sufficient (2 Corinthians 12:9 AMP). Move through life challenges with GRACE and Insight.

Affirm: Give me GRACE - Your GRACE is acceptance, trust, and peace. I let go of how I would have things to be and I trust that You will make all things right. My thoughts are of gratitude, love, and GRACE. Grant me the GRACE for the challenges I face (Romans 7:19 AMP). Because of Your GRACE and kindness, my soul is strong in Your power and GRACE. I thank You for Your Divine love, light, GRACE, guidance, mercy, and protection. You give me more and more GRACE and power of the Holy Spirit. I speak words of forgiveness, peace, and GRACE and GRACE returns to me 100-fold.

Be GRACE, teach GRACE - To Have GRACE is to Give GRACE.

Peace and Blessings

Day 8

HUMILITY as a Spiritual Practice (*Soul Qualities: The Art of Becoming, Chapter 19*)

The Adinkra symbol Dwennimmen (djwin-knee-mann) — ram's Horns; strength, humility, wisdom, and learning.

HUMILITY. Humbleness; meekness; modesty; gentleness. The horns of a ram are not used for strength or force. Akan Proverb: The ram may bully, not with its horns but with its heart.

We demonstrate HUMILITY by abstaining from any feeling of being better than others. Lack of HUMILITY and feeling self-important, negatively affects our relationships. The opposite of HUMILITY is haughtiness, greed, and unkindness. In every society and culture, there is pride before the fall (Proverbs 16:18 AMP). Throughout the scriptures, God opposes the proud and favors HUMILITY (James 4:6 AMP; Proverbs 16:5 AMP; Isaiah 2:12 AMP) - you cannot be unkind and humble.

Luke 2:1-20 AMP, gives an account of the birth of Jesus' HUMBLE beginnings; newborn Jesus wrapped in swaddling clothes in a manger surrounded by animals, because there were no private rooms available for Mary to give birth. Jesus demonstrated the 'how to' of HUMILITY by washing the feet of the disciples (John 13:12 AMP); listening and embracing children (Luke 18:16 AMP); and the HUMILITY of riding on a donkey (Matthew 21:5 AMP). HUMILITY, service, and kindness are close partners.

Service asks the questions: How may I help? How may I serve? HUMILTY is beyond service. HUMILITY is the manner in which we serve. Do you serve motivated by ego (complaint, judgment, criticism, selfishness, carelessness, arrogance)? Or by Spirit (peace, love, joy, mindfulness, patience, kindness, willingness) – *soul qualities*? Select at least three Acts of Service you currently enjoy with family, friends, co-workers, and acquaintances. Intentionally combine HUMILITY with service.

What does HUMILITY look like in today's world? HUMILITY is being willing and able to serve others to the best of your ability, without expectation of payment, reward, recognition, and complaint – with kindness. HUMILITY is knowing that you are not the only one - others exist. HUMILITY is being thankful for all things - big and small. When we are HUMBLE, we can become what God created us to be. Serving others, is serving God.

The Holy Spirit is compassion, love, kindness, peace, and patience. Demonstrate HUMILITY to others by the power of the Holy Spirit.

Peace and Blessings

Day 9

LOVE as a Spiritual Practice (*Soul Qualities: The Art of Becoming, Chapter 22*)

The Adinkra symbol Akoma (ah-ko-mah) — the heart; love, goodwill, patience, faithfulness, and fondness.

LOVE. God's concern for humankind; Unselfish, loyal, and compassionate concern for the good of another; I am my brother's keeper because I am my brother.

Two sacred Laws of the Universe: LOVE the Lord your God with all your passion and prayer and intellect. This is the most important, the first on any list. But there is a second to set alongside it: LOVE others as well as you LOVE yourself (Matthew 22: 37-40 AMP). We are taught in our youth about reverence and LOVE for God, but LOVE for Self is a learned behavior. Competition, bargaining, gains and losses - we LOVE others to get something for ourselves. We are at a deficit when we attempt to give LOVE to others and our cup is empty. We cannot give what we don't have. Violating the Law of Love results in dis-ease.

What does LOVING Self look like? When we LOVE Self, we are compassionate, gentle, kind, forgiving, and nonjudgmental. When we LOVE Self, we trust that what we do and say is in our best interest. When we LOVE Self, we tell the truth about what we do and why. When we LOVE Self, we take responsibility for all that we are and who we are becoming. LOVING Self means we value and celebrate who we are: human and Divine. Our Self LOVE keeps us full-filled, and when we are full-filled, we have the capacity to give LOVE to others. The more LOVE we give, the more LOVE we receive. Give and it will be given to you, pressed down shaken together and running over (Luke 6:38). When we fill our cup to capacity and the cup overflows, then we will have ample LOVE to give to others. At this level, we are able to LOVE others as we LOVE ourselves.

Divine LOVE is unconditional and detached from the outcome. Divine LOVE creates wholeness. and renews the mind - we see LOVE in everyone and everything. Acts of LOVE include patience, kindness, forgiveness, truth, trust, perseverance, sharing, and giving. Divine LOVE covers and sustains (1 Corinthians 13:4-7 AMP). The mind is a powerful device for growth, when we choose LOVE.

The heart is the center of our emotions, actions, and intentions. Be diligent and guard your heart, your heart is the wellspring of life. Wellspring is defined as source and supply, storehouse, bank, and treasury. The Ever-Loving Presence, the Divine, Creator of the Universe is our Source and Supply. When we are filled with LOVE, we can LOVE others like ourselves and guard them like the pupil of our eye. Make it a daily practice to LOVE and extend more of you to more people. LOVE is the fulfillment of the Law. God is LOVE. The Holy Spirit sees nothing but LOVE.

LOVE is all there is – LOVE is all we need. LOVE is enough, be LOVE in action, make practicing LOVE the goal in life.

Peace and Blessings

Day 10

PATIENCE as a Spiritual Practice (*Soul Qualities: The Art of Becoming, Chapter 27*)

The Adinkra symbol Osram (o-srahm) – The moon; faith, patience, understanding, and determination.

PATIENCE. The quality of being PATIENT; without complaint; an ability or willingness to suppress restlessness or annoyance when confronted with delay; steady perseverance; even-tempered care; diligence. Akan Proverb: It takes the moon sometime to go around the nation.

PATIENCE is having the capacity to accept or tolerate delay, trouble, or suffering without getting angry or upset. Getting angry, upset, pacing back and forth, checking the time, and patting our feet are indicators that we are IMPATIENT. Kindness and PATIENCE are close partners - the more we hurry, the less time we take to help others.

The fruit of the Spirit is love, joy, peace, PATIENCE, kindness, goodness, faithfulness, gentleness, and self-control. Against such things there is no law (Galatians 5:22 AMP). God's fruit prepares us to endure life challenges. Waiting with PATIENCE serves a greater purpose. Consider it a sheer gift, when tests and challenges come at you from all sides. You know that under pressure, your faith is forced into the open and shows its true colors. So, don't try to get out of anything prematurely. Let it do its work so you become mature and well-developed, not deficient in any way (James 1:2-4 AMP). PATIENCE is knowing that a delay is not a denial. Just as physical exercise strengthens our heart and muscles, PATIENCE develops and strengthens our spiritual muscles. Exercising PATIENCE is an opportunity for growth. PATIENCE is waiting with anticipation, and preparing for what's next; our destiny.

IMPATIENCE is the fear of not getting what we want. When we plant seeds, we don't dig them up every day - checking to see if it has roots. Our thoughts and desires are like seeds. Expectation, prayer, affirmations, faith, and PATIENCE are the nourishment needed for all things to come to full maturity. We cannot see a root growing beneath the surface, and if we are IMPATIENT, we miss the first sprout - the Blessing. In the midst of waiting, take the focus off of self and be of service to others. You are chosen by God, demonstrating behavior marked by tenderhearted mercy, kind feeling, gentle ways, and PATIENCE. You have the power to endure whatever comes, with good temper (Colossians 3:12 AMP).

Examine your 'PATIENCE Quotient '- PATIENCE is a learned behavior based on past conditioning and culture. The great news is we can unlearn behavior through awareness and making better choices. PATIENCE provides us time to make a course correction. Be glad of your trials to trust your faith (1 Peter 1:6 AMP; James 1:3 AMP) - PATIENCE and faith are close partners.

Be PATIENCE, teach PATIENCE, to have PATIENCE. Live your best life now.

Peace and Many Blessings.

Day 11

PERSEVERANCE as a Spiritual Practice (*Soul Qualities: The Art of Becoming, Chapter 29*)

The Adinkra symbol Wawa Aba (wah-wah ah-ba) – hardiness, toughness, and perseverance.

PERSEVERANCE. Steady persistence in a course of action in spite of difficulties, obstacles, or discouragement; continuance in a state of grace to the end. The wawa tree is hardwood, used for carving. Akan saying: He is tough as the seed of the wawa tree.

The process of life is not linear and seldom predictable. Think of a time when you experienced life's twists and turns. Our plans may not be in sync with God's Plan. The All Knowing, Omnipotent, and Creator of the Universe's Plan is always better. All things work together for the good of those that love God, to them who are called according to His purpose (Romans 8:28 AMP; Genesis 50:20 AMP). All leaves nothing out, and includes life's twist, turns, and challenges. In retrospect, and in God's timing, He reveals to us His purpose and plan for our lives - there is always more that will be revealed in God's time. We don't know what the future holds – but we know that God holds the future.

The challenges of life produce PERSEVERANCE; and PERSEVERANCE, character; and character, love in our hearts through the Holy Spirit (Romans 5:3-5 AMP). PERSEVERANCE exposes and tests the quality of our character – our faith. PERSERVERENCE and faith are close partners. Our faith is tested as fire tests gold and purifies it - and our faith is far more precious to God than mere gold; so, if our faith remains strong after being tried in the test tube of fiery trials, it will bring us much praise and glory and honor on the day of His return (1 Peter 1:7 AMP). We've all been through a 'fire' test, and when the test is finished, our faith is stronger. God uses situations and people to refine us.

What does PERSEVERANCE look like? Experiencing difficulties with family, friends, co-workers, associates, and strangers - seeing the good in others, acceptance, practicing love, trusting, and expecting the best possible outcome. As we PERSERVERE we are being prepared for what comes next – an onward and upward movement.

The good news about PERSEVERANCE is that it provides us an opportunity for change. When we become aware of our behavior, we can self-correct and stop circling around the mountain. We can change our habitual and automatic behaviors that do not serve us, others, or God.

Struggle builds character and brings out our greatest assets. We are God's handiwork - clay in the Potter's Hand - For we are His Workmanship, created in and for good works, which God has prepared that we should walk in them (Ephesians 2:10 AMP). Trust God and enjoy life while waiting with expectation for God's appointed time. Use life challenges as teaching tools. Spending time with God helps us to PERSEVERE. You cannot fail at life. The end result of PERSEVERING is the manifestation of our desires - the Blessing.

Affirm: God is in control - working out His plan for my life – Your Will Be Done on Earth as it is in Heaven.

How do you PERSEVERE when people and life challenges become difficult? Develop your own Spiritual practice – make your Spiritual practice personal.

Peace and Many Blessings

Day 12

SERVICE as a Spiritual Practice (*Soul Qualities: The Art of Becoming, Chapter 35*)

The Adinkra symbol Nkyinkyin (n-chin-chin) – selfless devotion to service and ability to withstand hardships.

SERVICE. The action of helping or doing work for

someone; contribution to the welfare of others; to provide someone with something that is needed or wanted; a helpful or useful act. The Akan symbol represents selfless devotion to SERVICE. SERVICE is changing one's self and playing many roles.

Even though I am free of the demands and expectations of everyone, I have voluntarily become a SERVANT to any and all in order to reach a wide range of people: religious, meticulous moralist, loose-living, the defeated, the demoralized – whoever…I've become just about every sort of SERVANT there is in my attempts to lead those I meet into a God-saved life. I didn't just want to talk about it; I wanted to be in on it (1 Corinthians 9:19-23 AMP).

SERVICE and humility are close partners. When we walk in the footsteps of the Master, we cannot go wrong. Jesus lovingly SERVED everyone He encountered in thought and prayer. Jesus, spiritually and physically, fed the multitudes, and counseled His followers with compassion. He assured us that we would do even greater things (John 14:12 AMP). SERVICE is living our Highest Potential by giving more to life than what we take; leaving people, places, and things better than we found them; creating peace; and being present for those in need.

Do you SERVE others with excellence, reverence, and creativity? Are you SERVING yourself to the best of your ability? Taking care of ourselves is paramount – eating healthy foods, drinking fresh water, breathing clean air, getting adequate sleep and movement, and communing with the Divine/God. We do our best SERVICE from a place of overflow.

What do you want others to say about you when you

transition? Write your obituary and then live it - live your Highest Potential!

How does your life SERVE you, God, and others? Develop your own spiritual practice – make your spiritual practice personal.

Peace and Blessings

Day 13

RELATIONSHIPS as a Spiritual Practice (*Soul Qualities: The Art of Becoming, Chapter 33*)

The Adinkra symbol Fi-Hankra (fee-han-krah) – brotherhood, safety, security, and solidarity.

RELATIONSHIP. The way in which two or more people or things are connected; the state of being related or interrelated; linkage. Create relationships based on brotherhood, authenticity, love, and compassion.

A RELATIONSHIP with the Divine is the most important RELATIONSHIP in our life. Our personal RELATIONSHIPS mirror our RELATIONSHIP with The Divine. To know God is to experience God through others. Choose to improve interactions with others through forgiveness (Matthew 18:22 AMP), kindness (Ephesians 4:32 AMP), peace (Romans 12:18 AMP), love (1 Corinthians 16:14 AMP), patience (Ephesians 4:2 AMP), nonjudgment (Matthew 7:1 AMP), and understanding (Psalm 119:130 AMP) – *soul qualities*. Honor yourself and others enough to be fully present in all RELATIONSHIPS.

The gap between human love and Divine love is an opportunity for growth. Human love is needs-based and conditional. Jealousy, anger, temper tantrums, and a need to be right, are ego-based behaviors. At the level of the ego (easing God out), we cannot love others more than we love ourselves – we cannot give what we do not have. Divine love is unearned, heart-centered, and unconditional. All RELATIONSHIPS benefit by practicing the fruits of the Spirit - the energy of The Divine, The Holy Spirit (Galatians 5:22 AMP).

What is the connection between RELATIONSHIPS, forgiveness, and boundaries? Our best selves are achieved through our RELATIONSHIP with others when we realize that the purpose of RELATIONSHIPS is to make us conscious - not happy. RELATIONSHIPS bring out our core issues disguised as love. Our response to others reflects core issues of unworthiness, abandonment, separation, and control. Forgiving others does not mean that we continue to accept inappropriate behavior. Awareness and discernment allow us to forgive, limiting our level of involvement with those who are careless and unkind. Choose to practice forgiveness, and love from a distance when others are callous. We are not required to continue to accept bad behavior. A higher level of awareness is lacking when people knowingly or unknowingly are unkind (Luke 23:34 AMP). People hurt others when they are hurting. It's never about you, but about how others feel about themselves.

Examine your RELATIONSHIPS and make all your RELATIONSHIPS an eight or better. Here are a few *soul inquiries* to consider:

Where are my RELATIONSHIPS located on a continuum of human love and Divine love? Who makes me a better person? Do I choose my RELATIONSHIPS based on what others can do for me? Is there a common pattern in my RELATIONSHIPS? Am I worthy of a better experience? Am I compassionate and forgiving? Do I serve others without expectation or reward? Am I grateful for my family and friends? Am I kind? Are my responses habitual and conditioned? Where is God in my RELATIONSHIPS?

Be willing and able to bring 100% of who you are to all your RELATIONSHIPS. Practice Divine Love with self, family, and others – and make your spiritual practice personal.

Peace & Many Blessings

Day 14

ACCEPTANCE as a Spiritual Practice (*Soul Qualities: The Art of Becoming, Chapter 1*)

The Adinkra symbol Akoma Ntoaso - (ah-ko-mah n-to-as-so) – joined and united hearts; agreement and togetherness in thought and deed.

ACCEPTANCE. The act of taking or receiving something offered; favorable reception; approval; receptive; the act of harmonizing; open to new ideas. A feeling of oneness and sharing a common spirit.

ACCEPTANCE is a knowing that allows us to be at peace. Trusting that all is well even when we cannot see how things will turn out. The pathway to ACCEPTANCE is peace - no stress, no fear, and no drama. When we practice ACCEPTANCE, events and situations pass through us with no resistance.

Our culture is overly concerned with other's people's opinions (OPP). Advertisement, music, peers, number of friends on Facebook, number of followers on social media, coveting and idolatry of others, and expectations of family and friends, dictate how we feel and what we ACCEPT in others and for ourselves. Who others expect us to be may cause anger, eating disorders, depression, unhappiness, physical ailments, anxiety, addiction, resentment, and grief. When others don't ACCEPT you, do not take it personal, it's not about you, it's about the other person. Have you heard the phrase, "It's not you, it's me?" Other people's drama has nothing to do with you — their drama is about what's going on in their lives. Be more interested in the Creator's ACCEPTANCE of you, than how others feel about you. Be who you are created to be — you are so Sacred.

What do you do to fit in? Do you ACCEPT the negative dialogue of others without offering an alternative perspective? What inappropriate behavior do you ACCEPT from others that does not support and honor your greater good? Fear stops ACCEPTANCE, and stress is a demonstration of non-ACCEPTANCE. Here is an Affirmation of ACCEPTANCE:

Affirm: I know my worth and I ACCEPT myself exactly as I AM. Conditions and circumstances are temporary and my potential is limitless. The stories I tell, are the stories I live. I AM devoted to re-writing my stories of greatness and goodness. I AM valuable to myself and others, I AM enough, and I share my good. Everything is working together for my good and the good of all concerned. I AM a perfect idea in the mind of The Ever-Loving Presence. The Holy Spirit lives through me and reveals everything I need to know this moment. I understand, trust, and ACCEPT the transformation of my life — I AM Blessed abundantly and all my needs are met. I open my mind and heart and ACCEPT all things good. I have the power and ability to create my ideal life. My life is my responsibility and the Holy Spirit, The Miraculous, the Creator of the Universe is guiding and directing my path. I AM at peace with myself and others. I know I AM going to be a great Blessing to someone today, because miracles are happening through me now. My life is a unique expression of Divine Energy – I see my faith and I AM ever so grateful - And So It Is.

ACCEPT that the Ever-Loving Presence is on your side. ACCEPT your good and affirm your Goodness – I AM GREAT- **I**ntegrity **A**ll **M**anifesting **G**raciously **R**ising **E**volving **A**ll **T**ogether - make your spiritual practice personal.

Peace and Many Blessings

Day 15

COURAGE as a Spiritual Practice (*Soul Qualities: The Art of Becoming, Chapter 9*)

The Adinkra symbol Akofena (ah-ko-fe-nah) – legitimized authority, heroic deeds, and courageous acts.

COURAGE. The quality of mind or spirit that enables a person to face difficulty, danger, pain, without fear; bravery; fearlessness; to act in accordance with one's beliefs, especially in spite of criticism.

COURAGE is asking the hard questions, the patience to wait for the answers, and responding when the answer is received. We do not have to be strong alone, GOD is our stronghold (Psalm 31:24 AMP). The sacred texts assure us, Fear Not – for I am with you – I will never leave you or forsake you (Isaiah 41:10 AMP). COURAGE is an internal process. Our purpose in life is to develop the divinity within - find the COURAGE.

As mentioned in *Thought as a Spiritual Practice*, negative thoughts are a source of anxiety, worry and fear. We become what we think about repeatedly. In the Hebrew scriptures, Job's life changed from abundance to desolation, he stated: for the thing which I greatly feared has come upon me, and that which I was afraid of is come unto me (Job 3:25 AMP). We experience a wide range of fears, real or perceived, based on our thinking – thoughts are powerful. The fear of being wrong, alone, not knowing, lack of control, fear of the dark, fear of heights, fear of cats, dogs, spiders, fear of success, fear of failure, and fear of the future. Fear damages our ability to move forward. The good news is that we have the ability to think on good things (Philippians 4:8 AMP).

What does COURAGE look like? Courage is demonstrated in one's behavior. To be vulnerable and to move forward, in spite of challenges and opposition is COURAGEOUS. Have the COURAGE to grow without question, hesitation, or complaint. Undo fear by recording and listening to Psalm 91 AMP, in the 1st person:

I live in the shelter of the Most High God and I rest in the shadow of the Almighty. I affirm, the Lord alone is my refuge, my place of safety; I trust Him. For He will rescue me from every trap and protect me and keep me safe. He will cover and shelter me from all harm. His faithful promises are my armor and protection. I am not afraid of disasters or challenges in the night or day. Tens of thousands fall at my side and around me, evil deeds do not come near me. I open my eyes, and witness how the wicked are punished. I make the Lord my strength, safe haven, and my refuge. No evil or disease will come near me, my family, or my home. The Most High God will order His angels to protect me wherever I go. The angels will hold me up with their hands so I won't stumble and fall and injure myself. I am protected from those who intend to harm me. My God rescues and protects those who love and trust Him. When I call on Him, He will answer me; He will be with me in trouble. He will shelter, defend, and honor me. He will reward me with a long life – delivering me from harm. The Most High God is my salvation. Amen.

COURAGE is required in becoming who we are created to be. Have the COURAGE to make your spiritual practice personal.

Peace and Many Blessings

Day 16

COMMITMENT as a Spiritual Practice (*Soul Qualities: The Art of Becoming, Chapter 8*)

The Adinkra symbol Fi-Hankra (fee-han-krah) – brotherhood, completeness, and solidarity; commitment to God, Self, family, and community. I am my brother's keeper. I am my brother.

COMMITMENT. A promise to do or to give; loyalty; the attitude of someone who works very hard; to give support; an agreement or pledge to do something in the future. Commitment promotes unity, and a sense of protection and security.

The process of COMMITMENT and moving forward can be challenging work. What does COMMTTMENT look like? How COMMITTED are you to You? Are you COMMITTED to your Life Vision? We tend to be successful when we envision the end result of our efforts at the beginning of a project. COMMITMENT takes time and discipline. Make a vow/a promise to your Higher Self - to have and to hold from this day forward!

We are masters of distraction, which keeps us from focusing on what we are feeling and what we need to do for ourselves. Decide what is priority in your life – and do it. If you are serious about your COMMITMENTS, you will write them down. Make journaling a part of your COMMITTMENT process. Seeing our challenges, vision, and goals on paper provides clarity and order. Clarity of purpose begins when we ask the question – "What do I want?' The Ever-Loving Presence, The Creator of the Universe wants to give you the desires of your heart. Ask, believe, and expect you will receive – seek and you will find (Matthew 7:7 AMP).

Develop daily practices and commit to them - kindness, gratitude, order, mindfulness, forgiveness, compassion - *soul qualities*. Overtime, practicing spiritual principles will come naturally. Select a spiritual principle and COMMIT one hour out of a 24-hour day to doing what you enjoy, and in the process, help someone else. Develop discipline and COMMIT to you - YOU are worth the effort. You are so Sacred.

Stay true to your COMMITMENTS by making your Spiritual practice personal.

Peace and Many Blessings

Day 17

One of the key elements of *Soul Qualities: The Art of Becoming* is spiritual practice – practice requires DISCIPLINE - DISCIPLINE comes from doing.

The purpose of DISCIPLINE is to regulate behavior. DISCIPLINE is more than thinking and speaking, DISCIPLINE is taking action. DISCIPLINE requires training, focus, and repetition. When we exercise DISCIPLINE, we improve a skill or behavior overtime - practice makes the master. What was difficult, becomes second nature. What area in your life requires DISCIPLINE?

Actionable principles we've covered within the past few weeks includes starting a GRATITUDE Journal (Chapter 18); FORGIVENESS (Chapter 15); Acts of Service (Chapter 35); mastering your inner dialogue through THOUGHT (Chapter 37); and creating Affirmative PRAYERS (Chapter 31). Practicing spiritual principles are easy to do, and easy not to do. DISCIPLINE comes from doing.

Today's soul quality is **DISCIPLINE**:

DISCIPLINE as a Spiritual Practice (*Soul Qualities: The Art of Becoming, Chapter 12*)

The Adinkra symbol Ani bre a gya (auh-ne bree ah jah) – patience, self-containment, self-discipline, and self-control.

DISCIPLINE. The Akan saying: Seriousness of one's deeds is demonstrated by one's actions, not appearance. The root word of DISCIPLINE is disciple. A disciple is a follower or student of a teacher, a leader - Jesus' disciples did not always think and do the right thing in all situations - but they were teachable. Self-mastery require DISCIPLINE.

Self-knowledge, self-control, self-censorship, and self-inquiry are the keys to a DISCIPLINED life. Knowing 'the why' of our behavior is a catalyst and motivator that keeps us focused on what we intend to accomplish. There is no magic formula for DISCIPLINE - DISCIPLINE comes from doing. True DISCIPLINE begins with our thoughts and a renewal of the mind (Ephesians 4:22-24 AMP). Focus, repetition, and consistent practice is the process of change.

Being DISCIPLINED does not always bring joy, but with training, DISCIPLINE results in the peace, fruit of righteous, right standing with God, and a lifestyle and attitude that seeks conformity to God's will and purpose (Hebrews 12:11 AMP). In your spiritual practice, let your 'why' be the driver - as you think in your heart of hearts, that is who you become (Proverbs 23:7 AMP). Stay motivated and find pleasure in your DISCIPLINE. There is a miracle trying to happen for someone through you today.

Below are steps for successful integration of spiritual principles into your daily life:

- **Select** a spiritual DISCIPLINE listed in *Soul Qualities*.
- **Become** that principle for a week.
- **Visualize** ways to practice the principle,
- **Study** the principle,
- And if you are really serious, you will **Write** it all down.

As you continue with your day, ask the question:

What spiritual practice provides opportunity to share my gifts? Be DISCIPLINED in your practice of forgiveness, gratitude, peace, love, service, humility, courage, and patience – make your spiritual practice personal.

Peace and Many Blessings

Day 18

PRAISE as a Spiritual Practice (*Soul Qualities: The Art of Becoming, Chapter 30*)

The Adinkra symbol Dono (dough-no) –celebration, praise, goodwill, and rhythm; The tension talking drum.

PRAISE. To proclaim the glory of God; to bless; celebrate; exalt; glorify; magnify; worship; to declare enthusiastic approval. The drum is a symbol of goodwill and elation. The sound of the drum intensifies the art of praise and worship.

Hallelujah, PRAISE the Lord! PRAISE God in His sanctuary; PRAISE Him in His mighty heavens. PRAISE Him for His mighty acts; PRAISE Him according to His excellent greatness; PRAISE Him with musical instruments, song, and dance. PRAISE Him with joy. Let everything that has breath PRAISE the Lord (Psalm 150 AMP).

PRAISE is service, devotion, and reverence to God. We also celebrate God through thoughts of gratitude, love, grace, and goodness produces the energy of joy and peace. Are you friendly and approachable? Are you joyful and enthusiastic? Do you love righteousness, integrity, and virtue? If so, God has anointed you with the oil of gladness (Hebrews 1:9 AMP). What if everywhere you went, you brought joy to the present moment. A friendly face is a demonstration of PRAISE.

There are as many ways to PRAISE and worship God

as there are people. The key element is to worship Him in Spirit and Truth (John 4:24 AMP); with heart, mind, and soul. We are the temple of the Living God (2 Corinthians 6:16 AMP). God dwells within us. God looks good in you and on you.

Below are daily acts of PRAISE between you and God:

- Give thanks for the simple things
- Give God the glory by always doing your best
- Dance with the Divine - the art of dance is worship
- Elevate the atmosphere with song and music
- Cultivate a feeling of thank-full-ness as you wake
- Display a joyful countenance and feeling throughout the day
- Be humble;
- Become your Sacred Self

PRAISE God through whom all Blessings flow.

Demonstrate PRAISE for the Creator of the Universe, The Ever-Loving Presence, The Miraculous, The Divine, Allah, Jehovah, Yahweh, The Holy One of God -– make your spiritual practice personal.

Peace and Blessings

Day 19

BALANCE as a Spiritual Practice (*Soul Qualities: The Art of Becoming, Chapter 5*)

The Adinkra symbol Krapa (khe-rap-ah) – Symbol of spiritual balance, good fortune, and spiritual strength.

BALANCE. A state of equilibrium; equal distribution

308

of weight; counterbalance. Spiritual balance is good fortune, spiritual strength, and positive vibrations.

A balanced life includes communion with God, family, friends, right livelihood, relaxation, movement, and sleep. There are 24 hours in a day and a majority of our time is committed to sleep (6 - 8 hours), work (8 -10 hours), with a remainder of 6 -10 hours of 'free' time per day. And if we are no longer at a traditional job – we are fortunate to have more time. When we experience enjoyable activities, time moves quickly. In contrast, with unpleasant activities, time stands still. Time is the movement of thought.

Are you enjoying your life? How do you manage your time? What activities would cause you to make the most of your time? A balanced life is having enough energy and time to do everything that you want to do within a 24-hour day. A balanced life requires planning, commitment, patience, and creativity. And if you are serious about balancing your time, you can purchase a monthly planner at the *Dollar Store* and write it all down.

Thought, energy, and time are connected. The process of recapitulation is a powerful tool in identifying energy loss, and the awareness of time. At the end of the day before sleep, account for your time. Think about the last 24 hours - waking, preparing for the day with family/work life, eating, interactions with strangers and coworkers. How did you feel with each activity? Did your discussions result in feelings of offense, defense, joy, or acceptance? Were you stressed, happy, sad; did you feel loved, connected, rejected? What thrilled and elated your mindbody? What sparked your creativity? Tune into your mindbody and become aware of what's draining or fueling your energy. What people, places, things, and thoughts encouraged, depressed, or stifled your energy? Pay attention to the feelings associated with your thoughts, words, and deeds. Thoughts and feelings are close partners. Do you know what makes you feel good? Plan to use your thought energy and time in doing what brings you joy. Include God, family, friends, right livelihood, relaxation, movement and creativity. Identify your timeless activities and intentionally plan a life of enjoyment. BALANCE and simplicity are close partners. Balance life with periods of stillness (Psalm 46:10 AMP) and activity.

Balance life to include the mental, physical, and spiritual by making your spiritual practice personal.

Peace and Many Blessings.

Day 20

Thank you for your willingness to participate in *Soul Journey: The Practice.*

We are at the half-way mark; day twenty. My prayer is that the Ever-Loving Presence, The Divine, has opened your heart and mind to a new paradigm, a new way of being with self and others.

Today's Soul Quality is TRUST:

TRUST as a Spiritual Practice (*Soul Qualities: The Art of Becoming, Chapter 38*)

The Adinkra symbol Funtummireku (fun-tum-me-rek-koo) is depicted as a two-headed crocodile representing oneness, unity, cooperation, trust, and shared destiny.

TRUST. A belief that someone or something is reliable, honest, and effective; TRUST God, TRUST the process of life, and TRUST that you will be guided and protected.

TRUST is a positive assumption and confident reliance on the character, ability, truth, and strength in someone or something, with no evidence of support. Where do you place your TRUST? Who do you TRUST? Do you TRUST only what you can see? Do you TRUST God? Can God TRUST you? Can you TRUST you? Are you TRUSTWORTHY? TRUST in the Lord with all your heart and lean not on your own understanding. In all your ways acknowledge Him, and He will make your path smooth and straight - removing obstacles that block your path (Proverbs 3:5-6 AMP). TRUST is a simple process; you either TRUST or you don't.

SELF-TRUST is the basis for all TRUST. SELF-TRUST calls into question our value and self-worth. Developing SELF-TRUST requires inner work – mastering your inner dialogue, making choices in your best interest, not being a people-pleaser, encouraging yourself with inspirational readings, sacred texts, Affirmative Prayer, and fasting from internal and external negativity. When we silence the negative tapes in our head, we can hear the voice of the Holy Spirit, The Ever-Loving Presence (Isaiah 30:21 AMP).

SELF-TRUST requires a process of commitment, discipline, and belief that you are supported.

Life happens to everyone. Think about your life experiences. What life challenges catapulted you into something you did not expect that not only benefited you, but others? The sacred scriptures tell the story of Joseph. His ten brothers threw him in a pit, and sold him into slavery because they were jealous of Joseph because he was favored by his parents. During Joseph's ten-year captivity, he demonstrated good character by being his best in every situation. As a result of sharing his gifts and talents, he became second in line to the king of Egypt. During Joseph's reign, there was a famine in the region, and Egypt supplied grain to all the nations, including his ten brothers who traveled to Egypt in search of food. With no malice in his heart, he provided food and shelter for his brothers and declared, "you intended to harm me, but God meant it for good" (Genesis 50:20 AMP).

Joseph is a perfect example of placing his TRUST in the Lord with all his heart (Proverbs 3:5,6 AMP). Continue TRUSTING until something happens, and be open to the guidance of the Holy Spirit. When you feel your back is against the wall, be faithful and know that God will support your efforts. The Divine, The Ever-Loving Presence has your back; God's got your back. He never leaves or forsakes us (Deuteronomy 31:6 AMP) and His Grace is sufficient (2 Corinthians 12:9 AMP).

Here is an Affirmative Prayer for you today:

Dear Father,

You are my Rock, my Fortress, and my Deliverer; I will not be afraid. What can man do to me? You are my God, my Strength and my Protection. I rely on You and I put my TRUST in You, for You have not abandoned me. In all my ways I know, recognize and acknowledge You. Your way has been tested and tried. Guide, direct, and make straight and plain my path. I TRUST You from the bottom of my heart. I listen for Your voice in everything I do and everywhere I go. You are the one that will keep me on track. I know Your Mercy and have experienced Your Kindness. I seek and inquire of You out of necessity. I am ever so grateful for

Your presence. In You I move, I live, and I have my being. Thank You, Father. Amen.

TRUST God, TRUST the process of life, and TRUST that you are guided, protected, and victorious – make your spiritual practice personal.

Peace and Blessings

Day 21

FREEDOM and thought are close partners. FREEDOM is contingent on decisions we make, based on our thought system. We choose between two thought systems – ego and the Holy Spirit. Ego is easing God out.

We are counseled on the role of the ego in the sacred scriptures. For out of the heart come evil thoughts - murder, adultery, sexual immorality, theft, false testimony, and slander (Matthew 15:19 AMP); We struggle not against flesh and blood, but against principalities, against powers, against the rulers of the darkness of this world, against spiritual wickedness in high places (Ephesians 6:12 AMP). The thief (deceptive intelligence/the ego) comes only to steal and kill and destroy our peace and joy (John 10:10 AMP). The flesh, the lower self, the ego wreaks destruction (Galatians 6:7 AMP).

In contrast, we are directed on how to respond to the distractions of the ego; deceptive intelligence. Be intentional and deliberate regarding your thought life by fighting the good fight of faith. Take hold of the eternal life and demonstrate your beliefs through practice (1 Timothy 6:12 AMP). Share and teach what you've learned with others, and never grow tired of doing good. At the proper time you will reap a harvest if you do not give up. Seek every opportunity to do good to all people (Galatians 6:9 AMP); when we sow to the Spirit – we reap eternal life (Galatians 6:7 AMP).

Submit to the authority of the Holy Spirit, resist and stand firm against ego/deceptive intelligence and it will flee from you. Be diligent and guard your heart, your heart is the wellspring of life (Proverbs 4:23 AMP). Wellspring is defined as source and supply, storehouse, bank, and treasury. The Ever-Loving Presence, the Divine, Creator of the Universe is our source and supply (1 Corinthians 8:6 AMP; Psalm 147:8 AMP; Matthew 6:26 AMP; Philippians 4:19 AMP; Matthew 6:31-33 AMP).

Today's Principle is FREEDOM:

Freedom as a Spiritual Practice (*Soul Qualities: The Art of Becoming, Chapter 16*)

The Adinkra symbol Adinkrahene (ah-dink-kra-hen-knee) – greatness, firmness, nobility; eternal nature of humanity.

FREEDOM. The quality or state of being FREE; the absence of coercion, or constraint in choice or action; ease; liberty; the condition of acting without compulsion. FREEDOM is unlimited possibilities.

And you will know the Truth, and the Truth will make you FREE (John 8:32 AMP). The opposite of FREEDOM is bondage. The emotional bondage caused by thoughts of fear, guilt, anger, strife, shame, hate, and doubt can be just as debilitating as physical ailments, hindering our FREEDOM to live a joyful and peace-filled life. FREEDOM is a state of mind. When we are FREE, we are in the presence of God; we help others without expectation of payment or reward; we are transparent; we are not easily offended; we are authentic; we live in the present moment; we transcend our self- importance; we are independent of other people's opinions; we can FREELY do a new thing; we are selfless - we simply live. Jesus the Christ is a true demonstration of FREEDOM. We are not separate from God, for in Him we live, move, and have our being (Acts 17:28 AMP). Truth is FREEDOM.

As discussed throughout our Soul Journey – the ego response is confusion, jealousy, conflict, offense, guilt, separation, judgment, abandonment, competition, and fear. A Course in Miracles (1975) suggests atonement when we decide wrongly.

Affirm: I must have decided wrongly, because I am not at peace, I made the decision myself, but I can also decide otherwise. I want to decide otherwise, because I want to be at peace. I do not feel guilty, because the Holy Spirit will undo all the consequences of my wrong decision if I will let Him. I choose to let Him (Schucman).

As you continue with your day, ask the question: What do I want?

The *FREEDOM Response* is the resolution to all conflict. The *FREEDOM Response* is the response of the Holy Spirit – peace, love, kindness, patience, gratitude, forgiveness, acceptance; *soul qualities*. The goal of a Spiritual life is FREEDOM.

Quiet the thoughts of the ego and hear the guidance of the Holy Spirit – make your spiritual practice personal.

Peace and Many Blessings

Day 22

CLARITY as a Spiritual Practice (*Soul Qualities: The Art of Becoming, Chapter 7*)

The Adinkra symbol Mframadan (m-fra-mah-dan) – preparedness and readiness to face challenges and weather the storm.

CLARITY. The quality of being easily understood in a very exact way; being easily seen or heard; state of being clear. Preparedness to face changes with faith and assuredness, knowing that you have what it takes to stand.

Who are you? Why are you here? Do you know what you want for yourself, and family?

If money were not a factor, what would your life look like? Where do you want to live? What type of business/ profession would you enjoy? What lifestyle and livelihood would you choose? How do you envision your health – physical, mental, and spiritual? Do you want to travel? These questions will prompt you to be CLEAR regarding how you see your life unfolding. And if you are serious about the process of becoming CLEAR, you will write it all down. You don't have to know how your wants will manifest. The first step is CLARITY – and think BIG!

Don't assume that others know what you want, and are willing and/or able to provide for your needs. When others do not meet our expectations, we respond with aggressive or passive aggressive behaviors. Acknowledge your feelings - this is an opportune time to gain CLARITY about core issues. Take time to sit down with paper and pen and ask yourself – What am I feeling? Have I felt this feeling in a similar situation? What do I want? Write down the dialogue in your head until the emotion is neutralized. Own what you feel and ask for CLARITY. Ask for HELP – Hello Eternal Loving Presence. The Presence is as close as our breath. If you need strength, direction, CLARITY – ask for it, and believe that you receive.

If you could ask God for anything, what would you ask for? King Solomon had opportunity to ask God for many things, but he recognized the value of wisdom (1 Kings 3:9 AMP), and Solomon's request made God happy. It's refreshing to know that The Presence wants to give us the desires of our heart (Psalm 37:4 AMP) – What are the desires of your heart? Always ask for what you want (James 4:2 AMP), and be specific.

Here is an Affirmation that will assist you with CLARITY: I acknowledge what I want and what I feel and I express my feelings clearly and directly, with kindness. I maintain CLARITY in the midst of chaos and confusion with the power of the Holy Spirit.

The goal of a Spiritual life is CLARITY (1 Corinthians 13:12 AMP) and the by-product of CLARITY is peace of mind. Make your spiritual practice personal.

Peace and Many Blessings

Day 23

ORDER as a Spiritual Practice (*Soul Qualities: The Art of Becoming, Chapter 26*)

The Adinkra symbol Mmara Krado (m-mah-rah crar-dough) – The seal of law and ORDER; ORDER is the first law of the Universe.

ORDER. To put in ORDER; arrange; ORDER suggests

a straightening out so as to eliminate confusion. ORDER is the arrangement or disposition of people or things in relation to each other according to a particular sequence. The first law of the Universe is the Law of ORDER – God is first. God is the Alpha and Omega, the First and the Last (Revelation 22:13 AMP). You are second, third family and friends, and fourth is work.

Cause and effect, laws of nature, and the Laws of Mind are governed by Divine ORDER. God established an operating system that consists of thought, speech, and manifestation. Thought is pure energy. Thought is pure energy. Thoughts are like seeds, planted in the mind. Sowing is thinking, affirming, and believing. What do you believe and why? Is your belief system based on past conditioning or habit? If you plant corn, don't expect to harvest beans. Likewise, planting love produces love; hate produces hate: and peace produces peace. All seeds produce after their kind (Genesis 1:11 AMP).

Divine ORDER and faith are close partners. As we think in our hearts, that is who we become (Proverbs 23:7 AMP). It's paramount to master your inner dialogue. When we are unaware of our thoughts/seeds, our lives are out of ORDER; chaotic. Do not be deceived, God is not mocked; for whatever we sow, this and this only is what we will reap (Galatians 6:7 AMP).

Here is a daily practice that will ORDER your life. The goal of this exercise is to ORDER the mind by ORDERING the physical environment. Our physical space is a reflection of the mind; our thoughts. You will need a journal to record your baseline assessment.

Observe what you see in your physical environment

and record it in your journal. Is your environment neat and clean or in disarray? Are items in place or out of place? Are things broken that need to be discarded? Make the necessary changes in your environment, organizing your physical space (home, car, purse, closet, drawers, desk, refrigerator, etc.). Second, develop a daily pattern for waking, eating, sleeping, prayer/meditation, and physical activity/movement. A daily pattern resets our circadian rhythm, our internal clock. ORDER and balance are close partners. Notice drama, confusion, and negativity throughout the day, and choose an appropriate response. Choose the *Freedom Response* of kindness, patience, courage, and mindfulness; *soul qualities.* Be mindful in all activities and have an intention to create peace. God is not a God of confusion and disorder but of peace and ORDER (1 Corinthians 14:33 AMP). Ask for the guidance of The Ever-Loving Presence, and be patient with self.

Affirm: I AM in Divine ORDER – Divine ORDER is mindbody alignment. My thoughts, words, and actions are in alignment with The Ever- Loving Presence, The Holy One of God, the Holy Spirt. My steps are ORDERED by The Creator of the Universe (Psalm 37:23 AMP).

Develop and maintain ORDER in the mindbody and Spirit – make your Spiritual practice personal.

Peace and Many Blessings

Day 24

DETACHMENT as a Spiritual Practice (*Soul Qualities: The Art of Becoming, Chapter 11*)

The Adinkra symbol Bi-nka-bi (bee-in-ka-bee) – freedom, peace, and avoidance of conflict.

DETACHMENT. The act of detaching; disengage; disunite. Freedom from prejudice, partiality, and other people's opinions. Detach from the past and live in the present moment, enjoying the here and now.

Social media platforms keep us connected to family, friends, associates, and work. In addition, we are entertained by other's lives: what they wear, what they ate for dinner, who they are dating. In today's media culture, we are famous by inappropriate behavior or by association. Our culture is obsessed with other people's lives. What other people think of you is not about you. People live in their own world and everything is all about them. DETACH from people's opinions, gossip, rejection, and negativity.

Here is an affirmation/declaration that if committed to memory, will guarantee a shift in your mind, heart, and spirit: I AM totally independent of the good and bad opinions of others, I am beneath no one. I am fearless in the face of any and all challenges (Chopra). This affirmation is powerful because it means that your greatness and goodness does not depend on compliments, validation, and acceptance from others. Within you is power and greatness. Live, move, and have your being in The Presence, The Miraculous, The Holy One of God (Acts 17:28 AMP).

Forgiveness and DETACHMENT are close partners. Our hearts have the capacity to love unconditionally and DETACHMENT or NONATTACHMENT gives us an opportunity to live in the presence of the Holy Spirit. Inappropriate behavior from others is minimized when we become aware of the role, we allow others to play in our life.

We can forgive ourselves and others, and choose the level and amount of energy (mental, emotional, and physical) we give. We are counseled to forgive, seven times seventy (Matthew 18:22 AMP). And if necessary, we can make a choice to love others from a distance. Live in the present moment, and don't dull the present with expectations of what or how it used to be, or how you think it should be. Let go of the hurt of the past, you survived it. Continuing to hold on to offense is a distraction, causing stagnation and delaying upward mobility. When we are distracted, we miss the joy, happiness, and Blessings of the present moment.

Know who you are in relationship to God, and whatever you think, say, and do, keep the Creator at the center of your life. We wrestle against the powers and rulers of darkness (Ephesians 6:12 AMP); deceptive intelligence. Fear, confusion, anxiety, and guilt are distraction to take away your peace and joy. DETACH from distraction (deceptive intelligence) and it will flee from you (James 4:7 AMP).

Live in the present, DETACH from social pressures of the past and future – and make your Spiritual practice personal.

Peace and Many Blessings

Day 25

MINDFULNESS as a Spiritual Practice (*Soul Qualities: The Art of Becoming, Chapter 24*)

The Adinkra symbol Fafanto (fa-fan-taw) – The Butterfly; tenderness, gentleness, honesty, and fragileness.

MINDFULNESS. A state of being aware of the present moment; consideration, discernment, and thought;

a heightened awareness of emotions or experiences on a moment-to-moment basis.

God is MINDFUL of His Creation (Matthew 6:25-32 AMP); The Lord has been MINDFUL of us. He will bless us (Psalm 115:12 AMP); What is man that You are MINDFUL of him, or the son of man, that You care for him (Hebrews 2:6 AMP). MINDFULNESS is being focused on the present moment, with full attention and awareness. It is comforting to know that God has not forgotten us. God loves and cares for us. We are commissioned to be MINDFUL of Self and others - Be careful how you live. Be MINDFUL of your steps...walk as the wise (Ephesians 5:15 AMP).

MINDFULNESS stimulates awareness and eliminates automatic and conditioned responses. When we are MINDFUL, we experience life with our total being; mindbody and spirit. MINDFULNESS asks and answers the question: Am I my brother's keeper? Yes, I am my brother. The Buddhist practice of MINDFULNESS is relieving the suffering of others through the art of deep listening, and kind, loving speech. MINDFULNESS encompasses many spiritual principles; awareness, kindness, clarity, intention, patience, simplicity, and peace.

Below are Acts of MINDFULNESS:

- Practice compassion, kindness, and generosity
- Give your time and attention
- Choose people over projects
- Protect others from physical, emotional, and sexual abuse

MINDFULNESS is living a God-realized, Christ-centered life, guided by the Holy Spirit. Are you available to be used by the Holy Spirit?

Develop a daily process of tapping into the healing power of MINDFULNESS – make your Spiritual practice personal.

Peace and Many Blessings

Day 26

NONJUDGMENT as a Spiritual Practice (*Soul Qualities: The Art of Becoming, Chapter 25*)

The Adinkra symbol Fofo (foo-foo) – warning against jealousy, envy, and negativity.

NON-JUDGMENT. The ability not to judge; not forming an opinion; discretion. The act of judging is unbecoming of good character. Jealousy, envy, gossip, and bullying reflects insecurity. Be more concerned about what God thinks of you. What others think of you and what you think of others results in division, strife, jealousy, and negativity; ego-based behavior.

JUDGE not, that you be JUDGED. For with the JUDGMENT you use you will be JUDGED, and with the measure you use, it will be measured to you. Why do you see the speck that is in your brother's eye, but do not notice the log that is in your own eye (Matthew 7:1-3 AMP)? What does JUDGING others say about us? Notice your self-talk about panhandlers, the homeless, and the less fortunate. We develop snap JUDGMENTS in regards to other people's misfortunes, and what they will do with the monies given to them. But for the Grace of God, we could be homeless or in a similar situation. When we JUDGE others by their external appearance, we are more likely to be critical of ourselves. A bully is self-important and is dependent on the discomfort of others. JUDGING is mental and emotional bullying. When JUDGING others, we don't have enough information. There is always something we cannot see that is hidden.

People are where they need to be. You are where you need to be. We are all on a spiritual path. We do not know the who, what, when, where, and why of God's process. We cannot see the entire scope of God's work (Ecclesiastes 3:11 AMP); God's plan is generational. As much as it depends on you, live peaceably with everyone (Romans 12:18 AMP).

NONJUDGMENT is an evolutionary practice that shifts our awareness. Instead of JUDGING, decide what you will give. If nothing else, give a hug, a compliment, or a Blessing. Do not neglect to extend hospitality to strangers, for by this some have entertained angels without knowing it (Hebrews 13:2 AMP). Commit to a day of NONJUDGMENT. To Have is to Give.

Affirm: Today, I will judge nothing that occurs, and throughout the day, I will remind myself not to JUDGE. I replace JUDGMENT with compassion and kindness. Namaste; I honor the place in you, where we are one.

The goal of NONJUDGMENT is to create a mindset where we enjoy life, family, work, and friends. Not JUDGING, just enjoying.

Create an atmosphere free of JUDGMENT – make your Spiritual practice personal.

Peace and Many Blessings

Day 27

SIMPLICITY as a Spiritual Practice (*Soul Qualities: The Art of Becoming, Chapter 36*)

The Adinkra symbol Asase Ye Duru (Ah-sa-see yeah doo-roo) – divinity of the Earth; nature.

Simplicity. The quality of being easy to understand or use; the state or quality of being plain; not fancy or complicated; clearness in speaking or writing; sincerity. God is revealed in His Creation, SIMPLISTIC and Beautiful.

We rejoice in living a life of SIMPLICITY, purity, and godly sincerity, not in carnal wisdom, but by God's Grace (2 Corinthians 1:12 AMP). SIMPLICITY is taking a direct approach to our connection with The Presence; free from dogma, rituals, and tradition. Believe in the All-Knowing power of The Presence by eliminating drama. Keep communication with others SIMPLE. Don't say anything you don't mean. You only make things worse when you lay down a smoke screen of pious talk, saying, 'I'll pray for you' or 'God be with you' and not meaning it. Let your 'yes' mean 'yes' and your 'no' mean 'no' - when you manipulate your words to get your way, you go wrong (Matthew 5:33-37 AMP). All of nature is SIMPLE and direct, except humans. We say one thing and mean another. SIMPLICITY is transparent, authentic, asking direct questions, free from denials or covers. Live your life in SIMPLE sentences - keep your stories SIMPLE minus drama. Clarity and SIMPLICITY are close partners.

Here are a few Soul Inquiries to consider when SIMPLIFYING your life: What SIMPLE things would make my life more enjoyable? Do I spend time doing the things I like to do? What five things would SIMPLIFY my life? What distracts me from what's important? What SIMPLE life lessons am I learning?

Spend time in nature enjoying the sunrise, sunset, flowers, trees, mountains, oceans, moon, and stars. God's creation is SIMPLE and elegant (Genesis 1:31 AMP). God is present in His Creation, and communing with nature brings light to the present moment. Evaluate your daily schedule and plan time for what you know and feel is important to you. The SIMPLE things are easy to do and easy not to do. Do the SIMPLE things.

SIMPLICITY is the key to happiness. SIMPLIFY life with more goodness; God by making your spiritual practice personal.

Peace and Many Blessings

Day 28

RESPONSIBILITY as a Spiritual Practice (*Soul Qualities: The Art of Becoming, Chapter 34*)

The Adinkra symbol Nkon Osnk Nkon Osnk (corn-song-corn-song) – unity, responsibility, and cooperation; A chain link.

RESPONSIBILITY. The state of being accountable for something within one's power; having the power to control or manage. Make a careful exploration of who you are and the work you have been given...each of you must take RESPONSIBILITY for doing the creative best you can with your own life (Galatians 6:4-5 AMP).

RESPONSIBILITY is being willing and able to RESPOND to everyone and everything with love and compassion. RESPONSIBILITY is to make our brother's and sister's problems our problems and solve them together. We are RESPONSIBLE for the development of our gifts. To him who much is given, much is required (Matthew 25:14-30 AMP). We are human and Divine (Acts 17:28 AMP) because the Holy Spirit lives within.

RESPONSIBILITY is the ability to respond with love, kindness, compassion, and equanimity. Collective work and RESPONSIBILITY are one of the seven principles of Kwanzaa, an African cultural celebration of family and community. Am I my brother's keeper (Genesis 4:9 AMP)? Yes, I am my brother. Akan saying: We are linked in both life and death. Being RESPONSIBLE means to choose the experience you want to create. Do not forget who you are and why you are here. We are here to shine our light and share our gift. Be RESPONSIBLE for that.

Be RESPONSIBLE for the energy you bring to others. You may be the only goodness that someone may encounter today. RESPONSIBILITY provides an opportunity to leave every person, place, and thing better than you found them. You know what you know to help someone else.

We are RESPONSIBLE for all that we are and who we are becoming. Demonstrate RESPONSIBLE choice – make your spiritual practice personal.

Peace and Many Blessings

Day 29

Welcome to day 29 of our Soul Journey. As a continuation of yesterday's principal on *Responsibility as a*

Spiritual Practice, we will continue our discussion on sharing our gifts and talents.

Practicing spiritual principles, the fruits of the Spirit (Galatians 5:22-23 AMP), are experiences in timelessness and eternity. The Holy Spirit provides us an opportunity to experience timelessness when we practice the qual; mindfulness, grace, joy, service, peace, gratitude, and freedom. We experience timeless when we live and walk in the Spirit.

In contrast, an ego response to experiences are unpleasant and disruptive. When our mind is consumed with repetitive thoughts of anger, abandonment, confusion, competition, guilt, rejection, defense/offense, separation, divisiveness, exclusion, pain, selfishness, revenge, fear, and strife, we are distracted. The ego is deceptive and is a master of distraction. The thief comes to kill, steal, destroy, (John 10:10 AMP) and wastes our time. We miss the peace and joy that is always present. Time is used as a teaching tool when we become aware of how ego-based behavior distracts us from practicing the qualities of the Holy Spirit.

The Holy Spirit is a return to God; a return to the qualities of the Spirit. The Holy Spirit is timeless and eternal.

Today's principle is Kindness:

KINDNESS as a Spiritual Practice (*Soul Qualities: The Art of Becoming, Chapter 21*)

The Adinkra symbol S E Ne Tekrama (s-e knee teh-kra-mah) – the need for friendliness, interdependence, and growth.

KINDNESS. The state or quality of being kind; good-natured disposition; considerate and helpful; passionate affection for another person; a feeling of warm personal attachment or deep affection. Friendliness and interdependence. Akan saying compares KINDNESS to the interdependence of the teeth and tongue.

Being KIND to ourselves is a prerequisite to how we demonstrate KINDNESS to others. KINDNESS is being considerate, helpful, humane, and friendly. KINDNESS is a fruit of the Spirit (Galatians 5:22 AMP). There is no greater act than KINDNESS because it embodies many principles in action; humility, forgiveness, patience, service, compassion, mindfulness, and peace. Flavor your actions with a pinch of KINDNESS - it only takes a little KINDNESS to make the difference in someone's day. Pay attention to the activities that you enjoy, and follow that energy. You will find your gift/talent/purpose when you do what you love. Share your gifts/talents with others. We learn what we teach.

KINDNESS is a learned behavior. We can be KIND and helpful to a stranger, and within a split second we can be mean and nasty to a friend or loved one. You cannot be authentically KIND if your cup is not filled to the brim. You cannot give what you do not have. We demonstrate KINDNESS by how we intentionally treat the people we know, and the strangers we do not know. See that none of you repays another with evil for evil, always show KINDNESS and seek to do good to one another and to everybody (1 Thessalonians 5:15 AMP).

Commit to a Day of KINDNESS by planning five or more acts of KINDNESS per day at least twice a week. Here are a few random Acts of KINDNESS:

- Give someone room to have a 'bad' day by offering words of encouragement

- When standing in line at the grocery store, allow someone to go before you
- Write a letter of encouragement to someone
- Do someone else's dishes
- In a 24-hour time span, smile and greet everyone you encounter
- Prepare someone's favorite meal

KINDNESS is priceless. Teach the qualities of the Holy Spirit with acts of KINDNESS practiced daily, weekly, and monthly — make your spiritual practice personal.

Peace and Many Blessings

Day 30

AWARENESS as a Spiritual Practice (*Soul Qualities: The Art of Becoming, Chapter 4*)

The Adinkra symbol Nyame Dua (n-yah-may doo-ah) — literal meaning, Presence of God; protection.

Awareness. The state or condition of being AWARE; knowledgeable; consciousness; cognition; informed; alert; and sophisticated. AWARENESS of and connection to a Supreme Being.

Studies in psychology and physiology have shown that AWARENESS is limited to what our physical senses can process at any given time. We have the ability to monitor and shift the constant stream of thoughts in our minds. Here is a simple AWARENESS practice: Think of a color. Become AWARE of the color in your environment. AWARENESS is intentional seeing and listening.

Be AWARE of a deceptive intelligence talking in your head — causing fear, feelings of competition, doubt, judgment, anxiety, and uncertainty. The endless dialogue in our minds has an opinion about everything. Witness the never-ending chatter, "I like that...I don't like that... What about me... Why didn't they..." These thoughts are vivid enough to release chemicals that activate cortisol and adrenaline in the nervous system, causing a fight/flight response - just by thinking. As a man thinks... (Proverbs 23:7 AMP). In contrast, studies indicate that affirmations, meditation, and stillness, triggers the nervous system to release calming chemicals of **endorphins** and oxytocin. AWARENESS occurs when we silence the mind - BE still and know... (Psalm 46:10 AMP).

The ego is in conflict with the Holy Spirit. Witness your ego dominated behaviors and transition to the Spiritual principles of the Holy Spirit. The soul is the Divine characteristic of the physical body. The role of the soul is to connect to Higher AWARENESS – The Holy Spirit. AWARENESS causes a shift in our thinking, and with time, soul-inspired thoughts replace ego-based thoughts. The goal is to modify the ego's role from a dominant to a subordinate status. Higher AWARENESS produces a Higher response (love, peace, kindness, goodness) in line with the fruits of the Spirit (Galatians 5:22-23 AMP) - *Soul Qualities*. Create a new paradigm by allowing the Holy Spirit to direct your lives.

Think on good things (Philippians 4:8 AMP), and be AWARE of how your mindbody processes information. AWARENESS is the first step to change. Keep track of your thoughts and with time, you will master your inner dialogue.

Shift your AWARENESS from ego and drama-based

to soul-inspired thoughts. Be willing and able to be guided by the Holy Spirit – make your Spiritual practice personal.

Peace and Blessings

Day 31

CHOICE as a Spiritual Practice (*Soul Qualities: The Art of Becoming, Chapter 6*)

The Adinkra symbol Mate Masie (mah-tee mah-see-uh) – being obedient; taking care of Self and making good choices.

Choice. An act or instance of choosing in awareness; choice is right action; something that is preferred or preferable to others; knowledge and prudence. The best part of something. Taking care and making a choice; to adhere to good counsel. A combination of knowledge, wisdom and obedience.

At this present moment, we have options regarding what to wear (color/style), what to eat/drink, where to go and how to get there, who to talk with, what to say or not say - we have a variety of options available to us depending on the decisions we made in the past, or the decisions we allowed others to make on our behalf. Forgive the 'CHOICES' others make and the 'CHOICES' you've made - forgive them because of lack of awareness (Luke 23:24 AMP).

Research studies show, that as adults, 25,000 hours of conditioning from childhood affect our thought processes daily. The next time you make a 'CHOICE' or decision, ask the question: Is my CHOICE a result of social conditioning, a habitual response, or past experience? If the answer is 'yes', then it is not a true CHOICE. True CHOICE only occurs in awareness. Confusion, drama, confrontation, and conflict is from the ego – deceptive intelligence. No one chooses dysfunction. Identify patterns of behavior that are habitual and/or conditioned, then list the *Soul Qualities* that you want to become –– CHOOSE the response of the Holy Spirit; CHOOSE life (Joshua 24:15 AMP; Deuteronomy 30:19 AMP).

The response of the ego is offense, guilt, separation, judgment, abandonment, fear, anguish, disorder, misinterpretation, criticism, selfishness, carelessness, retaliation, arrogance. The response of the Holy Spirit is always Peace – the Spirit only knows thoughts of Love, Peace, Knowingness, Joy, Mindfulness, Creativity, Service, Intuition, Patience, Responsibility, Forgiveness – *Soul Qualities.*

Make intentional CHOICES aligned with the Holy Spirit – make your Spiritual practice personal.

Peace and Blessings

Day 32

EVOLUTION as a Spiritual Practice (*Soul Qualities: The Art of Becoming, Chapter 13*)

The Adinkra symbol Nyame Nwu Na mawu (n-yah-may n-woo nah mah-woo) – the continuity and cycle of life.

Evolution. A process of gradual, growth, progressive change or development. Spiritual evolution is living the qualities of the soul – knowingness, peace, compassion, love - *Soul Qualities.* Spiritual intelligence is inner directed.

Darwinism dealt with man's linear EVOLUTION on a physical level from a single-cell organism to present day man. There is a Spiritual EVOLUTION of the mind - a renewing of the mind (Ephesians 4:23 AMP; Romans 12:2 AMP). This EVOLUTION creates a shift from ego-based consciousness, to a Higher consciousness consisting of mindfulness, compassion, love, forgiveness, kindness, wisdom, clarity, awareness, creativity - *Soul Qualities*. God has a Divine Design for everything and everyone. We can see His presence in nature, and sense His presence with stillness - your ears will hear a voice behind you saying 'This is the way, walk in it...' - Isaiah 30:21 AMP. Stillness/meditation is an EVOLUTIONARY process connecting us to The Presence – The Divine. With increased awareness, we are better prepared for the now, and for what's next. The Kingdom of God is at hand (Matthew 13:15-17 AMP; Mark 4:12 AMP) – awareness is at hand; our EVOLUTION begins with awareness.

We can be excited and captivated about the concept of Spirituality and awareness of Spiritual Principles when we see it in others. It's crucial to move from enthrallment to involvement by unveiling our conditioned personality and inappropriate reactions to life experiences. Spirituality is 2% awareness and 98% practice. If we are willing, we EVOLVE from awareness to practice.

Spiritual EVOLUTION is like throwing a pebble in a pond and watching the waves/vibrations move outward. Our EVOLUTION not only affects us, but everyone connected to us. In the process of spiritual EVOLUTION, choose to make your pebble far reaching. Greatness is finding and living our purpose. Ask the question – What is trying to EVOLVE in my life? Ask and you will receive – seek and you will find – knock and the door will be opened (Matthew 7:7 AMP; John 14:13,14 AMP).

Here is an Affirmation for you: **I**ntegrity **A**ll **M**anifesting **G**raciously **R**ising **E**VOLVING **A**ll **T**ogether - I AM GREAT, both human and Divine. I AM WILLING to be GREAT – come what may.

What experiences or states of higher consciousness have you experienced in your Soul Journey? EVOLVE into who God created you to be – make your spiritual practice personal.

Peace and Blessings

Day 33

PURPOSE as a Spiritual Practice (*Soul Qualities: The Art of Becoming, Chapter 32*)

The Adinkra symbol **Nkurumah** Kesee (n-kroo-mah Keh-see) – Greatness of purpose; good character.

Purpose. The reason for which something exists or is done; an intended or desired result; goal; the point at issue; resoluteness; intention. And we know with great confidence that God who is deeply concerned about us causes all things to work together as a plan for good for those who love God, to those who are called to His plan and PURPOSE (Romans 8:28 AMP).

Who am I? Why am I here? How can I help? How can I serve? What is God's plan and PURPOSE for my life? It's refreshing to know that God has a plan and PURPOSE for our lives. Are you willing and able to seek God's PURPOSE? Just as David served the PURPOSE of God in his own generation (Acts 13:36 AMP), Jesus epitomized

PURPOSE in action. As reported in the Gospels, His focus was in fulfilling His PURPOSE (Luke 4:43 AMP; John 12:27 AMP) - and He did not get distracted by deceptive intelligence (Matthew 4). Jesus focused His energy in doing what He came to do, and likewise, God has something for us to do. Ask the Divine, what will You have me to do today? Be willing and able to be led by the Holy Spirit. Want for others what you want for yourself – To Have is to Give.

Aligning with Spiritual Principles – *Soul Qualities*, shifts our focus from self-service to God-Service. We utilize our energy for God's PURPOSE when we become our best selves. Our PURPOSE is to demonstrate God's power, love, compassion, wisdom, and grace. Our PURPOSE is to create peace, harmony, and well-being. Our PURPOSE is to manifest the best of who we are by developing the divinity within us. Our PURPOSE is service and we serve because it is our PURPOSE. The Holy Spirit moves us to do not only what benefits us, but also what benefits others – the Greater Good. Greatness is finding and fulfilling our PURPOSE.

Here is a practice to assist with your life PURPOSE: Develop a Life PURPOSE Statement (LPS). An LPS provides a sense of awareness and direction. Develop several practices around your statement that resonate with you and trust that you will be supported. Place the LPS in clear view to be read daily, and do something every day, with heart, towards your PURPOSE. Be open to the guidance of the Holy Spirit. PURPOSE is eternal and is mastered through practice. Place yourself on a schedule – live your PURPOSE!

PURPOSE serves the soul and the soul serves The Divine. What have you come to life to give? Be willing to allow life experiences to move you closer to your PURPOSE.

336

Live a conscious and meaningful life with PURPOSE –
make your spiritual practice personal.

Peace and Blessings

Day 34

AUTHENTICITY as a Spiritual Practice (*Soul Qualities: The Art of Becoming, Chapter 3*)

The Adinkra symbol Nsaa (n-sah) – Akan saying: He who does not know the real design will turn to an imitation.

Authenticity. Real or genuine; not copied or false; true and accurate; not an imitation; excellence, bona fide. AUTHENTIC implies being fully trustworthy.

AUTHENTICITY is to know your truth, live from the heart, and to have the courage to show up with integrity, genuineness, honesty, and without pretense. Being AUTHENTICALLY courageous is meeting challenges and oppositions based on who you are – no pretense, transparent - being vigilant for righteousness (Proverbs 4:23-27 AMP).

AUTHENTICITY requires us to ask the hard questions: Who am I? Why am I here?' Am I double-minded? Do I create relationships based on AUTHENTICITY? How do I develop the courage to be AUTHENTIC in a culture that encourages me to fit in? What distracts me from being AUTHENTIC? Do people know my AUTHENTIC Self? What is the Truth of my being? What are my talents/gifts?

Our responses to these questions are based on object referral, external reference points outside of ourselves. Or self-referral, internal reference point - who we are at the heart and soul level. There is no other person like you. We are created to be a unique expression of The Divine, the

337

Ever-Loving Presence. Give your best without comparing yourself to others (Galatians 6:4 AMP). Are you willing to be the greatest You that You can be? Do not sacrifice your Real Self for a self-image – how and what others think you should be. Fitting in is the lowest level of existence. Being AUTHENTICALLY courageous produces a high vibration - be your AUTHENTIC Self.

AUTHENTICITY + Courage = Right Action. What we think, believe, say, and do is powerful. Know that you have what it takes to stand and act in accordance to your belief. The key to an abundant and peace-filled life is Right Action. Stand firm and be diligent in your Spiritual practices (Ephesians 6:10-18 AMP). Be more concerned about what the Creator of the Universe thinks of you than what others think of you. Be AUTHENTICALLY courageous by sharing your gifts and talents. You were given talents and gifts to share and to encourage others – be bold and vigilant in your practice – Live Out Loud!

Affirm: I AM AUTHENTICALLY courageous and I express my feelings clearly and directly with kindness. I stand in the truth of my AUTHENTIC Self and a I demonstrate integrity in thought, speech, and action. I stand strong and walk in a pattern of good works. I AM compassion, mindful, joyous, and jubilant. I rejoice and my vibration is high. I am a child of the Most-High God and I am here to serve and to do what brings me joy.

Develop the courage to be AUTHENTIC – make your spiritual practice personal.

Peace and Blessings

Day 35

VISION as a Spiritual Practice (*Soul Qualities: The Art of Becoming,* Chapter 39)

The Adinkra symbol Mframadan (m-fra-mah-dan) — elegance and preparedness and ready to face the changes of life.

Vision. VISION is a concept or image in the mind; insight; preparation; a deeper awareness and readiness for the future. When there is no VISION the people perish (Proverbs 29:18 AMP). Prophetic VISIONS are messages from God and reveal future events. Sometimes we question whether we are hearing the voice of the Holy Spirit or the ego. How do you know it's the Holy Spirit moving and speaking to your heart – your being? The Holy Spirit only knows peace, GREATNESS, and goodness.

The Creator of the Universe - God - gifted us with a Higher awareness and we are Blessed above all God's Creations with the ability to think, create, and fellowship with The Divine. Ideas, insights, and creativity are available to all - our sons and daughters will prophesy, and our young men will see VISIONS, and our old men will dream dreams (Acts 2:17 AMP). God has a Divine Design for our lives. Ask the question: What is my VISION and my genius?

What is your VISION for yourself and family? Do you have a limited or limitless VISION of your life? Are there others who benefit from your VISION? How will you fund your VISION? Michael Bernard Beckwith's book, *Life VISIONING,* is an essential guide on the how to of the life VISIONING process. We can enlarge our VISION when we see the end at the beginning. Take time to write about your 'Ideal Scene' in detail – breathe life into your VISION. Create a VISION Board. Plan monthly meetings to discuss what you ENVISION for the family with full participation from everyone. Create a theme, be enthusiastic, and have fun. Family VISIONING creates a sense of wholeness, harmony, and purpose. A Life Vision elevates us above our present life situations.

Do not reduce your VISION because others do not know or understand the VISION. Your VISION is possible. Believe, expect, affirm, and be open to the guidance of the Holy Spirit - there are unlimited possibilities waiting for YOU. Your Life VISION is sacred and is between you and God. You are so sacred.

Living a meaning-filled life requires VISION and Purpose. We come to life to express our gifts and talents, and we create our best life when we live as if The Ever-Loving Presence - God - lives in and as us (Acts 17:28 AMP). What does your VISION look like for yourself and family, and does your VISION include The Divine?

Your Life Vision benefits you and others – THINK BIG.

Peace and Many Blessings

Day 36

MEDITATION /STILLNESS as a Spiritual Practice
(*Soul Qualities: The Art of Becoming, Chapter 23*)

The Adinkra symbol Gye Nyame (jeh N-yah-mee) - The Akan symbol "Tis God Only"; or Except God; the Omnipresence and Omnipotence of God.

Meditation. To engage in thought; reflection; devout religious contemplation or spiritual introspection; silence within the mindbody and spirit. Connecting to the unlimited power of The Divine - the Supreme Being.

Meditation is a higher state of consciousness. In stillness, we tune into our internal guidance system. MEDITATION is the beginning of an intimate relationship with The Presence – be still and know the presence of The Divine (Mark 4:39 AMP; Matthew 8:23-27 AMP; Psalm 46:10 AMP). MEDITATION is giving our attention to the Divine – The Presence is deserving of our devotion. In a MEDITATIVE state, we dwell in the secret place of the Most High God (Psalm 91 AMP).

Affirm: The Ever-Loving Presence is the lover of my heart and the keeper of my soul.

Your MEDITATION practice is between you and God. Meditation is an evolutionary practice - your Spiritual evolution is as unique as your thumb print. Do not compare your practice with others – what The Divine has for you, is for you alone. 'Medi' means to heal, and MEDITATION is beneficial to our total well-being - mindbody and spirit. Stillness prepares the mind to receive direction from God; produces calmness, relaxation, and a sense of peace; increases coping skills; enhances the immune system; and heightens creativity and intuition. In MEDITATION, we are elevated to a higher frequency. Although there are unlimited benefits to practicing MEDITATION – the primary goal is communion with The Divine. The Divine always speaks to our spirit – the wind blows where it wishes, you hear its sound, but you do not know where it is coming from and where it is going; so, it is with everyone who is born of the Spirit (John 3:8). We can receive Divine guidance in the shower, driving, gardening, walking, or any activity. The

Word may come in an hour, one day, week, or month. Our responsibility is to open our heart and be receptive to the information and guidance of the Holy Spirit.

MEDITATION is a practice but also a way of being, affecting how we treat ourselves, and others. Our perspective shifts when we tune into God, a Higher Consciousness.

During MEDITATION, focus on the breath. Our life begins and ends with the breath. Just before the in-breath turns into the out-breath, notice the small gap. Be present in the gap and discover the true nature of silence. The breath is a movement of energy - master it. Know that God is working all things for your good and the good of all concerned (Romans 8:28 AMP) - and you cannot do better than ALL.

In MEDITATION, there are no thoughts, no-thing-ness, no stress - just you and The Ever-Loving Presence. The practice of MEDITATION and Prayer allows us to rest in His Presence. MEDITATION/Stillness and Prayer are close partners and practice establishes an inner Awareness and Peace.

Awaken to your inherently Divine consciousness – make your spiritual practice personal.

Peace and Blessings

Day 37

CREATIVITY as a Spiritual Practice (*Soul Qualities: The Art of Becoming, Chapter 10*)

The Adinkra symbol Ananse Ntontan (ah-nan-se n-to-n-tan) – craftiness; the use of the imagination; original ideas; vision and inspiration. A spider demonstrates its resourcefulness, CREATIVITY, and wisdom by weaving an intricate and elaborate web for survival.

Creativity. The state or quality of being CREATIVE; the ability to transcend traditional ideas, rules, patterns, relationships, and to CREATE meaningful new ideas; the process by which one utilizes CREATIVE ability.

The process of CREATION is thought, to speech, to manifestation. Words are things – words CREATE. You are a CREATOR, what are you CREATING in your life? Did you CREATE a Life Purpose Statement (LPS)? Did you CREATE a Vision Board to organize your life plans? Did you CREATE your Ideal Scene, the written scenario that maps your destiny? Have you taken the time to CREATE your Life Vision? Have you CREATED a Gratitude Journal? Have you CREATED a physical environment that is Orderly and peace-filled? Have you CREATED a specific time daily for Meditation and Stillness – communion with The Divine, The Ever-Loving Presence? Have you CREATED a program to practice Mindfulness, Acts of Kindness, and Service to others? Have you CREATED and recorded your Affirmations? Have you CREATED a space for FORGIVENESS in your heart? Have you CREATED a Thought Program to counter negative programming? Have you CREATED a process to make all your Relationships an eight or better? Have you CREATED Love and Peace in your heart?

We CREATE by our thoughts - karma are repeat thought patterns. CREATIVITY transcends karma. In CREATIVITY, a quantum leap occurs – something new and different beyond space and time. CREATIVITY is a higher level of Choice. Speak only about the things you want for yourself. Speak and write stories of Greatness, Goodness, and Abundance - this is the right use of the imagination.

Teaching, healing, and sharing is The Ever-Loving Presence way of CREATING – it is our way of CREATING. When we share, we expand our thinking and CREATE with our imagination. We CREATE room for more – more ideas, more abundance, and more possibilities (Isaiah 54:2 AMP) – to have is to give. CREATE a character that reflects your Higher Self; Christ-consciousness; God-Consciousness. Use your gifts and talents to CREATE Greatness and Goodness – the Kingdom.

Affirm: I have the power to CREATE. I am free and unstoppable.

CREATE a life of peace and harmony with self, family, friends, co-workers, community, and the world – make your spiritual practice personal.

Peace and Many Blessings.

Day 38

AFFIRMATION as a Spiritual Practice (*Soul Qualities: The Art of Becoming, Chapter 2*)

The Adinkra symbol Akoben (ah-ko-ben) – call to action, readiness; War Horn.

Affirmation. The act or an instance of AFFIRMING; state of being AFFIRMED; the assertion that something exists or is true; a statement or proposition that is declared to be true; a solemn declaration.

An AFFIRMATION is literally a call to action. Our voice vibrates and moves our mindbody from inaction to action. Words are things - words have power – words create

344

life. There is life and death in the power of the tongue (Proverbs 18:21 AMP). In Matthew 9:21 AMP, there is a noteworthy account of the use of AFFIRMATIONS – you may be familiar with the woman that was sick for twelve years with an 'issue of blood' that was incurable by the physicians of her day. The scriptures state, she AFFIRMED - she said to herself, 'If I could only touch the hem of his garment, I could be healed' - her faith made her whole. She no doubt, repeated to herself what she believed. AFFIRMATION is a powerful Spiritual practice. What we think, believe, say, and do is powerful. Thought, Faith, AFFIRMATION, and Right Action are the keys to an abundant and peace-filled life. Are you AFFIRMING that you can achieve your desires? Or are you a naysayer? The book of Proverbs (6:2 AMP) counsels that we are 'snared by the words of our mouth' – we can choose to speak words that liberate or entrap and keep us stagnate. Eliminate negative thoughts and AFFIRM your good. You don't need to know where your good will come from – just AFFIRM, have Faith, and do all you can do in the moment. Think of a time when you had difficulties and challenges and everything worked itself out – and fell into place. The Ever-Loving Presence, The Divine will take care of the details. Your job is to fast from negativity (worry, anxiety, and fear), and have Faith. You cannot add any time to your life by worrying about life challenges and difficulties (Matthew 6:27 AMP).

AFFIRMATIONS are for you – not for God. AFFIRMATIONS change how you feel about you. As repeated several times during our *Soul Journey*, 25,000 hours of conditioning from childhood affect our thought processes daily (Choice, #6). The mind requires repetition and reprogramming to make solid changes. Throughout the *40 - Day Soul Journey* there are many AFFIRMATIONS stated in the commentaries. In addition, located at the end of each chapter in *Soul Qualities: The Art of Becoming*, there is an AFFIRMATIVE Prayer – 40 AFFIRMATIVE Prayers. Record 10 - 20 minutes of AFFIRMATIVE Prayers, scriptures/sacred texts in the first person. Make your recordings personal by creating your own AFFIRMATIONS. If you are really serious, you will commit them to memory. Listen to and speak your AFFIRMATIONS with intention throughout the day, and overtime, you will change how you feel about you. AFFIRMATIONS replace the negative thought programs in your head – As you think, you are – you change your life by changing your thoughts. AFFIRM good things (Philippians 4:8), and speak only about the things that you want for yourself. AFFIRMATIVE Prayer is the right use of the mind.

Here is a sample AFFIRMATIVE Prayer:

Words are things - words have power. There is life and death in the power of the tongue. I AM whole through Faith. All my experiences are opportunities to grow in Faith, Endurance, and Patience. The Divine, The Presence is responsive to my needs – I AM a Divine pattern and AM surrounded by the Grace, Love, and Givingness of The Ever- Loving Presence. I AM Wisdom, Peace, Joy, and Love. The Spirit lives through, and around me. I experience Peace with uncertainty – ALL my needs are met. I AM at Peace with self, and others, and I Accept this Peace that surpasses all understanding. The Presence strengthens me, lifts me up to my Highest potential – I have access to more than I can see, say, and imagine. I AM ever so Grateful – You make ALL things new.

In all things I demonstrate a pattern of good works, I AM Perseverance and I demonstrate Integrity in thought, speech, and action. I AM Truth, Courage, and Willingness. I AM available to the power and Presence of the Holy Spirit, The Miraculous, The Divine. I express myself Clearly and directly with Kindness. I do all things with Gratitude, in Order, and I stand strong and walk in The Presence. I AM Compassion, Awareness, and Mindfulness. I Rejoice and Trust in The Presence and I AM Joyous and jubilant. I AM staying The Course and I submit to The Ever-Loving Presence and ALL IS WELL – and So It Is.

Thought Programming/AFFIRMATIVE Prayer, fasting from negativity, and Spiritual Practices will counter the 25,000 plus hours of conditioning from childhood and adulthood that does not SERVE or benefit you, family, friends, acquaintances, co-workers, community, world, or God.

As you continue with your day:

AFFIRM your goodness to Self, God, and others – make your Spiritual practice personal.

Peace & Many Blessings.

Day 39

We've covered 38 I /Spiritual Principles to date – what *Soul Qualities* or Spiritual Principles resonate with your mindbody and spirit.

We also discussed the relationship between the mind and body, in *Thought as a Spiritual Practice*. We cannot separate the mind and body – the mindbody operates as one unit and requires care for optimal well-being. Spiritual practice, fasting from negativity, and Affirmative Prayer, is essential in raising mental/emotional awareness. In addition, the body also requires care for total well-being. Thirty minutes of movement, and eating a rainbow of nutritious, fresh fruits and vegetables daily, fuels the body and combats dis-ease. Mindbody Soul Alignment (MBS) combines these five components (Spiritual practice, fasting from negativity, affirmative prayer, movement, and eating a rainbow of nutritious, fresh fruits and vegetables) and if practiced will arrest and reverse the aging process, energize the mindbody, and heighten awareness. You will impact your mindbody on a cellular level – and begin to live the best life you can imagine - you will not recognize yourself. Your physical, mental, emotional energy will align with Spirit. MBS Alignment will renew your life - if you are Willing. These things are easy to do – and easy not to do.

Today's *Soul Quality* is INTENTION.

INTENTION as a Spiritual Practice (*Soul Qualities: The Art of Becoming, Chapter 20*)

The Adinkra symbol Nyame Biribi Wo Soro (n-yah-may Bear-ree-bee who soh-row – God there is something in the heavens; hope and inspiration; direction during adversity.

Intention. The thing that you plan to do or achieve: an aim or purpose; a determination to act in a certain way; design and objective; to INTEND to accomplish or attain; INTENTION implies action.

In the Spirit, we are energy and information. We are Blessed and privileged above all creation by the Creator of the Universe with gifts and talents. Our Spirit (energy and information) radiates on a higher or lower frequency based on our thoughts. We can choose to radiate Love, Peace, Joy, Praise, Faith, Gratitude, and Kindness – guilt, anger, unforgiveness, deception, and confusion operates on a lower frequency. INTENTION is the energy behind every thought, word, and action, and our INTENTIONS are not always evident in what we say or do. We can give money to a friend because we want to help. Or we can give to a friend with the INTENTION to ask for a favor in the future. Both situations look the same, but the latter is based on manipulation (lower frequency). Examine your INTENTIONS – ask yourself what are my motives behind my actions, and be honest. INTENTIONS are from the heart. With God, transparency is not optional. God knows our INTENT - He would surely know, for He knows the secrets of every heart (Psalm 44:20-21 AMP).

We are responsible for setting INTENTIONS that benefit the greater good. Strengthen your INTENTIONS through association. As iron sharpens iron, so one friend sharpens another (Proverbs 27:17 AMP). Do you know the INTENTIONS of the people who are close to you? It's a good idea to know who you are in the trenches with - What is your INTENT for the people in your life – your partner, children, friends, relatives, associates, and coworkers? INTEND to do all you can do, for the good of all concerned, to the best of your ability (Romans 12:1 AMP; Ephesians 6:7 AMP). Spiritual growth requires setting INTENTIONS on how we live. What is your INTENTION for every area of your life?

Affirmative Prayer, Thought Programming, Kindness,

Mindfulness, and Gratitude shifts our Intention and attention. Here is an Affirmative Prayer for your life, today:

Dear Father: I thank You for every good INTENTION I ever had for myself and others. I thank You for Your inspiration, guidance, courage, and love that supports my INTENTIONS for my Life Vision. Thank You for allowing me to see the manifestation of my good INTENTIONS. Reveal to me my true INTENTIONS and create in me a clean heart. I focus my attention on the present - what I can do right now — at this moment and I Intend on the future as it unfolds. I trust You to work out the details and I am ever so grateful for Your Divine presence in my life. In You I move, I live, and have my being. You are my Father and I humbly give You all Glory, Honor, and Praise. Amen.

As you continue with your day:

Think and radiate the Light of The Ever-Loving Presence. Your INTENTIONS benefit the good of all concerned, the Greater Good — make your spiritual practice personal.

Peace and Many Blessings

Day 40

Thank you for your willingness and participation in *Soul Journey*. Which Spiritual Principles resonated with you throughout our Soul Journey?

Our challenge is consistent and sincere practice. Spirituality is 2% Awareness and 98% Practice. Awareness is our Divinity — we are human and Divine. Develop an individualized Practice that includes Forgiveness, Affirmative Prayer, intentional daily Spiritual Practice, and fasting from negativity. Share your gifts and talents with others – To Have is To Give.

Take a moment to think about how you spend your energy? We spend the majority of our energy on our external life. What are the 'labels' you allow others to place on you – the 'labels' you place on yourself? 'Labels' like friend, spouse, employee, business owner, gender, sexual orientation, religion, sister, job title, education, health, etc. And what is the story behind the 'labels'? There is always a story. Who would you be without the 'labels'? Who are you?

The WISDOM of Awareness is from the Holy Spirit, The Divine. With Awareness, we create a balanced lifestyle plan with purpose, and we cease to be entangled in the many 'labels' that keep us stuck in 'Doing'.

Today's Principle is WISDOM:

WISDOM as a Spiritual Practice (*Soul Qualities: The Art of Becoming, Chapter 40*)

The Adinkra symbol Nyansapo (n-yahn-sah-poh) – WISDOM Knot; the WISDOM of intelligence, ingenuity, and patience.

Wisdom. The quality or state of being WISE; knowledge of what is true and coupled with right action; understanding. In WISDOM we are established in Awareness – in Being.

If you could ask God for anything, what would you ask for? King Solomon had opportunity to ask God for many things, but he recognized the value of WISDOM (1 Kings 3:9 AMP), and Solomon's request for WISDOM made God happy. It's refreshing to know that The Presence wants to give us the desires of our heart (Psalm 37:4 AMP). WISDOM is a valuable asset. WISDOM is having knowledge of what is true, coupled with the ability to make right decisions. WISDOM is the principal thing (Proverbs 4:7 AMP). WISDOM and understanding are close partners.

The many benefits of WISDOM include peace, joy, and long life (Proverbs 3:17, 21 AMP) when combined with careful planning. Practicing Godly WISDOM consists of consuming live plants; fasting from negativity; drinking fresh water; deep breathing; adequate sleep; activity/movement; meditation/stillness, connection with The Presence/God, supporting relationships, laughter; reading literature that inspires the soul; balancing rest and activity; and right livelihood. The mindbody thrives on consistency. These lifestyle habits are easy to do and easy not to do. Take great care of you so that you are able to do what God called you to do.

Godly WISDOM from the Sacred scriptures makes us WISE (2 Timothy 3:15 AMP). Study and do your own independent investigation of the Truth (2 Timothy: 2:15 AMP). WISDOM and awareness are inseparable. Because our lives are routine, it's necessary to create opportunities to be filled full of The Spirit - by practicing Spiritual principles – *Soul Qualities*.

My primary reference in WISDOM traditions is the Bible – the book of Ecclesiastes, written by King Solomon, is practical and apropos in his council – Give your gifts and talents generously to many (cast your bread on the waters), for your gifts will return to you (Ecclesiastes 11:1 AMP). Give and it will be given to you (Luke 6:38 AMP) – To Have is to Give is the WISDOM of the Divine. Give your best. What miracle is trying to happen for someone through you today?

Demonstrate WISDOM by making your spiritual practice personal.

Peace and Many Blessings

LESSONS IN FREEDOM

Lessons in Freedom focuses on renewing the mind by changing our thought life, and the *Soul Quality* of Forgiveness. These sessions require you to record each session in your voice. You can purchase a voice recorder or utilize the recorder on your cell phone. The theory and practice around the recording are, for maximum affect, your mind and body respond to your voice. You are making efforts to override the internal and external negative thoughts that inundate you moment to moment by the media, people, past conditioning, and life situations. You tell yourself what you expect, and to expect change. As repeated in *Soul Qualities: The Art of Becoming*, 25,000 hours of conditioning from childhood affect our thought processes daily (Choice as a Spiritual Practice, #6). Words have miracle working power (Isaiah 57:19 AMP; Ephesians 6:17 AMP). The great news is that we have the ability to program thoughts that are beneficial. Our thoughts directly affect the mind and body and it's crucial that we master our inner dialogue. Renewing the mind requires repetition, and repetition is the key to mastery.

Record and listen to a recording at least twice daily: morning and evening. The recording primes the mindbody with affirmative thoughts – changing thoughts, changes our emotions, changes our lives. Real and sustainable change occurs in our thought life. Add sacred texts and affirmative prayers to the recordings when you are comfortable. Overtime, you will notice a change in tone/frequency of your voice. The change in your voice is energy transformation – your Goodness/Greatness.

The *Lessons in Freedom* session's central theme is Forgiveness. Begin the day with the reading/recording, and in the evening, listen to the recordings and examine all idle thoughts in opposition to the *Lesson* and not in your best interest. Then allow at least fifteen minutes recap the day. Use time to effectively to reprogram and renew the mind (Romans 12:2 AMP) by correcting years, decades of thinking that does not benefit you or others. Ask the question: Did I give/receive Forgiveness, Love, Freedom, Peace today? Am I willing to give/receive Forgiveness, Love, Freedom, Peace tomorrow? Journal your answers as a baseline, and revisit your answers for future reference and witness the change. As stated in *A Course in Miracles*, all things are lessons God (Creator of the Universe) would have us to learn. Learning is evident when behavior is changed.

In the *Lessons in Freedom*, you don't have to do anything other than be present, sit in silence, and listen. The mind knows how to process information, changes take place overtime. Our thought life keeps us in bondage. What does bondage look like? Disease (mental, emotional, and physical), guilt, envy, anxiety, lack, limitation, separation, judgment, and hate are the manifestations of bondage. Forgiveness is the key to Peace, Love, Wellness, and Freedom. Forgiveness is demonstrating the God in you, through practice by living as if God matters. Affirmative thoughts and Prayers are the right use of the mind.

Lesson 1

Why do I make attempts of Kindness and Forgiveness, only to attack others with actions of judgment, hate, separation, and offense - again? Why are the illusions of guilt and anger in my thoughts? My weakness is His strength (2 Corinthians 12:9-11 AMP). I now remember God's power and salvation in me, and I remain free of illusions. Forgiveness is the gift. Forgiveness is the answer to the illusion of separation, envy, guilt, and fear. Gratitude is the only appropriate response to Forgiveness (Matthew 6:12-14 AMP). Forgiveness, Gratitude, and Love equals Freedom - free indeed (John 8:36 AMP). I will not take back the gift of Forgiveness, even if it is not received. God acknowledges my gift. I AM as God created me to be - His Heart is in me and I AM ever so grateful. I Share with others the Holy Thoughts of God and my only function is Forgiveness.

I AM Grateful, Blessed and at Peace

Lesson 2

The salvation of the world depends on me. The will of God is unity on earth and restoring earth to Heaven's peace – on earth as it is in Heaven (Matthew 6:10 AMP). I accept the assignment of the Holy Spirit who knows who I am and who knows what is to come. God loves me and has not forgotten me. What will you have me to do today? I am humbled to hear Your Voice and accept Your assignment. I cannot fail because God is my Source – All things are possible to those who love God (Matthew 19:26 AMP) and called to His purpose for my life. Your will be done. God's Thoughts are the answer to all of my needs and desires according to His riches and glory (Philippians 4:19 AMP). Forgiveness is an earthly form of Love. Salvation of the world depends on my Forgiveness – my Love. This is my function here on earth as it is in Heaven – to Forgive and to Love.

I AM Grateful, Blessed and at Peace

Lesson 3

My condemnation is an illusion that injures and deceives me. It is done to me as I believe (Proverbs 23:7 AMP; Matthew 8:13 AMP; Matthew 9:29 AMP). My illusion has no value. Being free means freedom from negative thoughts that cause 'dis' – disease, discomfort, disorientation, distraught, disassociation, disguise. 'Dis" is my illusory reality. Forgiveness versus condemnation is like life versus death – I choose life (Proverbs 18:21 AMP). I am no longer condemned by my thoughts and speech (Proverbs 6:2 AMP). Perception is not my reality – perception is an illusion and Forgiveness is the answer to all illusion. Dr. Martin Luther King's famous *I Have A Dream* speech is a dream of Forgiveness that leads me to Peace, Harmony, Clarity, and Freedom. There is no other way, but Forgiveness. The simple lesson of Forgiveness is God's Plan for my salvation. My condemnation injures me, and my Forgiveness sets me free - on earth as it is in Heaven (Matthew 6:10 AMP). I choose to see the Light.

I AM Grateful, Blessed and at Peace

Lesson 4

Love is the way I walk in gratitude. My gratitude is to God who alleviates suffering, offers healing, and soothes my body, mind, and spirit with laughter and happiness.

I demonstrate my gratitude with Love. Who can I help and who can I serve today? Love makes no comparisons. I am not separate from others – I am not separate from God. Namaste. I give thanks for all things and I do not despise small beginnings (Zechariah 4:10 AMP), nothing is separate. You are my Source and supply and You will give me the desires of my heart (Psalm 37:4 AMP). I replace judgments and perceptions with peace and love. Forgiveness is total gratitude – gratitude is God's Way.

I AM Grateful, Blessed and at Peace

Lesson 5

I walk in the counsel of the Holy Spirit, standing for Goodness and Rightness. As I delight in the law of God, my thoughts are filled with goodness and greatness. Deceptive Intelligence and its negative distractions have disappeared, and my thoughts are of God's law of Love, Peace, and Forgiveness. I AM firmly planted and watered, because I walk in the Spirit. All my needs are met and I AM prosperous and overflowing in goodness and peace. My God fully loves, approves, and Blesses me. Everything I do prospers and comes to maturity (Psalm 1 AMP).

I AM Grateful, Blessed and at Peace

Lesson 6

I dwell in the secret place of the Most High and find peace and security in His presence. He is my Refuge and Fortress. He Covers and Protects me. His Faithfulness is a shield and a wall. Because He is the most powerful force in the Universe, I AM fearless. I AM Protected from all adversity, regardless of what happens around me. I keep my eye single and witness His Divine Power. His angels surround and protect me when I serve and am obedient to His Will. Wherever He leads me, I AM safe. My thoughts are of my Love for Him and I place Him at the center of my life. I confidently trust and rely on Him and I expect His Goodness. When I call on Him, He answers me. He will never leave or forsake me. In Him I live, move, and have my being (Psalm 91 AMP: Acts 17:28 AMP).

I AM Grateful, Blessed and at Peace

LESSONS IN AFFIRMATIONS

Affirmation: God is life, love, intelligence, substance, omnipotence, omniscience, omnipresence. I am a child or manifestation of God, and every moment His life, love, wisdom, power, flow into and through me. I am one with God, and am governed by His law. I am Spirit, perfect, holy and harmonious. Nothing can hurt me or make me sick or afraid. I manifest my real self through this body now. God works with me to will and to do whatsoever He wishes me to do, and He cannot fail.

Affirmation: I am moral, profitable, and ingenious extraordinaire, regardless of what any institutional transcript, or bank statement says (Dyer, W).

Affirmation: I am totally independent of the good and bad opinions of others, I am beneath no one, I am fearless in the face of any and all challenges (Chopra, D).

Affirmation: Why am I here? I am here to serve, inspire, love, and live the truth of who I am, and to do what brings me joy.

Affirmation: Fulfill Your highest thought in me and renew my mind (Romans 12:2 AMP). The Holy Spirit goes before me and shows me the way – Infinite Spirit shows me what to do. You abide in me now, from the center, to the circumference of my being. What I am seeking is also seeking me. What is the next step to take? Let Your will be done in me now (Luke 11:2 AMP). My answers are revealed in the stillness of my Spirit. Abide in me as I abide in You (John 15:4 AMP).

Affirmation: I am the one who sees from back in here somewhere. I look out and I am aware of the events, thoughts, and emotions, that pass before me. I am aware that I am aware (Chopra, D).

Affirmation: I acknowledge what I want and what I feel and I express my feelings clearly and directly, with kindness.

Affirmation: Namaste; The Light of God in me salutes the Light of God in you. I am not the only one.

Affirmation: I take full responsibility for my actions and forgive myself for all that I have knowingly or unknowingly done to hurt myself and any other individuals. I release myself from the bondage of un-forgiveness. I am free, free in the freedom that has always been mine. I claim it now. Guilt, shame, and blame are now neutralized by the unconditional love, compassion, and forgiveness which saturate my awareness, my heart, my entire being. Right here and right now I am cleansed of the toxin of un-forgiveness. I begin afresh and give thanks for this realization. I free myself and I free you from all blame of knowingly or unknowingly hurting me. Through the power of forgiveness all is well between our spirits. You are free and I am free. All is well between us (Beckwith, M., 2012).

Affirmation: I surrender to the power of truth and the presence of Spirit in my life.

Affirmation: Through the mirror of relationship, I discover my non-local self. I see the other in myself and myself in others (Chopra, D., 2003).

Affirmation: I am the one who sees out there. I am the observer, experiencer, the witness. I am changeless, timeless, invisible, and intangible. I am present at the seat of the soul. I look out and I am aware of the events and thoughts that pass before me with detachment. I sit in the seat of the soul; the seat of consciousness (Zukav, G., 2001).

Affirmation: I come from greatness, I believe in greatness, I am greatness. Unlimited possibilities are waiting for me.

Affirmation: My thoughts decide my destiny. I move toward what I dwell on, and I become what I think about. I am victorious. The way I think determines how I live. I am as great as my highest thought. My life is lived from the inside out.

THE BLESSING

I declare a BLESSING on my family and friends – A Generational BLESSING on my children's children of Peace, Awareness, Clarity, Courage, Creativity, Obedience, Discipline, Faith, Prosperity, Forgiveness, Freedom, Gratitude, Grace, Willingness, Humility, Wisdom, Kindness, Love, Order, Patience, Purpose, Service, Abundance, Balance, Protection, Acceptance, Authenticity, Awareness, Mindfulness, Non-judgment, Praise, Prayer, Responsibility, Trust, Joy, Strength, and Vision. God is able to make all grace [every favor and earthly blessing] come in abundance to me, so that I may always [under all circumstances, regardless of the need] have complete sufficiency in everything [being completely self-sufficient in Him], and have an abundance for every good work *and* act of charity (2 Corinthians 9:8 AMP).

And So It Is - Amen.

REFERENCES - SACRED TEXTS

Introduction: The Soul

2 Corinthians 13:5 AMP; Matthew 15:19 AMP

Acceptance

Matthew 6:25-27 AMP; Philippians 4:7 AMP; Ruiz, D. M. (1997). *The Four Agreements.*

2: Affirmation

Philippians 4:8 AMP; Proverbs 18:21 AMP; Job 22:28 AMP; Mark 11:24 AMP; and Proverbs 4:23 AMP.

3: Authenticity

Galatians 6:4 AMP; Psalm 139:23 AMP; 2 Corinthians 13:5 AMP; and Chopra, D. (2003). *The Spontaneous Fulfillment of Desire.*

4: **Awareness**

Proverbs 23:7 AMP; Philippians 4:8 AMP; Matthew 6:10 AMP; Psalm 46:10 AMP; Acts 17:28 AMP; Hanh, T. N. (2009) *Happiness*; and Zukav, G. (1989). *The Seat of the Soul.*

5: **Balance**

Chopra, D. (1993). *Ageless Body, Timeless Mind*; Mark 12:30 AMP; James 2:8 AMP; Mark 13:10 AMP; Matthew 28:18-20 AMP; 2 Timothy 2:15 AMP; and Proverbs 27:17 AMP.

6: **Choice**

Luke 23:34 AMP; Matthew 4:1-11 AMP; and Matthew 26:42 AMP.

7: **Clarity**

James 4:2 AMP; and Isaiah 65:24 AMP.

8: **Commitment**

Psalm 37:5 AMP; Hill, N. (1971). *You Can Work Your Own Miracles;* Chopra, D. (2004). *The Book of Secrets: Unlocking the Hidden Dimensions of Your Life*; and Proverbs 16:3 AMP.

9: **Courage**

Psalm 31:24 AMP; 2 Timothy 2:15 AMP; Chopra, D. (2009). *Reinventing the Body, Resurrecting the Soul; and 2 Thessalonians 3:13 AMP.*

10: **Creativity**

Philippians 4:8 AMP; Proverbs 4:23 AMP; and Hicks, E. & J. (2004). *Ask and It is Given: Learning to Manifest Your Desires.*

11: **Detachment**

Romans 12:2 AMP; Ephesians 6:12 AMP; Ruiz, D. M. (1997). *The Four Agreements: Wisdom Book;* and Dyer, W. W. (1995). *Your Sacred Self.*

12: **Discipline**

Philippians 4:7 AMP; and James 1:26 AMP.

13: **Evolution**

Matthew 6:10 AMP; Galatians 5:22,23 AMP; Ephesians 4:23, 24 AMP; 1 Peter 5:8 AMP; and Isaiah 30:21 AMP.

14: **Faith**

Hebrews 11:1 AMP; Romans 8:28 AMP; Luke 17:6 AMP; Matthew 9:2 AMP; Matthew 9:22 AMP; Matthew

9:29 AMP; Matthew 8:10 AMP; Matthew 15:28 AMP; Mark 2:5 AMP; Mark 5:34 AMP; and Luke 17:19 AMP.

15: Forgiveness

Proverbs 4:23 AMP; Proverbs 4:7 AMP; Luke 23:34 AMP; Hanh, T. N. (2009). *Happiness*; Matthew 18:22 AMP; Matthew 6:12 AMP; Beckwith, M. B. (2012). *Lifevisioning;* *and* Vanzant, I. (1992). *Tapping the Power Within.*

16: Freedom

Galatians 5:1 AMP; John 10:10 AMP; Galatians 5:13 AMP; Chopra, D. (2003); and *The Spontaneous Fulfillment of Desire.*

17: Grace

Romans 3:23 AMP; Luke 6:38 AMP; 1 Peter 4:10 AMP; Isaiah 30:21 AMP; and 2 Corinthians 12:9 AMP.

18: Gratitude

Dispenza, J (2017). *Becoming Supernatural: How Common People are Doing the Uncommon;* Proverbs 23:7 AMP; Philippians 4:8 AMP; and James 1:7,8 AMP.

19: Humility

1 Peter 5:5 AMP; Galatians 5:22-23 AMP; John 13:12 AMP; Matthew 19:14 AMP; Matthew 21:16 AMP; Mark 10:14 AMP; Matthew 21:5 AMP; Matthew 19:14 AMP; 1

Corinthians 9:19-23 AMP; and Schucman, H. (1975). *A Course in Miracles.*

20: **Intention**

Matthew 5:16 AMP; Psalm 44:20-21 AMP; James 4:8 AMP; and Matthew 18:20 AMP.

21: **Kindness**

1 Thessalonians 5:15 AMP; Matthew 5:44-45 AMP; 1 Peter 4:8 AMP; and Psalm 23:3 AMP.

22: **Love**

Matthew 22:37-40 AMP; and 1 Corinthians 13:4-8 AMP.

23: **Meditation**

Psalm 46:10 AMP; Mark 4:39 AMP; Acts17:28 AMP; Psalm 91 AMP; Romans 8:28 AMP; Romans 12:2 AMP; and Matthew 6:10 AMP.

24: **Mindfulness**

Psalm 8:4-5 AMP; Psalm 115:12 AMP; Hebrews 2:6 AMP; Ephesians 5:15-16 AMP; Hanh, T. N. (2009). *Happiness;* and Matthew 9:20-22 AMP.

25: Non-judgment

Matthew 7:1 AMP; John 10:10 AMP; 2 Corinthians 4:16 AMP; Proverbs 4:7 AMP; Dyer, W. W. (2007). *Change Your Thoughts - Change Your Life: Living the Wisdom of the Tao;* Philippians 4:8; Schucman, H. (1975). *A Course in Miracles;* Chopra, D. (2003). *The Spontaneous Fulfillment of Desire*; and Matthew 6:10 AMP.

26: Order

Genesis 8:21-22 AMP; Proverbs 23:7 AMP; Proverbs 6:2 AMP; Galatians 6:7-8 AMP; Matthew 17:20 AMP; James 4:8 AMP; Matthew 6:9-13 AMP; and Proverbs 4:23 AMP.

27: Patience

Colossians 3:12-13 AMP; Galatians 6:9 AMP; Romans 8:2 AMP8; and James 1:2-4 AMP.

28: Peace

Proverbs 4:23 AMP; James 1:7-8 AMP; and Philippians 4:7 AMP.

29: Perseverance

Galatians 6:9 AMP; Ephesians 2:10 AMP; 1 Peter 1:6-7 AMP; and Psalm 37:4 AMP.

30: **Praise**

John 4:23-24 AMP; 2 Corinthians 3:2-3 AMP; and Hebrews 1:9 AMP.

31: **Prayer**

James 4:2 AMP; Matthew 18:19 AMP; Philippians 4:16 AMP; Job 3:24-25 AMP; Mark 9:23 AMP; Luke 20:47 AMP; Romans 8:26 AMP; Ephesians 6:18 AMP; Job 42:10 AMP; Mathew 7:8 AMP; Colossians 4:12 AMP; and Mark 9:23 AMP.

32: **Purpose**

Romans 12:6-8 AMP; 2 Corinthians 4:16 AMP: Proverbs 20:27 AMP; Psalm 33:10-12 AMP; Proverbs 4:26 AMP; Romans 8:28 AMP; Isaiah 40:31 AMP; Psalm 32:8 AMP; and James 1:7-8 AMP.

33: **Relationship**

Matthew 5:43-45 AMP; Galatians 5:22-23 AMP; and Chopra, D. (2003). *The Spontaneous Fulfillment of Desire.*

34: **Responsibility**

Montapert, A. A. (1952). *The Supreme Philosophy of Man;* 2 Corinthians 5:10 AMP; and Galatians 6:5 AMP.

35: Service

Galatians 6:9 AMP; Romans12:3 AMP; and Luke 12:34-36 AMP.

36: Simplicity

Genesis 1:31 AMP; Matthew 5:34-37 AMP; and 2 Timothy 2:15 AMP.

37: Thought

Proverbs 23:7 AMP; Genesis 1:12 AMP; Philippians 4:8 AMP; John 10:1 AMP0; Romans 12:2 AMP; and Chopra, D. (2003). *The Spontaneous Fulfillment of Desire.*

38: Trust

1 Corinthians 12:8-10 AMP; Proverbs 3:5-6 AMP; Isaiah 30:19, 21 AMP; Vanzant, I. (2000). *Until Today; and* Psalm 138:8 AMP.

39: Vision

Proverbs 29:18 AMP; Joel 2:28 AMP; Matthew 6:33 AMP; Psalm 32:8 AMP; Matthew 6:33 AMP; and Mark 9:23 AMP.

40: Wisdom

2 Timothy 2:15 AMP; Proverbs 4:23 AMP; and Proverbs 4:7 AMP.

FAQ's: Soul Matters

Proverbs 27:17 AMP; Mathew 18:22 AMP; Matthew 7:6 AMP; Matthew 5:44 AMP; Luke 23:34 AMP; Romans 8:28 AMP; 1 Peter 1:6 AMP; James 1:3 AMP; Hicks, E. & J. (2004). *Ask and It is Given: Learning to Manifest Your Desires*; Job 4:8 AMP; and Philippians 4:8 AMP.

Soul to Soul: Additional Soul Inquiries

2 Corinthians 13:5 AMP

Blessing the Energy Centers

Root / Pure Wisdom

Proverbs 4:7 AMP; Matthew 6:10 AMP; 1 Kings 3:9-13 AMP; Psalm 37:4 AMP; Proverbs 3:17-18 AMP; 2 Timothy 3:15 AMP; and 2 Corinthians 13:5 AMP.

Sacral / Life Visioning

Proverbs 29:18 AMP; Beckwith, M. B. (2012). Lifevisioning: A Transformative Process for Activating Your Unique Gifts and Highest Potential.

Solar Plexus/ Affirmative Prayer

Joshua 23:10 AMP; Deuteronomy 32:30 AMP; and Romans 10:17 AMP.

Heart / Loving Forgiveness

Matthew 18:22 AMP; Schucman, H. (1975). A Course in Miracles.

Throat / Authentically Courageous

Matthew 10:31 AMP; Ephesians 6:14 AMP.

Third Eye / Creative Intention

Ephesians 5:13 AMP

Crown / Purposeful Response

Philippians 4:8 AMP

RECOMMENDED READING LIST

Akbar, N. (1995). Natural Psychology and Human Transformation. Tallahassee: Mind
Productions.

Beckwith, M. B. (2012). *Lifevisioning:* A Transformative Process for Activating Your Unique Gifts and Highest Potential. Boulder: SoundsTrue.

Chopra, D. (1993). *Ageless Body, Timeless Mind: The Quantum Alternative to Growing Old.* New York: Three Rivers Press.

Chopra, D. (1994). *Seven Spiritual Laws of Success: A Practical Guide to the Fulfillment of Your Dreams.* San Rafael: Amber Allen Publishing.

Chopra, D. (2003). *The Spontaneous Fulfillment of Desire*: *Harnessing the Infinite Power of*
Coincidence. New York: Three Rivers Press.

Chopra, D. (2004). *The Book of Secrets: Unlocking the Hidden Dimensions of Your Life*: New York: Three Rivers Press.

Chopra, D. (2009). *Reinventing the Body, Resurrecting the Soul: How to Create a New You.* New York: Three Rivers Press.

Collier, R. (1925). *The Secret of the Ages: The Master Code to Abundance and Achievement.* New York: Jeremy P. Tarcher/Penguin.

Dispenza, J (2017). *Becoming Supernatural: How Common People are Doing the Uncommon.* Carlsbad: Hay House, Inc.

Dyer, W. W. (1995). *Your Sacred Self: Making the Decision to Be Free.* New York: Harper.

Dyer, W. W. (2007). *Change Your Thoughts - Change Your Life: Living the Wisdom of the Tao.* Carlsbad: Hay House, Inc.

Hanh, T. N. (2009). *Happiness: Essential Mindfulness Practices.* Berkeley: Parallax Press.

Hicks, E. & J. (2004). *Ask and It is Given: Learning to Manifest Your Desires.* Carlsbad: Hay House, Inc.

Holmes, E. (1949). *Words That Heal Today.* Deerfield Beach: Health Communications, Inc.

Holmes, E. (2001). *Love and Law: The Unpublished Teachings.* New York: Jeremy P. Tarcher/Penguin.

Montapert, A. A. (1952). *The Supreme Philosophy of Man: The Laws of Life.* Englewood, Cliffs: Prentice Hall, Inc.

Murphy, J. P. (1963). *The Power of Your Subconscious Mind.* New York: Jeremy P. Tarcher/Penguin.

Ruiz, D. M. (1997). *The Four Agreements: Wisdom Book.* San Rafael: Amber-Allen Publishing.

Ruiz, D. M. (2010). *The Fifth Agreement: A Practical Guide to Self-Mastery.* San Rafael: Amber-Allen Publishing.

Schucman, H. (1975). *A Course in Miracles.* California: Foundation for Inner Peace.

Singer, M. A. (2007). *The Untethered Soul: The Journey Beyond Youself.* Oakland: New Harbinger Publisher, Inc.

Vanzant, I. (1995). The Value in the Valley: A Black Woman's
    Guide Through Life's Dilemmas.
Ney York: Fireside Book.
Vanzant, I. (2000). Until Today!Daily Devotions for
    Spiritual Growth and Peace of Mind.
New York: Simon & Schuster.
Willis, W. B. (1998). The Adinkra Dictionary: A Visual
    Primer on the Language of Adinkra.
Washington DC: The Pyramid Complex.
Zukav, G. (1989). The Seat of the Soul. New York: Simon
    & Schuster.

.

GLOSSARY

Acceptance. The act of taking or receiving something offered; favorable reception; approval; favor; the act of harmonizing.

Affirmations. The act or an instance of affirming; state of being affirmed; the assertion that something exists or is true; a statement or proposition that is declared to be true; a solemn declaration accepted, instead of a statement under oath.

Ancient wisdom. Sacred scriptures that include sources written regarding the Laws pertaining to a way of life that connects us to the Source – God. Sacred scriptures include the Bible, Dow Ching, MAAT, Koran, Vedas.

Attention. The act or power of carefully thinking about, listening to, or watching someone or something; notice, interest, or awareness; the act or state of applying the mind to something; a condition of readiness for such attention involving a selective narrowing or focusing of consciousness and receptivity; observation.

Authenticity. Real or genuine; not copied or false; true and accurate; not false or imitation; authentic, genuine, bona fide; authentic implies being fully trustworthy.

Awareness. The state or condition of being aware; having knowledge; consciousness; cognizant; informed; alert; knowledgeable; sophisticated.

Balance. A state of equilibrium; equal distribution of weight; something used to produce equilibrium; counterbalance.

Being, doing, having. A concept in Creative Visualization - be who you are, then do what you love to do, in order to have what you want. If you seek abundance, you must first find it within. If you want wealth, open your arms to gratitude. Be who you really are, do what you love to do and then ultimately, have what you desire. Being is the experience of being complete and at rest within ourselves. Doing is activity or creative energy. Having is being in relationship and accepting things and people as is.

Buddhism. Buddhism is a religion; the Buddha was said to be *enlightened* and "awakened." Buddha taught that awakening comes through one's own direct experience, not through beliefs and dogmas. Buddhism spread throughout Asia to become one of the dominant religions of the continent. The principles of Buddhism are universal (compassion and mercy; feeling what others feel).

Choice. An act or instance of choosing awareness; choice is right action; something that is preferred or preferable to others; the best part of something.

Clarity. The quality of being easily understood; ability to express; easily understood in a very exact way; the quality of being easily seen or heard. the quality or state of being clear.

Commitment. A promise to do or give something; to be loyal to someone or something; the attitude of someone who works very hard to support something; an agreement or pledge to do something in the future; something pledged.

Conscious breathing. Making a conscious effort to breathe slowly and deeply resulting in mind/body balance. Breath is powerful when focusing on an affirmation during inhales and exhales. Conscious breathing is used for stress reduction, improving breath related diseases, and training in mindfulness. Mindfulness and Awareness Trainings often use conscious breathing for training inner awareness and body consciousness.

Courage. The quality of mind or spirit that enables a person to face difficulty, danger, pain, without fear; bravery; to act in accordance with one's beliefs, especially in spite of criticism.

Creativity. The state or quality of being creative; the ability to transcend traditional ideas, rules, patterns, relationships, and to create meaningful new ideas and processes; the process by which one utilizes creative ability.

Deep listening. Deep listening or compassionate listening is the kind of listening that relieves the suffering of another person; listening with the purpose to help the other empty their heart; listening with compassion to help the other suffer less.

Detachment. The act of detaching; freedom from prejudice or partiality; disengage; disunite.

Direct Experience. The spiritual "seeing" of God is direct experience; real, vivid, near, constant, effective, intimate; the experience of being conscious of God's presence; to see God directly and intimately; going beyond learning about God and actually meeting God.

Discipline. Self-control; self-mastery; self-censorship; discipline leads to self-mastery.

Ego. A sense of one's self-importance; pride, self-righteousness; arrogance; ego is Easing God Out; the "I" or self of any person; distinguishing oneself from the selves of others; conceit; self-importance; the conscious mind, based on perception of the environment from birth onwards; one's image of oneself; the ego is the part of the psyche that experiences the outside world and reacts to it.

Emotional disturbance. An emotional upset or dis-ease that affects the physical body in response to thinking about unpleasant situations in the past, present, or future. Disturbances are caused by flight or fight reaction where a physiological reaction occurs - increased heartbeat, respiration, elevated blood pressure, and increased blood flow.

Emotional Guidance System. Classifying feelings or emotions on a continuum from good to progressively feeling better, and intentionally choosing to think of situations that create increasingly better feelings and emotions. The desired goal is to always feel good. Good feelings include abundance, prosperity, passion, love, enthusiasm and joy. Feelings and actions coincide. Feeling good aligns one with a desired goal.

Evolution. A process of gradual, growth, progressive change or development. Spiritual evolution is living the qualities of the soul – knowing, peace, compassion, and love; soul qualities. Spiritual evolution is inner directed.

Faith. Confidence or trust in a person or thing; belief in God or in the doctrines or teachings of religion; in faith, in truth; indeed.

Forgiveness. To grant pardon for or remission of an offense or debt; absolve; to cease to feel resentment against; to cancel an indebtedness or liability.

Freedom. The quality or state of being free; the absence of coercion or constraint in choice and action; ease; liberty; the condition of acting without compulsion.

God-consciousness/Christ-consciousness/Higher-consciousness/Source. Being conscious of a higher Self or God; the part of the human being that is capable of transcending the ego; state of consciousness that transcends personality and causality; being conscious that God is in everything and God is everything.

Grace. Simple elegance or refinement; the free and unmerited favor of God; the bestowal of blessings; an act of instant kindness, courtesy, or mercy; service.

Gratitude. The quality or feeling of being grateful; being thank-filled; appreciation; gratefulness.

Heart. The heart of hearts is the heart of the soul; intuition; feeling; the center of emotion in contrast to the head as the center of the intellect; courage.

Humility. The absence of any feelings of being better than others; humbleness; meekness; modesty.

Inner being. The Inner self, the subtle core present within every being; the inherent force that drives one to action; personal experience of God via the soul that disseminates absolute knowledge; the soul.

Intention. The thing that you plan to do or achieve; an aim or purpose; a determination to act in a certain way; purpose; design, aim, objective; to intend to accomplish or attain; intention implies action.

Intuition. The ability to understand something immediately without the need for conscious reasoning; a thing that one knows or considers likely from instinctive feeling rather than conscious reasoning; direct perception of truth; independent of the reasoning process; immediate knowing.

Journaling. To log data providing a record; to actively engage in learning through writing for future reference and reflection; record ideas and feelings; When students write in journals, they can record such things as ideas and feelings; journal entries are individualized.

Karma/Cause and Effect/ Sow and Reap. Every thought, word, and action produce karma; every action result in consequences; Grace saves us from our conscious and unconscious actions.

Kindness. The state or quality of being kind; good and benevolent nature or disposition; considerate and helpful; humane; passionate affection for another person; a feeling of warm personal attachment or deep affection.

Love. Unselfish loyal and compassionate concern for the good of another; God's concern for humankind; brotherly concern for others; goodwill. I am my brother's keeper; I am my brother.

Loving speech. Speaking in a way that helps relieve the suffering of others; not spreading gossip, malice, and dissention; speaking words that result in love and unity; loving speech is included in the Buddha's explanation of Right Speech; abstaining from false, slanderous and harsh speech; abstaining from idle chatter that negatively affect others.

Meditation. To engage in thought or contemplation; reflection; devout religious or spiritual introspection; to intend; silence within the mind, body, and spirit. Connecting to unlimited power - Supreme Being.

Mindfulness. A state of being aware; gentleness; consideration, discernment, and thought; a state of awareness of the present moment; heightened awareness of thoughts and emotions; experience on a moment-to-moment basis.

Non-judgment. The ability not to judge; not forming an opinion; discretion.

Oneness. The state of being unified or whole; a feeling of oneness; everything is part of a whole; originating from one common source; sharing a common spirit; the nature of existence.

Order. To put in order; arrange; to bring about order; order suggests a straightening out so as to eliminate confusion.

Patience. The quality of being patient without complaint; an ability or willingness to suppress restlessness or annoyance when confronted with delay; steady perseverance; even-tempered care; diligence.

Peace. A state of mutual harmony between people or groups, especially in personal relations; the mind free from annoyance, distraction, anxiety, and obsession; a state of tranquility or serenity; silence; stillness; refrain from creating a disturbance.

Perseverance. Steady persistence in a course of action in spite of difficulties, obstacles, or discouragement; continuance in a state of grace to the end.

Power. The ability to get results; power implies the ability to exercise force, authority, or influence.

Praise. To proclaim glory; to bless; celebrate; exalt; glorify; magnify; worship; to declare enthusiastic approval.

Prayer. A devout petition to God or an object of worship; a spiritual communion with God; thanksgiving; the act or practice of praying to God; a religious observance, either public or private.

Present/presence/ present moment. The state or fact of existing; the ability to project a sense of ease; feeling a divine spirit.

Process. A series of actions or steps taken in order to achieve a particular end; a continuous action, operation, or series of changes taking place in a definite manner; operation; procedure; a series of progressive and interdependent steps by which an end is attained.

Purpose. The reason for which something exists or is done; an intended or desired result; goal; the point at issue; resoluteness; intention, or goal for oneself.

Recapitulation. Recapitulation is an ancient technique for retrieving and healing energy. It also teaches how to prevent current energetic loss. The theory of recapitulation is simple. Every interaction you have in life is tied up with personal energy. The process of recapitulation assists in acknowledging, identifying and releasing negative energy.

Relationship. The way in which two or more people or things are connected; the state of being related or interrelated; linkage; connection.

Responsibility. The state or fact of being accountable for something within one's power; managing something within one's power; involving accountability as in having the power to control or manage.

Seed and harvest time - While the earth remains, seedtime and harvest, cold and heat, summer and winter, day and night, shall not cease (Genesis 8:22). It takes time to receive a bountiful harvest. The law of seedtime and harvest works in all parts of our lives. We plant seeds in our hearts, by reading, speaking, hearing, and meditating on our desires. In time, we are guaranteed a harvest, if we do not destroy our seed with fear and doubt.

Self-assessment/self-inquiry. The process of looking at oneself in order to assess aspects of the personality.

Self-correction. Adjusting to or correcting mistakes, malfunctions; the ability to correct oneself without external aid.

Service. The action of helping or doing work for someone; contribution to the welfare of others; to provide someone with something that is needed or wanted; a helpful or useful act.

Simplicity. The quality of being easy to understand or use; the state or quality of being plain; not fancy or complicated; clearness in speaking or writing; sincerity.

Soul. An immaterial force that gives the body life, energy, and power; spirit; life, vitality; being; essence; the soul is connected to the Source/God. God's power is so great that the soul's function is like a step-down transformer. The ability to receive God's power and presence because of the soul.

Spiritual Partner. A partnership of equals for spiritual growth; an accountability partner assisting in spiritual growth. In partnership, we observe and reveal to our partner the loving and unloving behavior in order to become our best selves.

Spirituality/spiritual principles. Basic principles; core truths. When embodied and practiced over time, spiritual principles change behavior and deepens our relationship with God, self, and others. Spiritual or soul principles create oneness.

Taoism. The Tao is a religious or philosophical tradition of Chinese origin. Taoism teaches that each person can discover the Tao on their own terms; embracing the joy in living with grace and style by following the heart.

Thought. An idea, plan, opinion, or picture, that is formed in the mind; the act or process of thinking; the act of carefully thinking about the details of something. Thought is energy.

Transpersonal. Transpersonal is a term used to describe experiences beyond personal and worldly events. Transpersonal refers to peak experiences, altered states of consciousness, higher awareness, and spiritual experiences.

Trust. A belief that someone or something is reliable, good, honest, effective; assured reliance on the character, ability, strength, and truth of someone or something.

Unconditional love. Affection without any limitations or conditions. Unconditional love is associated with true altruism; the type of love which has no bounds and is unchanging; not conditional or limited; absolute, unqualified, without any special exceptions.

Vedanta/Vedic/Vedas. The Vedas are among the oldest sacred texts originating in India, dating from 1700–1100 BC. Hindus consider the Vedas to be, authorless. Vedanta is one of the six schools of Hindu philosophy. The term Veda means "knowledge" and anta means "end".

Vision. A concept or image created by the imagination having no objective reality; discernment, insight, perceptiveness; wisdom; concern or preparation for the future.

Wisdom. The quality or state of being wise; knowledge of what is true or right coupled with right action; understanding; discernment and insight; wise sayings or teachings.

Witness (the). A person who sees an event take place; to see/ watch an event take place.